AMERICAN LONESOME

AMERICAN
LONESOME
THE WORK OF BRUCE
SPRINGSTEEN

GAVIN COLOGNE-BROOKES

LOUISIANA STATE UNIVERSITY PRESS

BATON ROUGE

Published by Louisiana State University Press

Copyright © 2018 by Louisiana State University Press

All rights reserved

Manufactured in the United States of America

First printing

DESIGNER: Michelle A. Neustrom

TYPEFACES: Whitman, text; Cervo Neue, display

PRINTER AND BINDER: Sheridan Books, Inc.

LIBRARY OF CONGRESS CATALOGING-IN-PUBLICATION DATA

Names: Cologne-Brookes, Gavin, 1961– author.

Title: American lonesome : the work of Bruce Springsteen / Gavin Cologne-Brookes.

   Description: Baton Rouge : Louisiana State University Press, 2018. | Includes bibliographical
   references and index.

Identifiers: LCCN 2018008741| ISBN 978-0-8071-6946-9 (cloth : alk. paper) |
   ISBN 978-0-8071-6947-6 (pdf) | ISBN 978-0-8071-6948-3 (epub)

Subjects: LCSH: Springsteen, Bruce—Criticism and interpretation. | Rock music—
   United States—History and criticism.

Classification: LCC ML420.S77 C68 2018 | DDC 782.42166092—dc23

LC record available at https://lccn.loc.gov/2018008741

For Nicki, Xenatasha, and Anastasia

A man sets out to draw the world. As the years go by, he peoples a space with images of provinces, kingdoms, mountains, bays, ships, islands, fishes, rooms, instruments, stars, horses, and individuals. A short time before he dies, he discovers that that patient labyrinth of lines traces the lineaments of his own face.
—JORGE LUIS BORGES, "AFTERWORD," *The Aleph*

Without work, the ship of human life has no sort of ballast.
—STENDHAL, *Souvenirs d'Égotisme*

Good art is always dangerous, always open-ended. Once you put it out in the world you lose control of it; people will fit it into their lives in all sorts of different ways.
—GREIL MARCUS, *Mystery Train*

CONTENTS

PREFACE
Looking in on Asbury Park

I t's been a long time coming but now, for a few warm September days, I'm finally here. I spent years of my youth roaming the States in search of who I
might become. But the Jersey Shore for me has been a place of the mind. The
nearest I've been was a cloudless night decades ago. Seen from a plane porthole,
a string of lights rimmed "the pitch-black nothing of the Atlantic."[1] Back then I
didn't know its significance as part of Bruce Land. The shot of Springsteen on
the back of *Greetings from Asbury Park, N.J.* is serrated like a stamp as if for the
album's postcard cover. It's unlikely he'd read William Faulkner back then, but
his instincts led him to mimic that southern novelist, who described the fictional
world of Yoknapatawpha County, Mississippi, as his "postage stamp of soil."[2] I've
approached the actual Asbury Park with unease and expectation. I'll never again
understand Springsteen's music and images in the same way, but the real place
will glitter with preconceived notions. I'll see in it what only a Springsteen listener could see: a place created by his artistry.

I haven't been in the States for three years or on the Eastern Seaboard for
six. The twenty-first century barrels on. Barack Obama's time in office is ending.
Within months of my visit, Donald Trump will be president. BA0189 from London to Newark is a Dreamliner, a new generation of planes that feel less cramped
inside, with more headroom and bigger lockers. You can tint your window to

cobalt blue. The touch screen is a virtual-reality arcade. You can spend the flight "bangin' them pleasure machines." But the past is still present. The TV in the Fairfield Inn breakfast room shows footage of the towers falling fifteen years ago today. I collect the car and set off beneath blue sky along the New Jersey Turnpike to the Garden State Parkway. Just as I pass signs for the New Jersey Veterans Memorial and for Asbury Park, the DJ plays "The Promised Land." I turn the radio up loud. Soon I'm rolling down Asbury Avenue and right on Fifth Avenue to the Asbury. Converted from a seven-storey Salvation Army building by Sunset Lake, it's the first hotel to open in the town in years. Situated at the end of a row of private houses right by Kingsley Street, beyond it are Ocean Avenue, Convention Hall, and the sparkling waves. Everything is quiet. The summer crowds have gone. The streets are empty. Michael Waters, a poet at Monmouth University in West Long Branch, tells me the Pony is dark this week, but I trust in serendipity. I'll view the Bruce Springsteen Special Collection at Monmouth, meet contacts, and expect the unexpected. "I never got into being discouraged," Springsteen once said, "because I never got into hoping."[3]

After my fill of WellFleet, Cape May Salt, 40 North and Chincoteague at the Oysterfest on Cookman Avenue, I stroll back along the boardwalk, past an old saxophonist playing to a bucket of dollar bills, and reach Convention Hall. This "first mansion" of Springsteen's rock-and-roll dreams has seen better days (BTR 456). One eroded strut appears to be buckling beneath the weight. The sea end of the balcony is boarded up. I climb the steps to the Beach Bar and watch the sun set the sand ablaze. Between the tables an old hippy couple dance to a Sinatra medley, a real death waltz. "I lost you to the summer wind," soothes Frank's voice across the beach, captured on record decades ago, slung out now to accompany the fiery sky. Down on the beach, a girl in pink impresses her parents with sunset cartwheels, spraying sand like stars. "Summer Wind" gives way to "It Was a Very Good Year" and "Imagination." On the wall of the Wonder Bar across Ocean Avenue, Tillie's Cheshire smile fades in an orange sky. Against "Sinatra's favorite color" (so I'll later read in *Born to Run*), "Angel Eyes" bows out to "Ebb Tide." Streetlights punctuate the darkness.[4] Autumn is a black ship on a dim horizon, barely perceivable but definitely there.

To cool my feet, I've ventured into "the murky Jersey surf," recalling the seashore rhythm of Springsteen's version of Tom Waits's "Jersey Girl" (BTR 116). The waves threaten to engulf, but the slope is deep and the undertow so strong this evening that they soon withdraw. I've been strolling the boardwalk down past Cookson to Wesley Lake and Southside Johnny's Ocean Grove in one direction and up to Deal Lake the other. Asbury has lakes each end and in the middle: Wesley, Sunset and Deal. Like spirits in the night, snatches of Springsteen lyrics populate the air. "By the time we made it up to Greasy Lake." A sunset makes a lake look greasy, and the greasers would have hung out at dusk. Contemplating what was once the circuit, the phrase "riding down Kingsley" comes to mind. In a different way from when I was a teenager, I still seek something in the night. I'm still the outsider. I'm not from the States. I'm not a musician. I'm not blue collar or working class, or any class, or really anything much. I'm not of Springsteen's era. I barely heard of him before 1980 and didn't see him live until 1981. Perhaps I'm therefore unqualified to write about him or have anything useful to add. Yet here I am, in search of that feeling only visiting a place evokes.

Asbury Park seems small. I'd pictured an immensity to match the music. The Asbury and another hotel, the Berkeley Ocean Front, are the only tall buildings by the boardwalk, and Convention Hall the only other notable building aside from the derelict Casino at the south end, where Mickey Rourke filmed scenes for *The Wrestler*. Head north through the cavernous area of shadowed shoppers ambling around souvenir shops and there's nothing but a locked building with no name and, at the north end, Asbury Tower, a high-rise providing affordable housing for low-income senior citizens. As for the other residents, nowadays tattoos are abundant among the young and on every visible patch of skin. Like anywhere, there are people of all shapes, sizes, and standards of fitness, from those with blubber from years of fried food and sugary drinks to joggers and power walkers vibrating the bleached boardwalk planks. "Please don't talk about me when I'm gone," croons Frank as if on a balcony stool, his trilby tilted to cover eyes the same sea blue as my father's. A Philadelphia couple confide over cocktails that they don't like Springsteen but are trying to like Asbury Park. ("*I don't hate it! I don't hate it!*" the girl might as well have been echoing Quentin Compson from Faulkner's *Absalom, Absalom!*)[5] But I find it beautiful on this fiery night and especially after more beer and what the Beach Bar sells as the Boss's Margarita.

My walk has dredged up debris from those days when Springsteen first became a local hero. I've found the Upstage—scene of his early break—where local musicians jammed into the small hours. I've found the Stone Pony, closed, as Michael warned me, but hard to miss since it's a low building on Kingsley with a large black pony painted on its white wall. A poster for the tribute band Tramps Like Us wilts in an outside wall cabinet. On my way from the Asbury to the boardwalk, past the turquoise, red-trimmed Wonder Bar on the corner of Ocean and Fifth Avenue, decorated with Tillie gazing toothily into the distance, turning right onto the boardwalk, away from Convention Hall, I've found a granddaughter of Madam Marie. Like Springsteen decades before, I later read, I've "sat across from her on the metal guard rail bordering the beach," and would have "watched as she led the day trippers into the small back room," had she found any takers. When she's beckoned me over I've turned down a reading.[6] A stroll from the beach stands the house where Springsteen lived while writing *Greetings*. From his top-floor room would be a view of Deal Lake to the left and the ocean to the right. That album makes sense of the environment, as does *The Wild, the Innocent & the E Street Shuffle,* whereas *Born to Run* is an impossibly large and melodramatic sound for such a low-key seaside setting.

This is the penultimate weekend of official summer, and back here at the Beach Bar the cartwheeling gymnast and dancing couple continue to make the most of a dying season, just as the people of New York and New Jersey did that Tuesday morning in 2001. For when winter comes in this part of the world it can do so with a vengeance. Meanwhile, the wagon train of Sinatra songs rolls on across the street-lit town. I came in search of Bruce but find that, tonight at least, the son of Hoboken remains, as Jack Nicholson put it to Springsteen, "King of New Jersey" (BTR 420). Ol' Blue Eyes breezes out "One for My Baby" across the shore as if here with us, " . . . and one more for the road." While such songs add to the melancholy of eating and drinking with strangers in a rusty bar far from home, they also help create an incredible sunset. As surely as day turns to night, time's wrecking ball will obliterate the daguerreotype dancers framed against the pillars and boardwalk lights, the Philadelphia couple who don't hate Asbury Park, and the girls at the next table, each tattooed with faces, symbols, and sayings, their skin imprinted with memories. "When you're smilin'," Frank's voice echoes out, "the whole world smiles with you." As I hear these words, I realize that sayings my mother deployed in response to my periodic childhood morosity come from songs she heard growing up. I drain my Margarita, bid farewell to the Philadelphia couple, and head back past the Wonder Bar. *Saturday Night Fever* is playing on the Asbury's rooftop cinema. From the street you can just see John Travolta's toothy grin, a more handsome echo of the now darkened Tillie.

* * *

After the night of the Sinatra sunset, I drive Monday morning to the Bruce Springsteen Special Collection. In January 2017 Monmouth University announced the creation of the Bruce Springsteen Archives and Center for American Music, but at the time of my visit the collection exists in the Springsteen House, a modest clapboard building separated from the campus by a wooden fence. To stand on the driveway is to be on the outside of campus and academia, looking in. The white clapboard house resembles a modest home. It contains mostly secondary material with the occasional primary item—a couple of letters, a handwritten set list, and, on a 2007 tour schedule, brief notes, one referring to a dentist appointment for Steve Van Zandt, the other Springsteen's reminder to himself that he must curtail a rehearsal to do the school run: ordinary people juggling life and work, making something of their lives. Assisted by a couple of students, John and Mariza, I peruse the material for four days. Outside the sun blazes, enticing me out each late afternoon to sit on the beach until dusk.

Eileen Chapman, who runs the Springsteen Collection as associate director of the Center for the Arts at Monmouth, drives me around one afternoon. She shows me the black neighborhood the residents burned down in the riots of 1967–68, watched by Springsteen from the roof of the Upstage. She tells me about all the jazz and blues clubs Gary Tallent would sneak into and how they closed down one by one. She rolls us past the Upstage, the Student Prince, where Springsteen met Clemons, and around the circuit. But as she talks I realize just how vast and empty are the gaps between buildings. The place has been all but bulldozed out of existence. It's not just that it's an empty beach town. It's that it's been emptied. What I'm actually looking at is a huge swath of space, much of it consisting of parking lots where bohemian life used to be. This explains an aspect of "Wrecking Ball." Maybe not much changes in America. I think of Joni Mitchell's "Big Yellow Taxi" and how they pave over paradise with parking lots. I never knew Asbury Park in the first place, and I doubt it was paradise, but you don't know what you've got until it's gone.

"So," I say, "you have to imagine the way it was."

"I don't," replies Eileen. "I see it. It's still here for me."

I've seen photographs of Stephen Zorochin's bust of Springsteen, complete with red bandana, and of the giant guitar on Belmont, but the only remnant I find near the boardwalk is a life-size poster of Bruce and band from the inside of the *Magic* album plastered onto the Ocean Avenue side of that nameless, windowless, virtually featureless building north of Convention Hall. Already, the band is fading into a past that no longer exists, and that's probably how it should be: new times, new bands. I find them on consecutive nights at the Wonder Bar. The second night it's Whiskey Shivers, a quintet from Austin, Texas. The banjo player, James Bookert, tells me he's "just started" on Springsteen and asks what he should listen to. I tell him to try everything, but he'll surely enjoy *We Shall Overcome: The Seeger Sessions* and *The Wild, the Innocent & the E Street Shuffle* before venturing toward the darkness on the edge of town and down to the river and so on.

O n my way out of Asbury Park I trace a loop beyond Monmouth University up to Rumson and Sea Bright, inland to Colts Neck, and then on to Freehold. To borrow the title of a novel by New Jersey writer Richard Ford, I'm seeking the lay of the land. But first I stop in West Long Branch to view the *Born to Run* house. If arriving in Asbury Park is disconcerting, that's nothing to encountering 7½ West End Court, where Springsteen wrote much of the album. In *Madame Bovary*, Flaubert talks of "the loftiness" of Emma's dreams and "the littleness of her house."[7] In her own way a romantic pragmatist, albeit a grossly misguided one, she works tirelessly to make her dreams reality. The novel is a tragicomedy never better summed up (unwittingly given the novel was as yet unwritten) by Flaubert's one-time lover, Louise Colet, in her comment that "love, like life, is a great comedy, unless you're playing one of the roles."[8] Springsteen's story, too, had he remained obscure, might have been tragicomic. Where the older Springsteen, in the 2016 *Vanity Fair* interview that preceded the launch of the autobiography, refers to his "Sisyphean" temperament, and attraction to repetitive activity, such as going to the gym and "lifting something heavy up and putting it down in the same spot for no particularly good reason," even the young Springsteen saw the comedy in the deadly seriousness with which he pursued his vision. "Someday we'll look back on this," he was able to write, "and it will all seem funny." I picture him gripped with an obsession to break through to a "promised land," to escape "a town full of losers," to "win," working his band to the bone in that squat beach house, so at odds with the grandiosity of the musical landscape with its giant Exxon sign, its highways and avenues, and the Big Man joining the band. "The Brain—is wider than the Sky—," writes Emily Dickinson in Poem 632. As I stand before this house, the roof of which looks touchable without stretching up, she reminds me that the mind is a universe. We can make of the world something dramatic however mundane our outward existence.[9]

Near the house I've waited at tracks for a freight train to cross the road. No wonder some of Springsteen's imagery involves trains whistling through sleepless nights. Maybe the sound of the freight train running through his head was literal. One song I can imagine being composed here is "Backstreets." This has indeed been a "soft infested summer," and today is a dog day, where high summer tilts into fall and the heat is like a precipice over which the season will plunge. While West End Court is a short, nondescript backstreet, wedged between Second and Ocean Avenue, beyond it lies the Atlantic like a blue ribbon, the very sea across which the pilgrims came to invent the America that Springsteen would claim his part in creating. The tiny house on a stub of a street is thus something of an illusion. The vision of immensity has its counterpart in the setting, with its beach house, and the possibility of feeling the summer weather could last forever.

The northern end of Ocean Avenue culminates in Sea Bright, a town along the narrow strip of land north of the university. This is where a local spied Springsteen pulling out of the beach parking lot in the days after 9/11 and called, "We need you, man."[10] I only see the beach, a few shops, and the parking lot (a theme of this trip), but it allows me to envision the moment. The strip of land lies between the sea on one side and Rumson and the Navesink River on the other. It further epitomizes the seaside culture to which Springsteen escaped from Freehold, and that gave him a community when his parents and youngest sister left for California. It's to that town that I now head, by way of Colts Neck and what may be Springsteen's horse farm along a road ending at fields and woodland. This I assume to be the meadowlands, where mosquitoes grow big as airplanes.

I arrive in Freehold that mellow evening knowing in advance that I might find nothing. It's quite a distance inland, and would have seemed even further in the 1960s, especially without a car. (Springsteen didn't learn to drive until into his twenties.) I park by 39½ Institute Street thinking that there must be something in this ½ and Springsteen's homes—as if his family were literally marginalized, fitted into spaces between more important ones. His second home where he lived from the age of five is a white clapboard house, with pale blue sides and blue shutters. Looming over the backyard is a water tower. I walk down Institute Street, turn right on South Street by the St. Rose of Lima School and up to 68 South Street where he lived as a teenager, prior to his ill-fated attempt to study at Ocean County Community College. Jon Stauff, vice-provost for global education at Monmouth, has told me that his father tried to teach Springsteen history, but this was merely a draft dodge. Springsteen had no interest. He dressed inappropriately (back then colleges had a dress code), carried his guitar around, unnerved other students, and eventually got kicked out. It was not, Jon told me, a good experience for teacher or student. In *Born to Run*, Springsteen explains that, even back then, they lived only "a block away from the Puerto Rican neighborhood" (BTR 30). "All you need do," he writes, is to walk down the main street of Freehold "on any summer evening to see the influx of Hispanic life" (BTR 402). On my way down South Street I pass Mi Casa, a shop proclaiming its dedication to *Productos Mexicanos y Musica Latina*. A Puerto Rican flag covers the inside of an upstairs window of the house next to 68 South Street. "There's just different people coming down here now," I can hear Springsteen tell his father, "and they see things in different ways." Yet it's striking how very Catholic this area remains. The Irish and Italians may have left, but other Catholics have taken their places.

Back down South Street and right on McLean, I'm in the vicinity in which five-year-old Virginia Springsteen, an aunt who never was, died beneath a truck on the corner by a Lewis Oil gas station while riding her tricycle one late afternoon in April 1927. Along on the left is the St. Rose of Lima Catholic Church at the start of Randolph Street. Beside it (of course) is a parking lot where 87 Randolph once stood, housing Springsteen and his parents and grandparents, with Virginia's faded photograph on the mantelpiece. Leaning against a tree I think of "Candy's Boy" on *The Promise*, a slow cut of what became "Candy's Room" on *Darkness on the Edge of Town*. In this version, Springsteen sings not, as in "Candy's Room," of "pictures of her heroes on the wall," but of "pictures of her savior on the wall." Candy thus becomes the equivalent of Raskolnikov's devout prostitute and confessor, Sonya Marmaladov. Again, Springsteen probably hadn't contemplated *Crime and Punishment* back then, but his subject matter was already converging with literary themes.

The church is redbrick, built in the 1920s. On the lawn is a white statue of the Virgin Mary with baby Jesus in her arms. Someone has stuck a red rose in the crook of her elbow. I envisage Springsteen driving past the parking lot, recalling what once stood here, and reflect on how very personal "Wrecking Ball" must be, both in terms of Asbury Park and this early home. "Yeah, we know that come tomorrow, none of this will be here," Springsteen tells me as we walk down the street. "Now, when all this steel and these stories, they drift away to rust / And all our youth and beauty, it's been given to the dust. . . ." This happens in Europe, too. I once found the house where Sylvia Plath and Ted Hughes vacationed in the then-fishing village of Benidorm. Surrounded now by skyscraper hotels in that holding pen of English migrants and partygoers, the cottage no longer gets much sun. In America, though, these drastic changes are perennial. William Styron writes, in *Set This House on Fire,* of a character revisiting Newport News in the Virginia Tidewater—coincidentally just across Hampton Roads Bay from Clarence Clemons's hometown of Norfolk. Recalling how he'd "known its gentle seaside charm," and shaken loose for himself its "own peculiar romance," he finds on his return that the magnolias have "been hacked down to make room for a highway along the shore," and "a Yankee-built vehicular tunnel" now pokes its "snout two miles beneath the mud at Hampton Roads." Seeking a recognizable scene, he stops at a garage and realizes that, right there, "several fathoms beneath the foundations of this Esso Servicenter," he'd once hunted for crawfish and "had almost drowned." All has been obliterated. His "great-grandchildren's cleverest archaeology" would "strive in vain to unlock that sun-swept marsh, that stream, those crawfish." This observation of destruction and construction, and of a landscape altered forever, stands as well for Bruce Land, even though, at other times, in unexpected ways, tantalizing glimpses of that past and links with that music still emerge.[11] By the time I'm loitering on Randolph it's between 5 and 6 p.m., the sun still warm through the trees. The church's electronic organ begins to grind out tunes I can almost place. Stroked by sun and shadow, I walk in tune, accompanied by the occasional percussive knock of a dead leaf on the hood of a car. Further from the church I fancy it might be "Hungry Heart."

I know what I'm doing during this foray into Freehold is not unlike what Springsteen did: going back to look at places where life was once lived. He'd drift past his family home, seeking out the root of his troubled relationship with his father, Douglas, later to be told by a psychiatrist that he was trying to right something that went wrong and that he would never be able to.[12] As men of that era point out, Springsteen is singing of the particular difficulties the Vietnam War years threw up between generations, and how fathers and sons were sometimes never reconciled. The crew-cut World War II veterans and the longhaired musicians could never understand one another. They held antithetical worldviews. The sons were demonstrable, the fathers not, even though they felt what they couldn't show. Of course, in my case, I'm not going back to my family home but to someone else's, as I've done before with other writers. I'm revisiting a past I could never adequately imagine, let alone know. So far as my own life is concerned I'm revisiting, to use a Springsteen title, "a time that never was." Empty spaces, shadows—that's the lonesome. Doing something practical—getting some work done, such as writing a book—that's pragmatism. Dusk gathers. I find the site where the Karagheusian Rug Mill once stood. I don't check out St. Rose of Lima Cemetery. I've had enough of hunting invisible game. It's dark by the time I return to the shore.

S o ends my brief time looking in on Asbury Park. I drive back to Newark International Airport, take the train over the Jersey swamps into Manhattan and, with a day or so before my flight home, revisit some of the places that have been part of my past experience of New York. These include the site of the World Trade Center, McSorley's Irish Ale House on East Seventh Street in the East Village, B. B. King's Bar and Grill on Forty-Second Street, and the Metropolitan Museum of Art on Fifth Avenue. Last time I was at the site of the twin towers it was Ground Zero. In 2002, there were still snapshots of victims on the railings of St. Paul's Chapel of Trinity Church on Wall Street. I recall, in 2010, the area swarming with protestors and police due to tensions related to a proposal for a new mosque nearby. Now, thanks to Daniel Libeskind's vision, the place is barely recognizable. "Architecture is communication," he suggests, "poetry in stone and in light and in gravity." The big hole in the ground, which became a building site, holds a vast, underground shopping mall with a white-ribbed roof resembling the remnants of the fallen towers. The sites of the towers are now Michael Arad's memorial, "Reflecting Absence." Created in collaboration with landscape architect Peter Walker, the area is a plaza of pine trees with an oblong cavity marking the parameters of each tower. The victims' names are carved around each rim, and water cascades down to a central sluice. Beside them is the 1,776-foot Liberty Tower, gleaming in sunshine or disappearing into mist.[13] The rising has happened. But beneath it, via a walkway through the subterranean granite that allowed Manhattan to materialize, is the cavernous Memorial Museum with its tribute to those who died and those who served in the rescue operations. Here I find another Puerto Rican flag—recalling the one in the window on South Street—this time in a glass case. It belonged to Sergeant First Class Jose O. Calderon-Olmedo of the U.S. Army. "Stationed around the world, including tours in Germany, South Korea, and in the Persian Gulf during Operation Desert Storm in 1991," the accompanying information explains, he died working at the Pentagon.

After this sobering visit, over McSorley's dark ale I sit in the almost empty spit-and-sawdust bar, contemplating the years I've been returning to New York, sometimes to visit friends, often to roam alone. I ask the barman how long he's worked there. Forever, he replies. How long's forever? Twelve years, he explains. I don't tell him I've been visiting McSorley's for over three decades, just that I was last there six years ago. He asks what took me so long. That night, I seek out the colorful cacophony of Times Square, then descend to B. B. King's, listen, over Samuel Adams draft, to Springsteen contemporary and blues musician Jon Paris, accompanied by Amy Madden on bass, and contemplate how Springsteen found his way through music, through making his guitar talk, to getting the world to hear him. Amy was playing at B. B. King's when I first ventured down there on that same trip six years previously. I chatted with the barmaid, a drama student married to a 9/11 fireman. As things got busier, she refused payment for my beers. The money wasn't the point; what mattered was the human touch in the heart of Manhattan. That's why I go back.

On the final day I'm at the Metropolitan, seeking as usual the silent wisdom of Rembrandt, gazing out in his sixties from his 1660 portrait in Gallery 634. Rembrandt's self-portraits may seem the very antithesis of rock. On one hand, the portrait hangs mute through the centuries, silent, unaware, inanimate, even though to look into those barely glimmering eyes makes it hard to accept that this isn't Rembrandt looking back at us. Rock, on the other hand, is ostensibly all present, all sound. Yet there's a link. On the train in from New Jersey I asked an old man with a knee brace—a Swede from Seattle, as it turned out—how he'd done the damage. "By living," he replied. Rembrandt's self-portraits are an uncompromising record of the toll of time. Witness a succession of such portraits and, with his merciless depiction of ripening features and the scars of experience, you see him age before your eyes. When I look at the 1660 portrait I recall a dream of walking the corridor to my parents' room one childhood night. They stood smiling in the doorway, but as I drew nearer the wallpaper began to peel, they began to age, and when I reached them, standing in the rotted doorframe, they crumbled to dust. Springsteen's body of work, however different, is equally about "the pain that living brings." His weary look on the cover of *Magic* speaks of the passing years. The artist and his assistants look out at us and say, we're getting old. Witness the aging process. Witness our mortality, mirroring your own. It's also true that just as this portrait I'm viewing is not Rembrandt, so the voice and sound and songs we hear, on record, are not Springsteen. Rembrandt made every brush stroke of the portrait, and Springsteen was involved in making the sounds on every song, but neither artist remains present in the artwork. It's not, therefore, all now, now, now in rock or in Rembrandt, but we're fascinated that the work came into being, that it records human activity, and that the moment of creation has vanished while the result will remain part of a present beyond our own time. Art, when seen or heard, becomes the property of the recipient.

Sitting on a bench in the Metropolitan, Rembrandt and I watch each other. I imagine approval in his expression, just as I look at Springsteen live, or hear his music, and think he somehow knows or acknowledges me. This is a powerful and enabling illusion fostered for decades. "The final belief," writes Wallace Stevens, "is to believe in a fiction, which you know to be a fiction, there being nothing else."[14] The brain cannot see. The eye and ear translate data into what's familiar from past experience. The past doesn't exist, and nor does the future, but we believe in all three things willingly, there being no sustainable alternative to doing so. What, I wonder to myself, is the connection between my attachment to Rembrandt and my attachment to Springsteen? What part of me responds to the silent image of the aging Dutch artist, in his dignified silence on the wall of Gallery 634, and the words and music of this American musician? I am the common factor. The art is the conduit. What matters is my relationship not with the unknowable artist but with the art.

Time to catch a plane. Walking down the Museum Mile stretch of Fifth Avenue from the Metropolitan, someone passes wearing a baseball camp stamped with the phrase, "New Era." I think of the Santa Fe wrap I had for breakfast, the burger and fries I had for lunch, the sushi I might have for dinner. I think of the pipe bombs in Manhattan and on the Jersey Shore that have caused consternation these past days. New York, like America, is a mélange of people from the world over. We're always trying to make sense of it, and of the world. A great artist makes you see aspects of it as they see it. Riding the 6 Train Uptown, everyone resembles a Rembrandt painting, with a Rembrandt mouth and eyes and skin. Then, around Fifty-Seventh Street, opposite me sits down Springsteen's very own Puerto Rican Jane, with a toddler on her knee. Her hair is dyed blond, and she has a bandage on her left wrist. Soon after that, as I switch to the Airtrain at Jamaica, I see that in writing about Springsteen I must include the lonesome and the communal, the images and the sounds, and notions of high culture and popular culture. Only by doing this can I describe his significance as an American artist of global renown. The way artists affect our perception of the places we visit, the people we see, the experiences we have, and the lives we lead is a very democratic process; I really mustn't care, I realize, about perceived hierarchies. I mustn't hold back from approaching the subject as I need to, from offering my vision, and from yoking together disparate ideas that might at first seem worlds apart. Being an outsider looking in is, I realize, precisely my qualification and reason for writing. To echo Sinatra, I must do it my way. Galvanized, encouraged, with a reason to believe, I fly home and write the book.

AMERICAN LONESOME

Quid terras alio calentes sole mutamus? Patriae quis exsul se quoque fugit?
Why do we seek climates warmed by another sun? Who is the man
that by fleeing from his country, can also flee from himself?
—HORACE, *Odes*, II, 16, 18

Someday girl, I don't know when, we're gonna get to that place
Where we really want to go
And we'll walk in the sun.
—"BORN TO RUN"

INTRODUCTION
Rock and Rembrandt

We should apologize when we talk about painting," wrote Paul Valery in an essay on the work of nineteenth-century French painter Jean-Baptiste Corot.[1] The same might be said of music. Bruce Springsteen early in his career implies as much. "People don't want to see things in black and white," he told Robert Hilburn in 1974. "Songs have to have possibilities." Like the writer, the recipient should "search out the songs." Discussion may be beside the point. Interviews "are like questions and answers when there is no answer, so why is there a question?"[2] Less talk, more listening. Yet more than for any other contemporary songwriter, talk of Springsteen has been voluminous. As Baillie Walsh's movie *Springsteen & I* shows, all kinds of people from all walks of life want to talk about Bruce. He's been the subject of numerous books and essays. No one apologizes. We're all participants in the drama, enjoying the performance and sharing our version of the experience. Most striking in the written work, as in Walsh's film, is the variety of expertise and responses. Springsteen is scrutinized across disciplines and cultural boundaries. The largest category is biography, critical or otherwise, from inside accounts provided by the likes of Dave Marsh, Robert Santelli, and Peter Ames Carlin, as well as the sketches in Clarence Clemons's tangentially informative *Big Man: Real Life and Tales* (cowritten with Don Reo, 2009), to outside investigations, offering very different versions of Springsteen

1

from one another and from those with direct access to what a friend of mine refers to as "the Deep Bruce Camp." Commentators like Christopher Sandford, Marc Dolan, and Clinton Heylin offer more than enough insight for those interested in versions of the man behind the work.

Beyond the biographies, the contributions are even more diverse. Historian and literature professor Jim Cullen's *Born in the U.S.A.* (revised 2005) explores the music in terms of American myths and symbols. Cultural historian and musicologist Daniel Cavicchi's *Tramps Like Us* (1998) and Pulitzer Prize–winning psychiatrist Robert Coles's *Bruce Springsteen's America* (2003), not unlike Walsh's film, adapt the interview method of Theodore Zeldin to suit differing purposes.[3] Cavicchi and Walsh focus on Springsteen's devotees whereas Coles documents his impact on a range of casual listeners. Other single-author books include journalist Eric Alterman's *It Ain't No Sin to be Glad You're Alive* (1999); music feature writer Geoffrey Himes's *Born in the U.S.A.* (2005), publisher Rob Kirkpatrick's *Magic in the Night* (2007); Unitarian minister Jeffrey Symynkywicz's *The Gospel According to Bruce Springsteen* (2008), historian Louis P. Masur's *Runaway Dream* (2009), and political columnist David Masciotra's *Working on a Dream* (2010). There are also fan memoirs, such as Jimmy Guterman's *Runaway American Dream* (2005), Robert Wiersema's *Walk Like a Man* (2011), and Caryn Rose's *Raise Your Hand* (2012). Variety is just as evident in essays, including those in volumes edited by Randall Auxier and Doug Anderson (2008); Roxanne Harde and Irwin Streight (2010); David Garrett Izzo (2011); and Kenneth Womack, Jerry Zolten, and Mark Bernhard (2012), and a volume of essays by attorneys in the *Widener Law Journal*. The same can be said of numerous stand-alone essays, web-based material, and chapters in books, from Martha Nell Smith on Springsteen's "sexual mobilities" to business professor Stewart Friedman's discussion of his leadership qualities as "the executive of a high-performing organization." Somewhere you can probably find Springsteen commentary by someone in most mainstream walks of life, and a version of Springsteen that designates him as possessing all manner of dispositions. As Joyce Carol Oates once said of her commentators, so could Springsteen: "All kinds—*all* kinds!—have written about my work." Matthew Continetti refers to "millions of Springsteens." "We narrate whenever we see," writes Portuguese poet Fernando Pessoa, "because seeing is complex like everything."[4]

Both Paul Valéry, as critic, and Springsteen, as songwriter, have more to say on writing about genres the primary appeal of which is something other than words. In terms of thinking about art, words can enhance what we perceive but are a poor adjunct when the art involves sound or vision. Like explaining a joke, the point can be lost; indeed, the point may be *not* to explain. "Maybe it's better *not* knowing," writes Springsteen, for artist as well as recipient.[5] Nevertheless, we love discussion. To quote that first line of Valery's essay on Corot perhaps misrepresented his sentiments. "On doit toujours s'excuser de parler peinture," he writes. "Mais il y a de grandes raisons de ne pas s'en taire. Tous les arts vivent de paroles." "One should apologize when we talk about painting. But there are big reasons why we should not stop. All the arts live through words." Despite his career-long skepticism of discussion of the art, Springsteen has joined the debate far more than most musicians. His views on a life shaped by music amount to a body of work in itself, culminating in the 512 pages of *Born to Run*. No doubt "music is primarily an emotional language," but then so is our articulation of living. Discussion is a natural response. We shouldn't be too earnest about this, even while we're also dealing with "what it means to be alive."[6] I'm always struck by how much Springsteen laughs in interview, especially in later years, sometimes at questions but more often at himself. As he advises young musicians in his 2012 keynote speech to the South by Southwest Music Festival in Austin, Texas, "Don't take yourself too seriously, and take yourself as seriously as death itself."[7] We read and listen to be both informed and entertained. Springsteen is not just a musician but also a storyteller and commentator on his culture and times. The Springsteen industry—the writing about the art—is part of that, and he has his say, as one more albeit "privileged" commentator.

He's also used his lyrics for this purpose, from "Growin' Up" to "Wrecking Ball." One song in particular, "TV Movie," is a wry comment on discussion of any artist's work—musician, novelist, painter, or circus performer. As is often noted of Springsteen, the upbeat sound cloaks downbeat lyrics: "I woke up last night shaking from a dream / For in that dream I died / My wife rolled over and told me / That my life would be immortalized / Not in some major motion picture / Or great American novel, you see / No, they're gonna make a TV movie out of me."[8] This is a good example of his willingness to deflate any sense that his work amounts to serious artistic achievement beyond its existence as popular music.[9] The joke of "TV Movie" is that falling into obscurity might not be the worst of fates. Attempting to reassure her husband that he'll be remembered, the wife stumbles into reminding him of the low level of his art. He's devoted his life to something that, if it brings any form of immortality, will do so at best in the star biography, remaindered after Christmas; in the "black velvet painting" that in

"Local Hero" he sees in the window of a "five and dime"; on tour T-shirts gathering dust in a middle-aged fan's attic, or in a TV biopic. For on one level what more does the career of a recording artist amount to? While Bob Dylan's receipt of the Nobel Prize for Literature suggests that times have changed, the melancholy truth might still be—as in any of the arts, with a few individual exceptions—that you devote your energies to something relatively insignificant. For all the exposure, adulation, and money—for all "the ramblings of fanhood" and multitude of books and essays by devotees linking you with such luminaries as Ralph Waldo Emerson, Walt Whitman, Flannery O'Connor, and Madonna Ciccone—all you've been is a passing minstrel, your pitifully popular output unworthy of intellectual attention.[10] Springsteen recounts in his Austin speech how he always told his children "that they were lucky to be born in the age of reproducible technology, otherwise they'd be traveling in the back of a wagon" and he'd "be wearing a jester's hat" (SOS 388). This contains truth, even if Keith Richards's view that "if there were anything better around he'd still be working the bars of New Jersey" says more about Richards than it does about Springsteen.[11] His light has shone in a specific era that's enabled his reproduced presence to grow exponentially. Opportunities accelerate daily to hear the music, watch footage, see photos, and hear and read about it in all kinds of forms. It's not least the stuff of a TV movie because we know how bad a biopic would be. If actors might be found to play Clarence Clemons, Steve Van Zandt, Danny Federici, Roy Bittan, Nils Lofgren, Patti Scialfa, and others, to play Springsteen would be almost impossible. But given time, and the loss of memory or first-hand experience, it will happen, just as it has for everyone from Moses through Ann Boleyn to the Beatles.

The persona of "TV Movie" is insouciant about his fate. They can switch his name, story, or ethnicity. They can make him do things he would never do, give his life a new ending, put him on prime time. "When it's over, what I did there will be what I done." His official story, distorted by narrative, mangled further when scripted for visual translation and acted out, will become the model that replaces the fact. "All that stuff on TV," says Lonnie, a friend of protagonist Samantha Hughes in Bobbie Ann Mason's novel *In Country* (1985), in which *Born in the U.S.A.* features strongly, "it's just fantasy. It's not real." But, as Springsteen points out, the imagined version takes on its own reality. "Ars longa, vita brevis," as Hippocrates' aphorism goes, "art is long, life is short." In *Born to Run*, Springsteen asserts that, "as real as the emotions called upon are," his art in performance is "theater" rather than "reality," and that "at the end of the day, life trumps art."

For Springsteen this is "always" the case (BTR 173). His point here has to do with the fact that he's implicitly advising young artists not to neglect their actual lives for their art and so lose out, as he feels he has done at times—only belatedly coming "to understand that music, a song, will always be there," whereas "your children are here and gone" (BTR 392).[12] Nevertheless, art, in its many forms, does triumph. *Born to Run*, the book, is a case in point. However candid the writer attempts to be, all autobiography contains multiple and unavoidable elisions and ambiguities. Given, too, that Springsteen is a professional storyteller, manufactured realities reflect manufactured realities in a surreal *mise en abyme*.[13] He states it in the first two sentences: "I come from a boardwalk town where almost everything is tinged with a bit of fraud. So am I." He's a long-standing member of the group of artists who "lie" to approach "truth," which is to say, all of us (BTR xi). Knowing this in "TV Movie," too, and appreciating the comedy involved, the speaker lightens up. Insouciance turns to validation. Maybe it's not such a bad fate after all. Why have your name "in a history book / Nobody's ever gonna see"? Someone will make a deal because he was "one of them kinds of stories / That everybody liked to see." Bring it on. Over a gravestone inscription or a soliloquy, he'll settle for a prime-time mini-drama. The coda to this may be "57 Channels and Nothin' On." If you can't find the remote to press Off, but have a gun and can afford to destroy your own property, you can always blast the screen.

Suitably, "TV Movie" was originally discarded as flotsam, only surfacing on *Tracks* (1998), the four-CD set of "outtakes" from across the years (BTR 277). Springsteen recorded it in 1983, just before *Born in the U.S.A.* transformed his image from cult hero to cartoon icon.[14] Humor and irony aside, it's the equivalent of the black-velvet painting or the TV movie itself. Maybe you caught it in the background. Maybe you didn't. But it speaks to Springsteen's position when it comes to commentary on his work. A man who could once upon a time write about history books nobody will read, or state, in "No Surrender," that he "learned more from a three-minute record" than he "ever learned in school," would seem to have at best as skeptical a view of the value of close study of material designed for live or recorded performance as he does of interviews. But, again, along with volumes of interviews, we have *Songs* (2003) and the revelations of *Born to Run*. For recipient as for artist, to analyze can be to enrich and expand, enabling us to reexperience the material in new ways.

* * *

So much for the context of this book, now to its genesis: if my approach revealed its form on that belated visit to the Jersey Shore, its seeds were sown in the whirlwind of youth, when all that mattered was to escape restriction and shape a life. If you're young, ambitious, and in some way hemmed in, by a parent, an environment, a country, your own apparent limitations or others' limited expectations of you, you get out. Music, and not least Springsteen's, is a well-known channel for that. In my case, despite being a high-school drop out, leaving at seventeen with poor grades, it led to a life teaching literature. I came to books not as a leisure pursuit but as a lifeline. They felt like a pull to safety. This book, in turn, will be unashamedly literary, as well as drawing on aspects of culture not routinely coupled with rock music. It simply reflects the way I think. Perhaps it's because I first listened to *Born to Run* as a teenager while reading Stendhal's seminal 1830 novel of youthful energy, *The Red and the Black*, that I associate the two. Both works are about that search for direction and self-realization. Stendhal's bullied, intelligent, sensitive, egotistical Julien Sorel finds employment with Monsieur de Rênal, seduces Madame de Rênal, flees Verrières for Besançon, flees Besançon for Paris, seduces a Marquis's daughter, and finds his place in the sun. Such things, attained, are not what he expects. Faced with fulfillment, he goes back and shoots Madame de Rênal. While the wound is not fatal, his refusal to express remorse leads to his execution. "I'm not a monster," he insists. "I'm the only one who knows what I might have done." Isolated in his cell, he asserts that he "didn't *live in isolation* on earth," and "had a strong sense of *duty*."[15] This is all very Springsteen-like to me, but although my comparison derives from a personal history of discovering literature and music at the same time, maybe it's not that strange to link Springsteen with Stendhal. One biographer tells us that Springsteen's manager, Jon Landau, pointed him toward not just John Steinbeck, Richard Ford, and others but gave him a copy of *Hamlet*. In the decades since, Springsteen has become an omnivorous reader, from Montaigne to Dostoevsky and Tolstoy, history to cosmology, classic to contemporary: he "does keep up." Out of the streets of fire he caught what Stendhal calls "the sacred fire," Cormac McCarthy simply "the fire"; and the New Jerseyan philosopher Richard Rorty, the "ever-building, ever-expanding fire" of the imagination: the desire to learn, to understand, to know. Stewart Friedman is spot on when he writes that "Springsteen is a teacher," and this is because, "personally and professionally," he thirsts "for useful knowledge" and has a desire "to change the world—to create something new that makes things better—and to change himself."[16] You start with what you feel within. You discover the contexts of how you came to feel that way. The young Springsteen wasn't so much born as made to run—made in both senses of the word: pressured into but also genetically able to do so. Circumstance and character produced this need: whatever "run" might mean, whether to race in the street, or find music and form a band.

This idea of the lonely journey touches on one part of what this book is about, Springsteen as an example of what Kevin Lewis calls "the American 'lonesome.'"[17] This idea, along with the linking of music and literature, has a personal side that requires a brief explanation. I spent segments of my youth traveling the country. On and off between eighteen and twenty-five I crisscrossed America into a cat's cradle. While seduced at times into imagining that I might make the country my home, I was always, as Springsteen has said of his own youth, "on the outside looking in." Like many young people, I felt that way in general. "I'm one of those," Springsteen has said, "who likes to retreat into the shadows." For many of his characters, it's terrifying to disappear, to be invisible, but the opposites are also true; it's stultifying to be too visible and deeply appealing to be, as Tom Buchanan disparages Jay Gatsby, "Mr. Nobody from Nowhere." "I'm Nobody!" writes Emily Dickinson in Poem 288. "Who are You? / Are you—Nobody—too? Then there's a pair of us! Don't tell! They'd banish us—you know."[18] My invisibility in America suited me. The journey involved interspersed time between leaving art school, an unglamorous spell as a registered "film artiste" (extra) that lasted long enough for me to barely feature in one of "the most expensive flops in cinema history" (*Heaven's Gate*), and university in England and the States.[19] I hitchhiked and rode trains, but my main mode of travel was the bus, from Greyhound and Trailways to regional lines like Bonanza in New England and Rabbit Lines in the Dakotas. Although my road trip continues, the first leg of this odyssey symbolically ended long ago and far away, at 3:00 a.m. on 11 August 1985 at the Trailways depot in Fort Smith, Arkansas. All of twenty-four, the age at which Springsteen produced his first album, I sent a postcard to my family ("Greetings from Fort Smith, AR") to commemorate reaching my forty-eighth conterminous state, and saying I'd be spending more time at home from now on. I was too young to realize that that "home," like the home we all grow up in, would soon dissolve. As for Hawaii and Alaska—my original aim, because they sounded sufficiently distant, like Outer Mongolia, the Moon, or Planet Nine—decades later I've yet to visit them and maybe never will. But some kind of journey felt complete.

Music accompanied me through almost all of those hours of watching America, but not Springsteen especially. The cassettes on my Walkman were eclectic, often recommended by others. Maggie from Omaha gave me Neil Young's version of "Four Strong Winds" ("Look for me if you're ever back this way," she said), so I traveled on from the prairies over the Rockies and westward with that and "Heart of Gold" and "Hey Hey, My My" and "Everybody Knows This Is Nowhere." At a stag party in the hills above Portland, Oregon, the groom played Willie Nelson on a loop, ingraining in me such songs as "Blue Eyes Crying in the Rain" and "On the Road Again." About as far southeast from Oregon as you can get, Danny in Jacksonville played me the Allman Brothers, as well as Lynyrd Skynyrd, who'd attended his high school, naming the band after their phys-ed teacher, Leonard Skinner.[20] Unlike the Allmans' "Ramblin' Man," I wasn't "born in the back of a Greyhound bus / Rollin' down Highway 41," but I took that Greyhound south. "Free Bird," "Tuesday's Gone," and "Simple Man" accompanied me to the Everglades. Heading back up through the country, the shadow of Aretha Franklin sat by me one rainy night in Georgia. A stranger in a bar in Traverse City, Michigan, punched into the jukebox Bob Seger's "Night Moves," "Main Street," and "Against the Wind."

One addition to my collection, however, turned out to be anachronous. Boarding a Maple Leaf Greyhound after a summer working in a Vancouver bookstore, I found a discarded cassette of Supertramp's *Crime of the Century*. It provided a soundtrack through Washington, Idaho, Montana, North Dakota, Minnesota, Wisconsin, Illinois, Indiana, Ohio, Pennsylvania, and New Jersey to the Port Authority in New York, and then (since I had a Greyhound Pass) in my "hotel room"— the midnight bus to D.C., hour stopover and dawn ride back to Forty-Third Street to roam Manhattan before flying home from Newark on the short-lived budget airline PEOPLExpress. It was all I had so I played it night and day across thousands of miles. No song intermingled more with my dreams than "Rudy," on his "train to nowhere, halfway down the line." He'd never get there, but he felt fine. Harry Chapin had told me, in "Greyhound," "it's got to be the going not the getting there that's good." Supertramp told me that I was not the only one traveling alone. "Where you goin'?" an old black man asked one year in the depot in Albuquerque. "I'm trying to get home," I replied. "We *all* tryin' to do that!" he chuckled. But years later I discovered that I'd misheard "Rudy." In the background a station announcer lists place names, including Reading, Didcot, and Chippenham. The sounds are of London's Paddington Station. The track Rudy is on is not some desolate railroad through prairies and badlands, as I imagined, but the Great Western Railway through my hometown in Wiltshire. Moreover, heading out of Chippenham to Bath and Bristol it crosses a bridge over the A4. If you ever take this ride, look through the window on your left and you'll see a road named Rowden Hill. In a lay-by, a hundred yards from the bridge, stands a memorial the size of a small amplifier with a black metal plate attached. Inscribed in white around a depiction of a red Gretsch guitar, is the statement: *1938–1960 Eddie Cochran—Cherished Memories.* This marks where a car wreck fatally injured the young, Minnesota-born, Californian performer and cowriter of "Somethin' Else," "Three Steps to Heaven," and "Summertime Blues." Cochran died in Bath the next day, Easter Sunday, 17 April 1960, less than a year before I was born.

By chance, the countryside where I grew up, on the borders of Surrey and Sussex, had two signs of what Springsteen refers to as "The British House of the Second Coming." Besotted with America, it never occurred to me that when Springsteen first flew over, he'd be thinking: "The Beatles, the Stones, the Animals, the Yardbirds, the Kinks, Jeff Beck, Clapton, Hendrix, the Who—we were heading for the isle of our heroes" (BTR 226). But the fact is that as an adolescent I occasionally saw Eric Clapton's red Ferrari zip along the sun-dappled roads between his home in Ewhurst and ours in Okewood Hill, and less than a mile away, at a crossroads for Ewhurst, Cranleigh, and Horsham, stood not Robert Johnson's devil but British actor Oliver Reed's house, in the driveway of which squatted a full-size model of a rhinoceros given him by the Who drummer and fellow self-destructive hell-raiser, Keith Moon. But my mind was elsewhere, and, for me, the music that mattered, along with literature, cinema, and art in general, only existed in far-off lands, and most romantically in America. I was doubly wrong. It wasn't just that signs of "The British House of the Second Coming" were in my neighborhood, but that I would end up living in a town where art and everyday life intersect.

This is a reminder, too, that despite his global appeal Springsteen is very much a local writer. For all John Lombardi's claims that his success up into the 1980s owed much to the fact that his "images were utterly familiar"—generic because, like his listeners, "he lived vicariously"—they have also often been very specific to northern New Jersey. "A regionalist in the best and broadest sense of the word," as June Skinner Sawyers puts it, he not only, in his words, used his "own localism" to make his locality our locality, and vice-versa, but employed it as a source of dynamism in his work: "as a strength and as something to get away from."[21] He's spoken of the radio feeling like "a magical device," providing a gateway to other worlds.[22] Had that late song "Hunter of Invisible Game" existed during my days of seeking, it would have resonated. At the end of the recording the sound takes on a tinny quality. Springsteen foregrounds the artifice. But the immediate moment of recording ripples outward and invites response. (As the lines go in "Bobby Jean," "in some motel room you'll hear a radio playing and you'll hear me sing this song.") In an early interview Springsteen jokes that if you were to open up the back of the radio you'd find the band in there.[23] The point is that music, most of which we listen to away from the actual performers in time and space, is present in our lives. "It avails not, time nor place—distance avails not," wrote Whitman.[24] "Music on the radio is a shared fever dream," writes Springsteen, "a collective hallucination, a secret among millions and a whisper in the whole country's ear," and it's true that it "kept me alive and breathing throughout my teens" just as it did him (BTR 183–84). It's simply that I used to assume that the singer of "Summertime Blues," of all singers and all songs this one in particular, lived an era ago and a world away. Yet Cochran's voice is part of the present and the written or sung word is here right now, to be made use of. Rudy may be on a train to your town. Springsteen's music belongs to us as much as to him. I learned more on the road than I ever learned in school, and university only supplemented that education. In maturity, however, I discovered that I'd merely been growing out of adolescence into adulthood, seeking to escape and to define myself in relation to others. Springsteen became part of that when, at a Poconos summer camp in 1980, a counselor from New Jersey, David "Dogie" Gelman, gave me *Greetings*. I associate that early listening not with the United States but with "the dirty streets where I was born," and rainy drives to night school with *Born to Run* or *Darkness on the Edge of Town* in a tape deck on my dashboard. The tapes of those two albums wound tighter until *Darkness*, in the middle of "Adam Raised a Cain," snapped.

If the lonely journey relates to one aspect of the book, another aspect is the communal. The book's genesis, like Springsteen's art, involves both. Indeed, for psychiatrist Anthony Storr, these are the "two opposing forces" operating "throughout life." On one hand we're driven "toward being independent, separate, and autonomous." On the other hand, we experience a "drive for companionship."[25] For Springsteen, one expression of this division is writing versus performing. As he explained in 1984, they're "two different jobs entirely, with very little to do with each other, which is why you have people who make really good records and don't perform well, and people who perform well and don't make good records." To cut a record is a "reflective" process, whereas to perform "is a very physical experience, very tied to the moment" (TAD 139). His songs reveal both impulses. For every public-focused song, let's say "Rosalita" or "Mary's

Place," there is a reflective song, such as "Breakaway" or "The Wrestler," along with plenty of hybrids. To focus on writing over performance or vice-versa would warp the picture. Nevertheless, the fact that many have written on Springsteen, however fired by witnessing his work as a performer, is absolutely down to his reflective work of creating songs and records. Without that, there'd only be biographies and less of them, and no contemplative, self-written autobiography.

Perhaps the latter is enough to ensure his position as a figure in American literature—certainly it places him in the autobiographical tradition. But he was in the mix anyway on the basis of his songs. In American culture, and now perhaps beyond, if Dylan's Nobel Prize is anything to go by, it's a given that great art can spring from a popular source. Just as American society was founded (founder though these ideals do under some administrations and in some regions more than others) on the notion of welcoming the stranger, so too a distrust of hierarchies as "invidious"—the view in particular of educationalist John Dewey—is not only part of the democratic impulse but also part of the American ethos that, regardless of where you begin, you can create a meaningful life in your own ways and on your own terms.[26] Novelist John Gardner once wrote, "most great American art is an elevation of trash." Out of the apparently unremarkable can come something deep and original. To use Gardner's examples, "New Orleans tailgate funeral jazz," while it might have been mostly "mediocre," ultimately produced the "art of Ellington, Gershwin and the rest."[27] Springsteen's art exemplifies this transition. Through aside or performance he publicizes songs that would otherwise be lost among the driftwood of the rock-and-roll seashore. "All the music I loved as a child," he told Mark Hagen in 2009, "people thought it was junk." But he saw something that the older generation missed. "People were unaware of the subtext in so many of those records," he said, "but if you were a kid you were just completely tuned in, even though you didn't always say—you wouldn't dare say it was beautiful." The older Springsteen stands by that judgment. "Why are they beautiful? Well, they're beautifully sung, beautifully played, and the mathematics in them is elegant" (TAD 361). Hence he takes these musical traditions and produces something, as Richard Ford puts it, "of a different order."[28]

Springsteen's career, therefore, has been all about bringing to an art centered on community, connection, and participation a depth of reflection and craft hitherto unusual in a popular art form. His work's mass appeal, live and in recordings, across the world and in numbers that dwarf the appreciators of so-called high art, might seem distasteful to the guardians of hierarchy. But for the rest of us it simply relates to his artistic significance. To discuss his work, therefore, in the context of such art or thought—by which I mean classic American and European literature and philosophy but also other responses to life, including music, painting, or film—feels entirely appropriate. When I do this, it's not because I laughably think he's the Rembrandt of Rock or the Emerson of Entertainment (or "the Bard of Asbury Park," as Roxanne Harde and Irwin Streight lightheartedly describe him in introducing *Reading the Boss,* a comparison that a reviewer calls "hyperbolic, hagiographic, hilarious," though I found it interesting) but simply because I'm moved by Rembrandt's work and by Springsteen's. I grew into adulthood as attached to one as the other, unaffected by views that art contains stratifications. Ludicrously ignorant or deluded as connoisseurs or the self-appointed intelligentsia might designate such comparisons, the two kinds of emotional and intellectual response are not poles apart.[29] Both are examples of work by human beings who communicate with us about our mutual experience. True as it may be that, as he admits, "a lot of what the E Street Band do is hand-me-down schtick," albeit "transformed by will, power and an intense communication" with the audience "into something transcendent," he has also made great art out of popular music in that many obviously see life differently as a result (BTR 453). To transform an audience's understanding of an art form's possibilities is something individuals have done across centuries—and from Dickinson to Miles Davis to Dylan it's also typically American.

H aving, I trust, established the context and genesis of the book, here's a word about its shape. I've called it *American Lonesome: The Work of Bruce Springsteen.* The main title relates to this sense of isolation that is often the catalyst for creativity. The subtitle came later on. Originally I had in mind the phrase "passionate pragmatism." But "work" is a better summation. What interests me, beyond the sense of isolation any of us can feel, is the communal process that all art is ultimately aimed at, and that we turn to art to seek out, whether it's audio, visual, sensual, written, or a combination of these, and I include here the art of criticism. In his comments at a rally for presidential candidate John Kerry in 2004, Springsteen quoted Paul Wellstone, one-time Minnesota senator, saying, in Springsteen's words, "the future is for the passionate, and those that are willing to fight and to work hard for it."[30] I had the "passionate pragmatist" phrase in mind beforehand, but it was hardly a surprise to find Springsteen referring to passion, and of course, Wellstone enmeshes it with labor. This relationship between work and drive, especially the drive to connect, feels akin to his immersion in the crowd—still body surfing the mosh pit when I saw him in Paris in 2016, and no doubt since. The emphasis on a committed social work ethic echoes his role as a writer whose worldview relates to classical pragmatist ideas carried forward in Richard Rorty's neo-pragmatism, and evident in writing beyond the United States, for instance in European literature.[31] As the many books and essays on him indicate, his presence in American life transcends music and crosses boundaries. In some quarters (rock-and-roll criticism) he's canonical, in others (literary criticism) he's not. But pragmatists don't care much for categories; they care about the effect of the ideas they have and the work they do, alone and with others, on their own and others' lives. I'm therefore harnessing multiple approaches to an overall vision that broadly aligns with the reflective process of writing and recording, and the more spontaneous process of performing. I agree with John J. Sheinbaum that Springsteen's art has a "deceptive simplicity" not adequately describable in conventional approaches. Reading the huge body of criticism, thorough and stimulating though much of it is, it's striking how to see him in one way is to sideline another way. Labeling him "a pure singer-songwriter" may "place him in the tradition of American working-class heroes" but at the same time sidestep his rock-and-roll side and "longstanding collaborative music making," while to construct notions of "pure rock-and-roll authenticity" equally limits his contribution in other modes. But in the end, as Sheinbaum argues, "we're confronted with a multifaceted persona, and challenged by sublime musical passages that incorporate a multiplicity of visions."[32]

I hope not only to explain something of Springsteen's appeal but also to address his role as a performer: a physical as well as cerebral artist. Dave Marsh criticizes the tendency among "people who write about music" to fixate "on Springsteen as a songwriter, by which they always mean lyricist." "Way too much current analysis of Springsteen's work," in Marsh's view, "relies on looking at pages, rather than listening to sounds." For Marsh, "one reason that Springsteen gets celebrated in literary terms is that it's a lot simpler for a writer to describe him that way, and another is that literature remains in our official culture the highest caste of all art forms." In his view "the Bruce-is-literature types" don't take into account that Springsteen's mastery has less to do with "technical prowess" than with an understanding of "the vernacular of music."[33] While the pragmatist perspective gives short shrift to the idea of "types," preferring to recognize individuals, Marsh may be right. My background and interests predispose me to think of Springsteen in relation to literature. I don't pretend to know much about Springsteen's "use of multiple bridges." But I appreciate that you can "overemphasize plan," and that improvisation, process, and performance are as important in thinking about Springsteen as his words and stories.

Pragmatism, therefore, which I see as integral to his emphasis on work, would seem to consolidate the relationship between his intellectual and emotional journey, his American perspective, his previous commentators' eclectic approaches, and his significance both in terms of his art and craft and in terms of the effect of his art on recipients. The pragmatist qualities evident in his art help explain his appeal across disciplines. Others have touched on this. Randall Auxier refers to the debates between Rorty, Cornel West, and Hilary Putnam. Heather Keith discusses Herbert Mead and John Dewey.[34] For me, Springsteen's connection with pragmatism seems central. It clarifies his work's cultural significance. As for his importance as an American writer, views on what this means may vary, but I agree with those who think that his craft, artistry, multiple themes, and phenomenal output stand comparison with many highly regarded figures, as I'll show in discussing writers from Douglass to Ford. Cullen and Dolan, for example, intimate that his work rewards literary analysis. In particular, though, I take my cue from Robert Coles's quoting of Walker Percy saying that Springsteen is "a writer as well as a composer." Although doubts have been raised about Coles's rendition of his conversations with Percy, the novelist's explicit testimony in a letter to the musician echoes implicit testimony from others. As Cullen notes, he features as an empathic commentator on clinical depression in Elizabeth Wurtzel's 1994 memoir, *Prozac Nation*, and provides a soundtrack to Samantha Hughes's adolescence in Mason's *In Country*.[35] But Springsteen's own statements reveal him to be a driven, self-taught thinker who, while not, as he puts it, raised "in a community of ideas—a place where you can sit down and talk about books," nevertheless has taken his place in the great circle of remarkable American artists (TAD 221). He may have begun as "the product of Top 40 radio" (S 65), but his influences include his ubiquitous interest in American cinema, all manner of music from jazz, blues, and country to gospel, swing, and Celtic ballads, and writers as diverse as Steinbeck, George Orwell, Flannery O'Connor, Ralph Ellison, and—as the 2014 *New York Times Review* interview revealed—Tolstoy, Dostoevsky, Whitman, Chekhov, and Marquez.[36]

His autobiography, too, reveals more than a passing acquaintance with these wider cultures, as well as in numerous ways exemplifying the pragmatist impulse. While it's more common to discuss pragmatism in terms of American "authors," the notion of art as action is embedded in the philosophy. The fact that Springsteen is a performer and recording artist as well as a writer merely makes him a different kind of figure from other writers we might see in pragmatist terms. Without "dogmas" or "doctrines" except an "attitude of orientation," writes William James, philosophical pragmatism is always open to revision. Heir to Emerson's call to "trust thyself," driven by passion, and inspiring passionate interest, Springsteen has helped to realign this "attitude of orientation" with powerful results.[37] To witness his work, his processes, and his observations is to see that he's both a communal and a sui generis artist. A storyteller as well as a lyricist, he's developed his vision and evaded category. That, as well as refusing to categorize others, is a pragmatist hallmark.

This book, then, is written in the contingent, idiosyncratic, highly personalized tradition of pragmatism itself. With each of the following chapters I've had in mind *Tracks*, *The Promise*, and *The Ties That Bind*: a simultaneous narrative drive forward coupled with a doubling back to revisit paths and possibilities. Springsteen describes *Tracks* as "the alternate route" through his work.[38] For the most part, each chapter suggests differing paths through his music. What connects them is a sense of temporality: of time past, passing, and cyclical, and the experience of time as more complex than a linear approach would suggest. The chapter treatments of time, therefore, include conventional trajectories but also contemplations of the past in the present and the present in the future. Chapter 1 provides a narrative of the overall direction of Springsteen's career. Discussing lonesomeness and community in Springsteen's world, I offer a working definition of a common human experience of perhaps special pertinence in American culture, given its landmass and history. I then draw on the writings of Emerson, James, Dewey, Rorty, and others to provide an explanation of pragmatism and to define my take on it in relation to Springsteen, viewing his career, haphazard and oscillating though the journey is, from lonesomeness to community.

Chapters 2 and 3 provide an American literary context in discussing "Classic Solitudes" in terms of nineteenth-century writing from Frederick Douglass, Nathaniel Hawthorne, Herman Melville, Henry David Thoreau, Emily Dickinson, Walt Whitman, and Mark Twain, through to "Contemporary Solitudes" expressed in the work of Flannery O'Connor, Walker Percy, and Richard Ford, all with links to Springsteen discussed by others, as well as Richard Wright and Joyce Carol Oates, whose links with him I suggest. I also touch on film regarding this tendency, including movies Springsteen has been interested in, such as *The Searchers, The Night of the Hunter, Badlands,* and *The Last Picture Show.* To situate Springsteen's writing within broad contexts of American solitudes is not to lose sight of the personal origins of this impulse. It's always been evident that he's drawn from a well of emotion that contains a high proportion of melancholy, but the autobiography reveals the severity of his bouts of clinical depression. Like many well-known American writers, he's found a way to turn these feelings into something of social value. Introspection is ultimately about connection. For Springsteen, this has been a reason to continue believing in the value of what he does.

Chapter 4, "Of Time and *The River,*" is a meditation on witnessing Springsteen and the E Street Band live. I contemplate the nature of his concerts—in some cases witnessed first-hand, in others seen and heard on recordings, and in yet others only heard as recordings, each of which is a different kind of experience. The narrative takes us from early to later performances, for the most part those available on DVD or CD. The shows I've attended over the years, from *The River* Tour of 1981 to *The River* Tour of 2016, have also had a permanent effect. In writing about performance, time once again becomes a concept to contemplate. Springsteen's concerts are famously long, yet they hasten to their end as surely as waves to shore. "Tick . . . tick . . . tick," he writes. "I had no time for time." On stage he long hugged the illusion that he could "master time, stretching it, shortening it, advancing it" (BTR 273). Well, while there's no escaping it, Jorge Luis Borges reminds us in "A New Refutation of Time" that it's simultaneously a reality—the substance we're made of, a river that both sweeps us along and that's made of us—and a delusion, in that "the difference and inseparability of one moment belonging to its apparent past from another belonging to its apparent present is sufficient to disintegrate it."[39] Springsteen's concerts, like most peak experiences, imprint themselves indelibly so as to begin as a "now" but immediately exist as a "then." My meditation revolves around their combination of fantasy and life-renewing energy, and their peculiar blend of ephemerality and—on rare occasions individually, but for numerous individuals—lifelong resonance.[40]

Springsteen's description of his concerts as "theater" rather than "reality" is an oversimplification. Art and life are not separate entities. In Borges's words, the mind itself "is a kind of theater." Concerts are also, therefore, a source of practical renewal and realignment of perspective.[41] If romanticism can be a form of escapism, I argue in chapter 5, it can equally be a form of pragmatism. Returning to focus on the first half of his career, the chapter gauges the difference between escapist romanticism and pragmatic romanticism to show how Springsteen's work ultimately aligns with the latter—in other words, the belief that if we articulate our thoughts in positive ways we can improve our own and others' lives. As part of this discussion I explore the different perspectives of Bertrand Russell and William James on whether what James called "The Will to Believe" is a romantic (and irrational) notion or a pragmatic one rooted in the immigrant experience and its need for survival mechanisms to cope with loneliness and the desire for community. Springsteen's art facilitates a reflection on the practical consequences of belief and the relative utility or futility of art as a means for producing practical results.

Chapter 6, "Multiple Selves," focuses on the second half of Springsteen's career and his complex rendering of varied personas. I compare James's and Springsteen's transforming awareness of the fragility of identity, in Springsteen's case manifesting itself gradually from his third album onward. To write about multiple selves requires experience and maturity. Springsteen's first two albums are notably un-experimental in this regard. While Springsteen may be right that most of his work "is emotionally autobiographical"—how, on some level, could it not be?—the viewpoint in early work is basically the writer's (BTR 267). "Meeting Across the River" on *Born to Run* anticipates a change. While the willingness to take on other viewpoints continues through subsequent albums, the one-dimensional image created by the success of *Born in the U.S.A.* brought these issues of identity to a head both in Springsteen's personal life and most obviously in *Tunnel of Love*. After a brief return to the first-person self of *Human Touch* and *Lucky Town* (reprised in *Working on a Dream*), Springsteen, in maturity and parenthood, returns to the mode of multiple selves from *The Ghost of Tom Joad* onward.

Chapter 7, "After Springsteen," ends the book with a consideration of his legacy both in the effect of his music on our lives and beyond our own time. Aside from recordings, this may amount to something as grand or dubious as biographies or made-for-TV biopics, or as ineffable as influence or memory. A performer deeply aware of the varying degrees of lonesomeness in all lives, Springsteen has emphasized many of the key elements of pragmatism. In recapitulating aspects of that argument, this final meditative chapter involves contemplating

Springsteen while in Berlin, Rome, and elsewhere in order to address the way in which he's increasingly faced the fact of his own mortality, and of the finitude of the individual journey. For all the power and joy of performance, in the end there's nothing left but the recordings and the effect of the output. I therefore consider his achievement not only in his impact on the generations who have experienced his evolving performances and recording career, but also in that effort beyond our time.

My approach may already diverge from expectations of a book on Springsteen. I hope so. Given all the writing that has come before, and given my particular perspective, I can't envisage any other way to write honestly about the man and his work. I see no need to repeat biographical details or add to conventional expositions. One aspect of the E Street Band that we respond to is the sense that they're fans who became stars. This feels true of Springsteen, scaling the gates of Graceland, and it feels true of Van Zandt, Clemons, and the rest. "Springsteen's musicians," writes Simon Frith, "stand for every bar and garage group that has ever got together in the fond hope of stardom." In *Big Man*, Clemons provides fantasy conversations with one of his heroes, Norman Mailer. "He was my companion on so many plane rides and in so many dressing rooms over the years," writes Clemons, "that I began to believe I knew him." "Why don't you write about us?" asks Clemons. "Nah," says Mailer. "It's been done to death." "There must be a fresh angle," says Clemons, whereupon Mailer launches into a diatribe about fans as "fanatics" who "pore over the minutiae of everything E Street like demented archaeologists." Such "crazy, rabid fuckheads" (says the imaginary Norman) "would crucify me if I said anything that didn't conform to the God like status they've endowed upon you."[42] Contrary to Clemons's fantasy of Mailer's viewpoint, those of us interested in Springsteen and his place in American culture are probably well-balanced global citizens who needn't be told what we already know. Many of us are also too old to mind someone holding a different opinion of an artist. I assume readers know the biographical facts, the lyrics, and may be acquainted with the usual areas of discussion—though such knowledge isn't essential. I won't repeat them unless pertinent to my argument. The aim, to combine Thoreau with Robert Frost, is to avoid the beaten paths in search of a road less traveled.

My life's the same story, again and again
I'm on the outside looking in.
—"OUTSIDE LOOKING IN"

People really invest themselves in you
and you invest yourself in them.
—SPRINGSTEEN, INTERVIEW, 2004

1

LONESOMENESS TO COMMUNITY

The narrative Bruce Springsteen has created during his career contains a tension between lonesomeness and community. This tension never subsides. The loner aspect of Springsteen's personality and worldview has always been apparent. But there's also an impulse toward community both in the journey from youth into artistic maturity, and in characters' stories across the decades. Springsteen's work articulates the American lonesome while equally qualifying him as an American pragmatist. "It's always public and personal simultaneously for me," he says.[1] Driven ultimately by social engagement, he's mined his experience of solitude to create an oeuvre of significance to his era. To use Wendell Berry's description of Springsteen's fellow New Jersey writer William Carlos Williams, his career amounts to decades of practicing "citizenship," by which Berry means "the unceasing labor of keeping responsibly conscious" of his time and place. He's accomplished, as Berry writes of Williams, "a sustained and intricate act of patriotism in the largest sense of the word—a thousand times more precise and loving and preserving than any patriotism ever contemplated by officials of the government or leaders of parties."[2] His instincts have kept him on this broad path from early in his career.

Related to these two ideas, and to facilitate investigation of Springsteen's significance as an American writer and musician, this chapter sets up two definitions and a narrative. The definitions are of American lonesomeness and of the passionate pragmatism at the heart of Springsteen's work, and the narrative is of his journey from a deep-rooted sense of alienation to a community-oriented perspective. All creative output is uneven, and the art is not the artist. In choosing "to trust the art and be suspicious of the artist," Springsteen echoes D. H. Lawrence. The human being is likely to be as much of a "stumbling clown" as everyone else (TAD 314).[3] There's our image of the artist, the artist's self-image, and there's the messy life lived.[4] Barack Obama is supposed to have joked to Michelle Obama that he opted to become president because he couldn't be Bruce Springsteen. "Sometimes," Springsteen once said, "I wish I was Bruce myself" (TAD 318). Like all of us, the artist himself is flawed and has floundered at times in shaping his mature vision, but few who read the interviews, ponder the songs, or attend concerts are likely to question his professional integrity. Through his work, we get the best he can offer, and the broad sweep of that is built on opposing impulses that construct a narrative from youth to maturity.

As Walker Percy evidently indicated to Robert Coles, in seeing Springsteen as "a writer, as well as a composer," he "knows how to improvise through music, through poetry, through his public talking: he's able to connect with, communicate with, us hearing him. You feel what he's saying is his very own, deeply felt letter being sent to you—and there he is: putting it on the line the way writers do."[5] Springsteen's lyrics and interviews illustrate his concern with literary as well as compositional craft in creating song storylines as well as a loose narrative within and between albums. The result has been an evolving parallel universe that sustains both artist and audience. In a 2010 interview, he reflected on an early decision to do this. Already successful as a performer, he grew aware that when it came to recording more was needed. There would always be plenty of other bands and others who "play guitar well" or "front well." To stand out he concentrated on "the imagining of a world," the creation of a personal "fingerprint" that would affect the lives of members of that audience. "All the filmmakers we love, all the writers we love, all the songwriters we love, they put their fingerprint on your imagination and in your heart and on your soul" (SOS 350–51). "Inspired" by the work of others, he wanted "to inspire" (TAD 262).

Yet for all this, Springsteen's writing contains a strong sense of the lonesome. Kevin Lewis argues that "lonesome" is a notably American word and that "the American lonesome" is a state of mind peculiar to the national culture. Lonesomeness has connotations of loneliness but also of solitude conducive to reflection. "In part the word has created the experience," he writes, "and the experience has come to be reflected in the word." "Where the meaning of 'lonely' is uniformly negative," the "meanings of 'lonesome'" can "layer a positive upon the negative."[6] Lonesomeness involves a sense of "taking confident possession of oneself on a crest of savored, transcended melancholy."[7] It's obvious from what he talks and sings about that Springsteen has used music to fill a void and believes he can connect with his audience by having the void facilitate the connection. "I know how deadly important my job is to me," he told Bob Costas in 1995. "What if I didn't have that job? Or what if I couldn't do that job after I did it for 20 years or 25 years?" (TAD 186). "If you don't have that underlying emotional connection," he told Chet Flippo in 1984, "then you don't have anything" (TAD 144). In the same interview he talks of his own experience of solitude. Explaining *Nebraska*, he reflects on characters suffering "a spiritual crisis" that renders them "isolated" from society, job, family, even friends, "to the point where nothing makes sense." "That loneness," he says, is "the beginning of the end" (TAD 145).

One explanation for a preoccupation with this feeling is personal. Springsteen is describing symptoms of depression, a tendency to which he's been open about in recent years and explicit about in the autobiography.[8] Such feelings of isolation produce many metaphors, from William Cowper's eighteenth-century description of being "buried above ground" through Sylvia Plath's bell-jar image to William Styron's portrayal, in *Darkness Visible: A Memoir of Madness* (1990), of depression as "a storm of murk." Springsteen's mixture of metaphors surpasses any of these in its nightmarish depiction of the illness. Depression brings with it "torrents of self-loathing." It has him "face up against the wall" he's been "inching toward for a long time." It spews "like an oil spill all over the beautiful turquoise-green gulf" of his "carefully planned and controlled existence," a "black sludge" that threatens "to smother" him (BTR 308–9). It's "a freight train bearing down, loaded with nitroglycerin and running quickly out of track" (BTR 484). Horrifying as these images are, the severity of his condition unless controlled by antidepressants is not unexpected. His lyrics are full of references to deathly isolation, from two mentions of suicide in "Born to Run" to the pilgrimage to the dry riverbed in "The River" to a dream of dying in "Valentine's Day," to imagining being buried in "We Are Alive." For Elizabeth Wurtzel, author of *Prozac Nation*, "Stolen Car" captures "the essence of depression." It's easy to think of the characters in *Nebraska* in terms of Styron's observation that, subject to a madness "chemically induced amid the neurotransmitters of the brain," the person's "aggrieved, stricken, and muddied thought processes," while usually "turned agonizingly inward," can induce "violent thoughts regarding others."[9] This may help explain the "Nebraska" protagonist's response that he did what he did because "there's just a meanness in this world." Similarly, when in "State Trooper" the driver pleads that no trooper stop him an implication is that to do so might lead to murder, suicide or both.

Indeed, *Nebraska,* as Dave Marsh and Springsteen himself have suggested, for all its political concerns, is laceratingly personal. Marsh refers to Springsteen's "private demons," while Springsteen told Mikal Gilmore that he'd always considered it his "most personal record" because it captured the "tone" of his childhood.[10] With regard to solitude, two pertinent songs are "My Father's House" and "Highway Patrolman." In both, the speaker's focus on a loved one highlights his isolation. There can hardly be a more forlorn song about father-son alienation than "My Father's House," not least in the son's inability to penetrate the father's angry pride. The house stands "shiny and bright," "so cold and alone," and the song ends with no suggestion that either the father's or the son's sins will be atoned. Something of that same yearning for an elusive closeness is apparent in "Highway Patrolman," the story of Joe Roberts, the good brother (as he sees himself) and Frankie, a Vietnam veteran and petty criminal. After a car chase to the Canadian border, Joe pulls over and watches Frankie's "taillights disappear." As with the "lunar landscape" of a New Jersey morning on "Open All Night," this is a depiction of personal and cosmic loneliness akin to Joyce Carol Oates's image, in her 1996 novel of a father's banishment of a daughter, *We Were the Mulvaneys.* As the father drives away, Marianne watches his taillights shrink and fade. "Smaller and smaller," they resemble "rapidly receding suns." Whatever your personal relationship with a family member, especially where circumstances keep you apart, to view the matter in terms of a human lifespan set against the eternity and immensity of the Cosmos concentrates the mind.[11]

Springsteen refers not only to isolation but also to feelings in youth of being an outsider and of having to work things out for himself. "An outcast weirdo misfit sissy boy," even aged seven, he received "the bullying all aspiring rock stars must undergo," that "playground loneliness that is essential fuel for the coming fire" (BTR 15). He experienced a basic rite of passage for those who are troubled by their place in society and by their sense that others expect them to conform. Nor is it self-deprecation. In an unpublished reminiscence, Joe de Pugh, the model for the pitcher in "Glory Days," describes how he and his teammates nicknamed Springsteen "Saddie," because the cool and the outcasts were known as the Bad and the Sad, and Springsteen sat on the bench and "hardly ever played."[12]

Hard as it is to assert your identity, and harder still when you're labeled a loser, one way to achieve this is to escape the world you're brought up in and find a new one. This needn't mean physical travel, though since, in Saul Bellow's words, "travel is mental travel," it often does. But equally, one can stay put yet, the brain being wider than the sky, burrow deep within oneself. "Had I not been lonely none of my work would have happened," said British painter L. S. Lowry. Art provides both the opportunity to express isolation and to escape it.[13] If Bellow found it through travel, Dickinson through poetry—her letter to the world that never wrote to her—and Lowry through painting, Springsteen found it through music.

But expression of isolation and escape from it are often inextricable. A band in itself can be a community formed by misfits. "Musicians are funny," Springsteen notes. "When you're home, you're never a real connected part of your own community, so you create one of your own" (TAD 198). Destined for an itinerant existence, they exemplify the lonesome. Those with a lonesome mentality turn it into a source of inspiration. Of being in the studio Springsteen said in 1981 that he wished he was "somewhere strange, playing," because this made him "feel most alert and alive" (TAD 125). Moreover, it's striking to note him saying four times in a few sentences, in 1975, that he likes to keep to himself, and add that his father "was always like that" (TAD 62). "From my youth," he admits, "I had a tendency to be isolated psychologically" (SOS 173). Not knowing "how to join in," he stood back and "watched the way things interrelated" (SOS 270). This sense of apartness drew him to what, in his Austin address, he calls the "outsider art" of rock and roll (SOS 388). But rather than stay within that narrow world he's defined this experience in broader terms. Feeling like an outsider is often a common factor "with people who then go on and take their own thoughts and formulate them in some fashion," he suggests. "It's usually a result of a variety of dysfunctions that you've managed to channel into something positive and creative rather than destructive" (SOS 270).

Dwelling in solitude as a place of reflection is particularly a characteristic of youth, and to move from a sense of isolation to a sense of community is usually about maturing. But it's rarely straightforward. The young test out who they might become. Like Julien and his mountain grotto in *The Red and the Black*, the young can be insanely ambitious yet happiest developing dreams alone. Subsequently most find their place. As their lives change, so do their perceptions. Lonesomeness may remain with maturity, merely changing shade and shape. The lonesome young may well become the lonesome old, or the older singer or listener may simply recall that lonesome youth. After all, how do we understand the young unless we put ourselves back into the mode that was once our core being? We might revise our response to a given song, or we might disassociate ourselves from it. The meaning of a song might change if it's crafted to contain possibilities. Equally, we might keep singing or listening as a form of independent or communal nostalgia. This wouldn't be pernicious, but we should see it for what it is. Shared lonesomeness creates a sense of the communal. Willa Cather ends her novel *My Ántonia* (1918) with the words, "whatever we have missed, we possessed together, the precious, the incommunicable past."[14] Like many a compelling phrase, this cracks on examination. We all possess the past. We may even possess aspects of that past together, and be unable to communicate it to others, yet the past we possess is never shared in detail. Our own past is a lonesome thing. Even if together, we're solitary sailors on a flotilla of yachts dotted on an ocean. Perhaps, then, the past is incommunicable even to those who in theory share it, and not just to those who weren't there. The character in "The River" speaks of how he and Mary would dive in the reservoir before the dreams of youth dissolved, and how they still return to the dry riverbed, he pretending amnesia and she indifference. "You shall not go down to the same river twice," counsels Heraclitus. Borges explains the "dialectical dexterity" of this statement "because the ease with which we accept the first meaning ('the river is different') clandestinely imposes upon us the second ('I am different') and grants us the illusion of having invented it."[15]

Springsteen's career encourages a sense of this dichotomy, apparent to many people at any time in life, between being an individual and being part of the crowd. This is true not just in terms of the individual creating and performing the song before escaping to the next town but also of the individual attending the concert and contemplating it in solitude. Perhaps it's not just Springsteen but all of us who are by nature loners yet seek community. We're strange animals and the work embodies our contradictions. The river becomes a metaphor for togetherness, then solitude even in company, and finally for the flow of time, where elsewhere (as on *Live in New York City*) it becomes the river of hope and the river of life. Springsteen stands on the bank between solidity and fluidity—"the edge of the stage," as Stevan Weine puts it, "worked so intensively for forty years," "a concentrated point on the edge connecting and dividing the individual and the world"—reminding us that we can accommodate the lonesome by sharing.[16] When he performs "Born to Run," the lights go up on the audience. The singer and Wendy are the nominal "we" while the band and crowd form another collective. Yet this most melancholy of songs mingles major chords with minor, and the lyrics are full of yearning. As Springsteen put it of his music and the band's performances in those early days, it was "*desperate* fun" (TAD 200). But the "loneness" he refers to can give way to lone*someness*. On one hand, country music, among Springsteen's multitude of influences, might be, in Cecelia Tichi's words, "a grieving music for a lonesomeness bred in the American bone," and at times tending toward "mawkish self pity," on the other hand, to turn a negative into a positive is an American ideal. For both Tichi and Lewis, the lonesome is rooted in the immigrant experience. Tichi describes this in terms of the "gut-level loneliness" of being separated from one's family, friends, and culture. For Lewis, "this feeling state" grows out of the historical contexts whereby "religious inclinations have had to find expression or release where they will" in the face of frontier experience, "post-Enlightenment scepticism," and an erosion of "the authority of traditional doctrine-based religions." He thus writes of the American "cultural imperative to reinvent religion." The lonesome, he argues, relates to the "yearning for belief in a transcendent reality, a yearning not capable of being fulfilled more than a tantalizing, fleeting moment, but at least for that."[17] Springsteen nails it in a title: "Gotta Get That Feeling." American culture does this best in what he calls "the dream world of popular music" (TAD 412).

As noted with "My Father's House," and other *Nebraska* songs, Springsteen doesn't always provide the possibility for a positive interpretation, but the idea of something positive coming out of a negative can exist in ostensibly bleak material. In "State Trooper," for instance, the desperate voice hopes that "somebody out there" will hear him. A "last prayer" doesn't bode well, but it's a phone-in show and the radio suggests other listeners. A song can save a life. "State Trooper" is a companion to "Stolen Car" on *The River*, in which the isolated individual feels it's better to be caught, and thus become something, if only a convict, than to travel so far into "this darkness" that he'll "disappear." Discussing "Stolen Car," Springsteen reveals the extent to which he blends the personal with the cultural. "If you don't connect yourself to your family and to the world," he says, "you feel like you're disappearing. I felt like that for a very, very long time. Growing up, I felt invisible." "To be caught" on the radar as a felon is the most muted positive imaginable. But it's a version of a far more prevalent force, both in American culture and in Springsteen's work: a life-affirming, ultimately communal impulse. "The heart of almost all my music," he explains, is "the struggle to make some impact and to create meaning for yourself and for the people you come in touch with" (TAD 254). Beginning with that "outsider art," Springsteen has, as he told Percy's nephew, always been "looking inward and reaching out to others" (TAD 231). His career has thus evolved through passionate engagement, first with his art form and later with wider areas of interest. From the experience of being on the outside looking in—and mentally on the inside looking out—to discovering meaning through music, to finding that his private experience had value through communal expression, he found his path.

The idea that "lonesomeness," in the midst of a "loneness" that threatens pure negation and annihilation, has within it a core positive, a *some*-thing felt by and between all his listeners, is the "hungry heart" that pulses through Springsteen's work. It's where his version of the American lonesome merges with his passionate pragmatism. I use this particular "-ism" advisedly. In 1972 Springsteen described his abortive attempt to study at college. "I got there and tried to take psychology," he said, "and I kept opening a book and seeing myself in all these different -isms. I thought, I can't get into that."[18] We should honor our young selves. They will always be a part of us. In maturity we may still feel that records taught us more than we learned in school. But not all "-isms" are alike. The young Springsteen was reacting to categorization. All young rebels resemble that most lonesome of youths, Huckleberry Finn. Like Huck, many too are at heart conservative. They're responding to a world that has gone awry from their instinctive morality. They don't want to adhere to hollow conventions, accept falsities, be confined, or swallow a belief system served up for them by circumstance or accident of birth. Nor do they want to face the brutality of fathers unable to come to terms with failure. The last thing they want is a curriculum leading to that euphemism for conformity, "sivilization," which too often contains acceptance of inequality, greed, and racism. The nineteenth-century rebel seeks escape on a raft. The twentieth-century rebel finds "the key to the universe in the engine of an old parked car." He wants to be free, to fake his own death, debunk to Jackson's Island (or escape the Jackson Cage), and "light out for the Territory ahead of the rest."[19]

But pragmatism is paradoxically all about escaping "-isms" of the incarcerating kind. It celebrates the fluid energy of the river rather than the solid conventionality of the bank. It's never been about bowing to authority. It's akin to the very rebelliousness that rejects most "-isms." One might almost call it a constructive anarchism. A multipurpose philosophical tool, it is reshaped by pragmatists for the task at hand. To be a pragmatist is to have a secular sense that what we believe will affect how we act, and hence that idealism is pragmatic. This amalgam of positive perspectives began, in American terms, with the ideas of Emerson and then Whitman; Charles Sanders Peirce coined "pragmatism" as a term; William James articulated it as a way of thinking; diverse American thinkers and writers from Dewey and Rorty to Wallace Stevens and James Baldwin developed it. Since then it has continued to resonate into the twenty-first century.[20] Brother of novelist Henry James, William James has something in common with Springsteen in his outsider status. In the words of Louis Menand, "he was not a product of a particular school or academic tradition, or even a practitioner of a particular scholarly discipline," so he "could honestly feel that he was responsible for his beliefs to no one but himself. This not only lent passion to his convictions," it also enabled him to ignore convictions if they began "to operate as prejudices." He started out rebelling against his father, whose beliefs in "the unchanging reality of an unseen world, indifference to temporal moral distinctions, and anti-individualism" were anathema to him. He thus designed pragmatism to undermine such conceptions of "a closed and predetermined universe." Hating notions of "an undifferentiated oneness," he "thought the universe should be renamed the 'pluriverse.'"[21] Springsteen has been an eclectic reader for decades, and influenced as much by this as by music. Robert Santelli said to him in 2013 that, when he worked with him on *Songs* in the 1990s, he was amazed at the books in his study on "American history, politics, art, and music." In response, Springsteen admitted to being "quite a student" (TAD 426). He'll therefore have imbued many ideas from American philosophy and be familiar with some of these figures. Certainly his work shares many of their preoccupations and tendencies.

The idea of the lonely journey—the American lonesome—is integral to Springsteen as an American pragmatist: in Stewart Friedman's terms, "a teacher" who has come to this by way of "his own experience." This sense of an individualistic worldview self-made out of available materials is one of pragmatism's most appealing aspects. Pragmatists don't function as a group. They merely share traits. Idiosyncratic thinkers, they rely on intuition as well as evidence, and borrow ideas to suit a purpose. Typical of James was his belief that "a risk-assuming decisiveness—betting on an alternative even before all the evidence was in— was the supreme mark of character" set against his view "that certainty was moral death."[22] "Pragmatists," writes Rorty, "realize this way of thinking about knowledge and truth makes certainty unlikely. But they think that the quest for certainty—even as a long-term goal—is an attempt to escape the world."[23] Springsteen's homespun, contingent worldview therefore exudes both the American lonesome and a particularly passionate form of pragmatism.

Lonesomeness and pragmatism combine in expressing the value of charting your own path using whatever's at hand. Emerson was a family friend during William James's childhood. His ideas, epitomized by his celebrated essay "Self-Reliance," clearly influence James's formulation of pragmatism. "Emerson's method," writes Menand, "was to skim works of literature and philosophy, of all types and from all cultures, with an eye to ideas and phrases he could appropriate for his own use." His conviction was "that organized study deadens the mind, and that genuine insight arises spontaneously." You should "believe your own thought," writes Emerson. "What is true for you in your private heart is true for all."[24] That we work from the inside out, that intuition is preferable to dogma, and that consistency might amount to falsity, are all central tenets of his writing. There's no point in arguing pragmatism into false coherence, of trying, in Rorty's words, "to find a way of making everything hang together." Instead, the point is to use the concept as a magnet for attracting other sources to create a narrative that may in turn stimulate the ideas of others, growing from their own experience and interests.[25]

In critical terms, what matters for pragmatists and neo-pragmatists is invariably what an artist's work does rather than any lowered or elevated status an establishment assigns it. This view tends to see the importance of an artist, in Giles Gunn's words, "in relation to the questions they continue to keep alive and insistent." For Gunn, this is why opening up the canon "to more and different authors" is so important. It is to alter "the way culture represents its own resources to itself. Until new texts and new authors are brought into functional relations with established ones," he argues, "culture doesn't really change." Pragmatists thus celebrate the "world of difference between thinking of canons as treasuries to be protected and hoarded and as savings to be invested, portfolios to be managed and risked."[26] In Rorty's pragmatist utopia, "there will be *no* dominant form" of culture. "High culture will no longer be thought of as the place where the aim of the society as a whole is debated and decided, and where it is a matter of social concern which sort of intellectual is ruling the roost. Nor will there be much concern about the gap that yawns between popular culture, the culture of people who have never felt the need for redemption, and the high culture of the intellectuals—the people who are always trying to be something more or different than they presently are." We'll have dropped notions of "a standard against which the products of the human imagination can be measured other than their social utility," and will judge such use by taking "fully to heart the maxim that it is the journey that matters."[27]

While philosophical pragmatists have no bosses, they tend to hold similar values. To borrow definitions set out by John Stuhr, these include a rejection of "distinctions made in thought" such as supposed oppositions between intellect and emotion or oneself and other people; a fallibilist, pluralist belief that "varieties of experience" are valid, and a sense of radical empiricism, James's term for the conviction that "experience is an active, ongoing affair." They also tend to think in experimental, melioristic terms, and proceed with "a method of enquiry" that assumes "human action can improve the human condition."[28] When I think of supposed oppositions, such as intellect/emotion, I recall Springsteen's comment that music is primarily an "emotional language" but intimation that emotion and intellect are entwined. I also think of Springsteen's class awareness, and the once-common assumption that rock music must be a lesser art, and so recall Dewey's view, in Menand's words, that such oppositions reflect "class bias." When I think of fallibilism, I reflect upon Springsteen's willingness to revise beliefs (or, to use his vernacular, from "Long Time Comin'" on *Devils & Dust,* not to "fuck it up this time"). When I think of pluralism, I note the common ground he finds with diverse others. Radical empiricism is evident in his comments—echoing Emerson's to let "the inmost" become "the outmost" and to "trust thyself"—that ultimately you must "trust yourself" and "the world will catch up" (TAD 213). He's experimental in his willingness to try different formats. Danny Federici described him as "the kind of guy who just says, 'Oh—that was yesterday.'"[29] More to the point, he revises, reworks, and recasts ideas. The spare rhythm of "Open All Night" from *Nebraska* transforms in his 2006 Dublin show with the Sessions Band into a 1940s-style big-band extravaganza. When I think of meliorism, I reflect that, for all the dark material, he's never been "much of a cynic" (SOS 152). When, finally, I contemplate community and the social, I'm aware of how even the most downbeat of songs, such as "This Depression" on *Wrecking Ball,* imply the possibility of help-at-hand. "Baby, I've been down but never this down," is the shocking opening to a song that never transcends the emotion. Yet the singer is confident of emotional support. Even in songs such as "State Trooper," "My

Father's House" or "Dead Man Walkin'" a community element exists in that Springsteen gives voice to people often denied it in American culture, and the speakers assume listeners.[30]

In sum, art, from a pragmatist perspective, is seen to have a social *use*. "Our beliefs are really rules for actions," writes James. American poets often echo this. "The necessity, the *usefulness* of poetry!" exclaims Wendell Berry. "The people I love best," writes Marge Piercy in "To Be of Use," "jump into work head first."[31] "I wanted to be good at doing something that was useful to other people, and to myself," said Springsteen in 1984 (TAD 134). "One of the main motivations for me was to try to be useful," he repeated in 1995. "I was trying to find a fundamental purpose for my own existence" (TAD 172). By 2012, opening the *Wrecking Ball* tour in Atlanta, he was describing himself as "the custodian" of "people's feelings and memories" and the band as "a purpose-based organization." In other words, pragmatism is all about moral purpose, testing beliefs and ideals in terms of their practical, beneficial effect.[32] As for what might be meant by "use," in Rorty's words, "pragmatists—both classical and 'neo-'—do not believe that there is a way things really are." Rather, "they want to replace the appearance-reality distinction by that between descriptions of the world and of ourselves which are less useful and those which are more useful."[33] This doesn't mean they have answers to questions about what the descriptions might be useful for, or by what criterion a definition might be judged to be better. Pragmatists have no abstract agenda defined in advance. They deal with specific situations. Thus they tend to adhere to what Rorty calls "polytheism," which amounts to an abandonment of the idea of locating an unchallengeable script "which will tell all human beings what to do with their lives, and tell them all the same thing."[34] Usefulness, therefore, always depends upon the concrete situation.

It's no coincidence that, as an American, Springsteen has a worldview that echoes the tendencies of pragmatism since the latter articulates, in Stuhr's words, "attitudes, outlooks, and forms of life embedded in the culture from which and in which it arose." Springsteen's adherence to the pragmatist principles of revisionism, fallibility, energy, movement, pluralism, meliorism, and usefulness feeds his prolificacy. Equally apparent is the neo-pragmatist emphasis on language as the shaper of worldview. Few other singer-songwriters have ever produced not just album after album but also version after version of song after song and then whole back catalogues that contain such a stream of material, including versions of well-known songs, songs that didn't make it onto albums, and hybrid songs drawing on ideas and rhythms from other artists that then become Springsteen's own. However different the mature artist is from the young artist, his work has always tended to reflect the ideals and actualities of his country—or at least, as he puts it, "that big country" he feels his audiences, American, European, or otherwise, carry "in their hearts" (TAD 211). "The country of one's dreams," writes Rorty, "must be a country one can imagine being constructed, over the course of time, by human hands." "With these hands," runs the refrain from "My City of Ruins." Such language, common to Rorty and Springsteen, about "what a nation has been and should try to be" is not about "accurate representation," in Rorty's words. Rather, it's an attempt "to forge a moral identity."[35]

If Springsteen's work has long revealed a pragmatist worldview, *Born to Run* is a culmination of it. Very much a reader- rather than self-serving autobiography, its impulse is to be useful—whether to fans wishing to understand "the Boss," young musicians wishing to make the most of their craft and avoid pitfalls, workaholic parents who need reminding of priorities, people coping with depression who can gain from knowing they are not alone, or any of us in our roles as sons, daughters, siblings, or spouses. "The writer has made one promise," he writes near the end, "to show the reader his mind. In these pages I've tried to do that" (BTR 501). It's obvious from the confessional element of the book that this is not designed to impress but to help readers to "strengthen" and "make sense of" their own lives (BTR 505). The book is shot through with the belief that we can use our imagination to shape our senses of ourselves. In the "Badlands" phrase, "Talk about a dream / Try to make it real." The first thing to do is to find a language. Out of the language comes the idea. Out of the idea comes the reality. Out of experimentation we find that future. A hypothesis is not merely something to prove but to provide new possibilities. "My first act of free will shall be to believe in free will," writes James.[36] The word or phrase, denoting an idea, can lead to the belief and then the action. "Faith," he writes, "creates its own verification."[37] Decades after James, Springsteen asserts: "Mister, I ain't a boy, no I'm a man / And I believe in a promised land." Attitudes have concrete results. This is what James, to use one of his essay titles, called "The Will to Believe." Such idealism tends to bypass the fact that beliefs can be destructive as well as constructive, depending both upon what one might mean by "a promised land," or what one might put faith *in*. But, writes Rorty, "any philosophical view is a tool which can be used by many different hands," and in its melioristic form this one shapes Springsteen's career.[38]

These beliefs explain Springsteen's willingness to change sound and image across the decades. They explain his willingness to embrace multiple styles and influences, from the joyous blend of rock and jazz—part Duke Ellington, part Elvis, part Van Morrison—that provided live entertainment on the Jersey Shore in the early 1970s, through the operatic romance of the *Born to Run* era, the moodier period of *Darkness, The River,* and *Nebraska,* and the more socially and politically engaged, Guthrie-inspired music of *The Ghost of Tom Joad* to the eclectic mix of *Wrecking Ball* and *High Hopes.* As many have noted, Springsteen is, in June Skinner Sawyers's words, an unabashed "synthesist." "There has never been an artist so aware of the rock 'n' roll heritage," writes Greil Marcus. As Ann Douglas points out, he "learned his trade through" what she calls "saturation—he calls it 'assimilation' as opposed to study—in the cheapest media outlets of rock, the AM radio station and the single." More than that, it was, for me, startling to discover that the origins of "Backstreets," and the extended versions at late-1970s concerts, owed so much to Van Morrison's *Astral Weeks,* and that even the late wails on "Born to Run" strongly echo those of "Madame George." But such echoes are everywhere in his music. If Van Morrison refers to a "Mansion on the Hill" on "Cedar Avenue," there's also, to borrow from Geoffrey Himes's more extensive selection, Hank Williams's "Mansion on the Hill," Roy Acuff's "Wreck on the Highway," Tim Hardin's "Reason to Believe" and Woody Guthrie's "Tom Joad." American pragmatists accept, in Rorty's words, "the contingency of starting points," and that our identity is part of a continuum. To do so "is to accept our inheritance from, and our conversation with, our fellow human beings as our only source of guidance." Without a solid base of the kind that dogma claims, we live our lives in a river of language-created realities. What therefore ultimately matters "is our loyalty to other human beings clinging together against the dark, not our hope of getting things right," let alone a deluded sense of creating new ideas, or tunes, unconnected with what has come before.[39]

Springsteen expresses these sentiments in numerous utterances in conversation and from every pore during performance. He speaks often of his dialogue with his audience and sense of continuity with the music of the past. That he's people-oriented, "isolationist" tendency aside (TAD 157), is self-evident. But he's spelled out on many occasions what he tries to achieve. He put it best to Mark Hagen in 1999. Everyone carries idiosyncratic, personal memories "for no explicable reason," he says. These memories live with you throughout your life and "are an essential part of who you are." "For some reasons on that particular day you had some moment of pure experience that revealed to you what it meant to be alive. How important it is, what you can do with your life." "The writer's job" is therefore to collect and create such moments from personal experience, to imagine them into cohesion and to present this to others "who then experience their own inner vitality," and "their own questions about their own life, and their moral life" (TAD 255–56). In other words, artists first of all try to make sense of their own lives, but if they do it well then that has a similar effect on the lives of others. His vision is of the artist as teacher, teaching first himself and then allowing us access to what he's learned. As he said in 1995, he's always been "interested in becoming part of people's lives, and having some usefulness—that would be the best word." "To try to be useful" (as well, of course, as dreaming of "the Cadillac or the girls") would, after all, fulfill that need to find "a fundamental purpose" (TAD 172).

W hile it's true that lonesomeness and community are oscillating poles in Springsteen's music, one can also see his early career as a journey from one to the other. Starting with feelings of alienation, he discovers that he can turn these feelings into an art that celebrates community and proves beneficial to others. The process has two stages. One is to recognize this as a way forward. The other is to make it real. As is the case with most young people, he begins without a fully realized sense of what he's doing or why. In time, he begins to express a message of community on stage. But he admits that, for all his talk "about community," his personal immersion in the process is another step (TAD 161). This in itself is an example of the pragmatist belief that putting a goal into words can lead to an emotional, intellectual, and professional reality. Achieving this eventually transforms Springsteen from being a mere writer and performer to a position where he becomes an articulate spokesperson for his society.[40] Perhaps he always felt, as he told Will Percy, that what he "was doing was rooted in a community—either real or imagined" and that his "connection to that community" is what made his work matter (TAD 212), but it wasn't until he had a stable personal life that he "was driven to write more outwardly—about social issues" (TAD 223). The pivotal album is *The Ghost of Tom Joad*, but the process begins much earlier, both through his own desire to make his life and work more significant, and through Jon Landau and others encouraging him to open himself up to wider cultural influences. Continuing from the 1980s into the twenty-first century, it's deepened into a consistent attitude toward the role of the songwriter in the community, both in his actions and in songs from "Streets of Philadelphia" to "Wrecking Ball." Although "The Ghost of Tom Joad" was inspired by John Ford's 1940 movie version of *The Grapes of Wrath*, and as late as 2014 Springsteen was embarrassed not to have read *East of Eden*, his alignment with Steinbeck's active concern about migrants illustrates a tendency that's become more obvious in artistic maturity, to assert what David Masciotra describes as a "progressive political vision."[41]

Springsteen's art had long functioned as social commentary, but by the late 1990s he was consistently aware of this. Only from *Darkness*, notably in "Factory," did he begin to refer to the workplace itself, but in "Youngstown," on *Tom Joad*, he documents a specific ironworks founded in northeast Ohio in 1803 by James and Dan Heaton. He notes its role as a maker of Union cannonballs in the nineteenth century and tanks and bombs in the twentieth, and he situates one blast-furnace worker's story within a cultural, geographical, and historical context. By the end, he's taken us from the Monongahela Valley of West Virginia and Pennsylvania and the Mesabi Iron Range of Minnesota to Kentucky's Appalachian coalmines and from the Civil War through World War II to Korea and Vietnam. At the same time, he's given voice to the American worker as deliberately as that quintessential cultural witness, Studs Terkel.[42] The same can be said for later songs like "Jack of All Trades" and "Wrecking Ball." That the impulse toward specificity had been growing is apparent from the excised "Glory Days" couplet that has a boy observing how his father no longer works "at the Metuchan Ford plant assembly line" but "just sits on a stool down at the Legion Hall."[43]

Tom Joad marks Springsteen's maturation beyond mere awareness of his immediate environment into a sense of his story as part of American history and culture. Early in his career, his travel motif is predominantly about individual dreams of escape. The heroes of "4th of July, Asbury Park (Sandy)," "Born to Run," and "Thunder Road" see their hometown as restrictive. They'll find personal success elsewhere. From this, Springsteen moves, via the sense of entrapment, family ties, and reluctant separations evident in such *Darkness* and *River* songs as "Factory" and "Independence Day," to something quite different. His theme in *Tom Joad* is forced migration and communal responsibility. Characters try to connect with each other. In "Galveston Bay" a Vietnam veteran spares a Vietnamese immigrant who's killed two Texan Klan members in self-defense. As Jim Cullen puts it, the song's resolution offers "the ultimate definition of brotherhood: love that transcends boundaries."[44] Similarly, "Sinaloa Cowboys" and "The Line" raise questions—again far from the early work—about the interrelationships between friendship, responsibility, family, and community.

Curiously, Steinbeck critic Warren French's analysis of the change in the character of Tom Joad describes the kind of change evident in Springsteen's perspective as this new emphasis emerges. The change, writes French of Joad, is from an "individual concerned only with the survival of his touchy clan into a visionary" who becomes "an inspiring influence to his unity."[45] Springsteen, like Joad, moves from self-as-rebel-hero to being that "inspiring influence." Again, like Joad, he absented himself from his original community when, as "a southern Californian in the early nineties," he echoed his parents' migration to the West Coast.[46] But his return spoke to his attachment to place as a marker of identity. That "a fella ain't no good alone" is as relevant to Springsteen's career as to Steinbeck's novel.[47] Individuals mature when they see themselves as part of a larger context. The change between Springsteen's youthful and mature visions is put in relief on his 1989 video anthology. Introducing a 1987 live version of "Born to Run," he advises his audience, "Nobody wins unless everybody wins." "This is the beginning," writes Steinbeck, "—from 'I' to 'we.'"[48] American myths of individualism strike at the heart of notions of community, and this is evident in both *The Grapes of Wrath* and *The Ghost of Tom Joad*. Those Springsteen listeners who prefer romantic rebellion to an emphasis on community, may, as Christopher Sandford suggests, "feel that he never quite recovered from watching *The Grapes of Wrath* on TV," but, as he introduced a 1988 acoustic version of "Born to Run" in the same anthology, he realized that, having "put all those people in all those cars," he would "have to figure out some place for them to go." "Individual freedom," he came to acknowledge, "when it's not connected to some sort of community or friends or the world outside ends up feeling pretty meaningless." For what does it mean to "win"? What does it mean to "succeed"? To quote Spanish film director Pedro Almodóvar, "success has no smell or taste, and when you get used to it, it doesn't exist."[49] Real as they may be, feelings or manifestations of personal achievement are more temporary than family and community.

Springsteen's changing statements between the early 1970s and late 1990s corroborate the evidence of the songs. In a 1974 interview with Michael Watts, appropriately entitled "Lone Star," he admitted, "the main thing I've always worried about is me." He "had to write about me all the time because in a way you're trying to find out what that 'me' is." This is a youthful question. "Is there anything more interesting," asks a young character in Joyce Carol Oates's *You Must Remember This,* "than who you finally turn out to be"?[50] In maturity you're more likely to be interested in what you *do* with who you've turned out to be. By 1992 Springsteen had moved to the next stage. His relocation to California would seem to have been part of that. He'd lived in New Jersey for a long time, he told David Hepworth, and had written a great deal about his past. Having taken this as far as he could, he was now writing instead about "people trying to connect to each other, and that happens everywhere." Connection, as he says of "With Every Wish" on *Human Touch,* means "dealing with a life with consequences." "What does it mean to be a husband?" he asks. "What does it mean to be a father? What does it mean to be a friend to somebody? When you finally get a good look at the world as it is, how do you not give in to cynicism, not give in to despair?" His answer is that you recognize "a world of love and a world of fear," and that the two go hand in hand.[51] Springsteen's later albums have plenty to say about lonesomeness; you don't outgrow your nature or leave your formative experience behind. But he rejects extended escapism in favor of confronting "the pain that living brings." Out of the world of love and fear comes the world of responsibility. Beginning with his own early wrath he comes to see class anger in context. As enmeshed in the capitalist system as one can imagine, he's part of the system he critiques. As Simon Frith put it, at the height of his popularity in the *Born in the U.S.A.* era, Springsteen came to represent the "pop commodity" that "stands for the principle that music should not be a commodity."[52] But the contradictions of his songs and story have largely to do with the contradictory American ideals of equality and individualism. His intelligence enabled him to negotiate that period and establish a deeper role as a cultural commentator.

Beyond the similarities between Joad's maturation in the novel and Springsteen's through the 1970s to the end of the 1990s, *Tom Joad* is also notable for a new approach. It shows Springsteen reflecting on the roots of his profession. The translation of Steinbeck's words and Ford's images from movie into lyric sees him returning to storytelling as folk art. It pays homage to Guthrie and other folk singers of the 1930s and 1940s.[53] Not least in its depiction of alienated labor in "Youngstown" and itinerant labor in "the New Timer," it calls to mind Steinbeck's campfire guitarist both in its ruminative rhythms and in subject matter, marking a return to music as intimacy. This is also why *Tom Joad* is markedly warmer and more companionable, for all its dark subject matter, than *Nebraska,* which it superficially resembles. The bleaker, harder songs of that earlier album reflect a destructive form of contemporary solitude. "Johnny 99" would hardly weld our imagined group of migrants, let alone lull their children to sleep. Nor is there any of the sense some might feel about *Nebraska* that the emphasis on the humanity of the criminals—albeit because the album critiques both the death penalty and incarceration without parole—leaves an uncomfortable silence about the multiple tragedies of the victims and their bereft loved ones. The characters in *Tom Joad* are for the most part decent individuals in dire straits.[54]

If this shift from lonesomeness to community pivots on *Tom Joad,* thereafter community is a watchword for every studio album, *We Shall Overcome: The Seeger Sessions* included, except *Working on a Dream,* where the communal aspect has to do with the narrower if equally important matter of everyday involvement with family and friends. *The Rising* is one of Springsteen's most important albums in this regard. In the wake of 9/11 there was a need among people, and a response from artists, musicians, and writers, to articulate their emotions. Jonathan Safran Foer responded with *Extremely Loud and Incredibly Close,* Don DeLillo with *Falling Man.* There are examples in painting, in film, in poetry, and in music.[55] Springsteen responded with skill and sensitivity. In the words of Cornel Bonca, in an exceptionally considered study of the title song in this context, "more than any other pop product produced since 9/11," it "suggests than an artist can transcend pop's typical puerility, commercialization, and superficiality to deliver an enduring piece of art." Bonca hears "a man who has listened to the silence at the heart of the massacre, has honored it, and then proceeded to transform it into music." In doing so, Springsteen provides not only "a vital, vibrant testament that popular culture can transcend its usual limitations," but also shows that responses "needn't be merely part of the noise, but truly be a help to those trying to get beyond it."[56]

Springsteen also responded by consolidating the reuniting of the E Street Band for their first studio album since 1984. The album heralded his renewed sense of purpose as rooted in the communal even as lonesomeness is, for self-evident reasons, a central theme. For Geoffrey Himes and others, *The Rising* songs "are strangely vague and apolitical," and most "could just as easily have been describing the aftermath of a hurricane or earthquake as a terrorist attack by right-wing religious fundamentalists." But such observations, as Roxanne Harde argues, underestimate the meanings and manifestations of the "political." "Several songs bring up and dismiss the thought of vengeance or discuss the costs inherent in taking revenge," writes Harde.[57] They thus take a political position, as does Springsteen in featuring Sufi Muslim musicians on "Worlds Apart." The majority of listeners bring to the music images of 9/11, and Springsteen need only hint at those images for them to form. Such obliqueness enables him to blend acknowledgments of personal tragedy with a range of emotions we might feel. While several of the songs were written earlier, in the wake of 9/11 *The Rising* provides music as a catalyst for renewing strength. Cullen calls it "a profoundly religious document." I prefer to think of Springsteen simply using religious language as an artistic device. Rorty describes religion and philosophy as "relatively primitive, yet glorious literary genres" in a world where those of a secular mind-set accept that there's no "intrinsic reality to be discovered," no "nonhuman authority" to which human beings owe respect, only useful ways of describing things and useful work to be done in bettering individual and collective lives. Hence the refrain, "with these hands."[58]

Springsteen followed *The Rising* with *Devils & Dust*, which is as concerned with foreign policy and with the experiences of soldiers abroad as with America at home. "Devils & Dust" itself picks up from "Further On (Up the Road)" on *The Rising*. The voice of a soldier heading for war with grim concentration becomes the voice of a soldier in the midst of war, uncertain of what he's being asked to do, and of the effect on him and his comrades if what "you do to survive / Kills the things you love." The lyrics are both abstract and visceral, yet the "field of mud and bone" is indeterminate in setting or scenario. Other songs, notably "Reno" and "All I'm Thinkin' About," depict the search for companionship. But two standout songs on the theme of lonesomeness and community are about mothers and sons. "Jesus Was an Only Son" and "Black Cowboys" mirror each other. One depicts a son dying young and leaving a grieving mother, the other depicts a son leaving a dying mother. The first dramatizes the human story behind the Christian myth. We see Jesus as a child, walking with his mother on Calvary Hill, and Mary soothing him to sleep, then in the Garden of Gethsemane, praying "for the life he'd never live," and finally comforting his mother by reminding her that "the soul of the universe willed a world and it appeared." "Black Cowboys" is equally about mutual tenderness. Rainey Williams's mother has protected him in the Bronx and fed his imagination with a book about "the black cowboys of the Oklahoma range," and in turn he grows up to support her as she falls into addiction and perhaps prostitution. But, echoing *The Grapes of Wrath*, the song tells of his need to say farewell and move to distant lands. The smile Rainey has depended on has "dusted away." Through her chest he hears "the ghost of her bones." The final verse produces such a sense of lonesome reverie that I listened to it again and again to overcome being hypnotized by the clacking rhythm of the train tracks. As with Supertramp's "Rudy" on that "train to nowhere," we take the journey, drifting through Pennsylvania and Indiana, awakening "to muddy fields of green, corn and cotton." The "red sun" slips "over the rutted hills of Oklahoma," and the moon strips "the earth to its bone." In terms of *The Grapes of Wrath*, the irony is that the boy is escaping *to* Oklahoma, the starting point of Steinbeck's novel. Our dreams start out in our head. We invest a land with meaning. It's not the land that's turning to dust, but his mother. He's heading for the place of his childhood dreams, the land of the black cowboys who are no longer there, and the final word reminds us of his mother on whose bones he's laid his head. Like Tom Joad, he must leave the parent and find his own identity. Like 1920s folk singer Jimmie Rodgers who, in Greil Marcus's words, "simply hopped on a train"—a "mystery train" no less—he's "every boy who ever ran away from home." More than this, he's all of us, heading from our place of origin with high hopes.[59]

Throughout his career, Springsteen has shown suitable devotion to the matriarch, often having his mother, Adele, attend concerts. As with Elvis, his mother would seem to have been his first great fan. There's a photograph of him at a New York show, aged sixty-two, serenading her aged ninety just as he did in Hyde Park a couple of years later, in 2013. The most personal and touching tribute to his mother is "The Wish" on *Tracks*, about her purchase (taking her cue from Grace Presley perhaps) of his first guitar. Along with "Jesus Was an Only Son," "Black Cowboys" runs a close second in the mother-son depictions. Its emotional impact is reminiscent of that final movie scene between Ma and Tom. "We ain't the kissing kind," she says, yet embraces him. Tom recedes from the camera while his mother looms in the foreground, her hand momentarily reaching out. To hear the song is to have such images in mind. But "Black Cowboys" is about more than mother-son bonds. It's about the creative imagination. Rainey is off to reenvision the world. I picture Steinbeck in his study, crafting this great American novel and, after scribbling away month after month, finally coming to those words of Tom Joad's, "I'll be there." I see Woody Guthrie in that fleapit hotel, Hanover House, on the corner of Sixth and Forty-Third on 23 February 1940, penning his own "God Blessed America" in answer to Irving Berlin's "God Bless America" and so composing verses that led to "This Land Is Your Land"—"the wheat fields waving and the dust clouds rolling." Steinbeck couldn't have known that his sentiments would inspire Guthrie and Springsteen. But a few scrawled words and there you have it, a kind of immortality: proof, in a way that ghosts—not least those of Tom Joad and his family—do exist; proof that the American lonesome instigates an equally powerful pull toward community, both between people in their own time and with the voices of the past, recalled and rearranged in the present, enlarging the circle of American art.

The path established in the *Tom Joad* era and consolidated in *The Rising* and *Devils & Dust* continues through *Magic, Wrecking Ball,* and *High Hopes* to the present. While "Girls in Their Summer Clothes" speaks to unrequited attraction, "Radio Nowhere" is about connection through music. The singer seeks his "way home." The sound he hears is "bouncing off a satellite" in "the last lone American night." He spins "'round a dead dial" in search of "a world with some soul." Sheer rhythmic noise will sometimes do, "a thousand guitars," the "pounding drums." "Making the Loud Noise" drowns out what Blaise Pascal calls "the eternal silence of these infinite spaces."[60] The same is true of *Wrecking Ball,* the title track of which combines this requiem for a community with a squaring up to mortality. It sets the speaker in that community, even as the wrecking ball in question is also what Philip Roth calls "the truncheon of old age."[61] "Bring on your wrecking ball" thus becomes existential defiance as well as a musical shield. We're all "burning down the clock." Gone is the exuberance of youth, but gone, too, or at least tamed, is that sense of lonesomeness without remedy. In the long run, no *Wrecking Ball* song will be more poignant than the final one, "We Are Alive." The band and its contemporary audience will disappear. But the dead reside in the living. "They" becomes "We." "I'm basically a traditionalist, and I like the whole idea of a rock and roll lineage," Springsteen said in 1995. "I always saw myself as the kid who stepped up out of the front row and onto the stage—who would carry the guitar for a while, and then pass on the rock and roll flame" (TAD 174). This sense of community acknowledges not only continuity between living beings but also with past eras. Musically exuberant, "We Are Alive" ends with a whistle, a whistle in the dark perhaps but a whistle nevertheless. Something remains. Others will inherit and use the music. Springsteen continues to take new directions, whether in the reinvigorating of American folk songs in *We Shall Overcome* or in *High Hopes,* with its mixture of material including the title song by Tim Scott McConnell; "Just Like Fire Would," from an Australian punk band, the Saints; "Dream Baby Dream," by Martin Rev and Alan Vega; and "The Wall," acknowledged as stemming from an idea of Joe Grushecky's and dedicated to Walter Cichon, missing in action in Vietnam in 1968. Together with new versions of older songs, "American Skin (41 Shots)" and "The Ghost of Tom Joad," and newly composed material one of which, "Down in the Hole," features his own then-middle-school children, Evan, Jess, and Sam, on backing vocals, this merging of the old and new, personal and public, could hardly be a better expression of the communal that has arisen over the decades out of the lonesome.

We must reserve a backshop, wholly our own and entirely free, wherein to settle our true liberty, our principal solitude and retreat.
—MICHEL DE MONTAIGNE, "OF SOLITUDE"

2

CLASSIC SOLITUDES

R evealing as Springsteen's autobiography is about his life, career, and craft, *Born to Run* is not least a confirmation of his qualities as a writer. Maybe he overuses capitals and occasionally rocks and rolls down anecdotal byways, but from that first description of childhood memories of Randolph Street through the compassionate portrait of his father to his relative honesty about his own failings, it's shot through with incisive descriptions, character sketches, observations, and judgments. This is no surprise. Robert Coles reports Walker Percy saying that some of his novelist friends told him they wished "they could write a story that had the power and the appeal of Springsteen's musical storytelling." Bob Dylan told his son Jacob that Springsteen "can block out a novel in two lines." Writers and songwriters have long admired Springsteen's way with words. He doesn't feature in Percy's fiction, but the novelist notes T. Coraghessan Boyle's story, "Greasy Lake," and the influence on it of "Spirit in the Night."[1] With Richard Ford, the admiration is mutual. Springsteen observes that *The Sportswriter, Independence Day,* and *The Lay of the Land* "nail the Jersey Shore perfectly" while Ford admits that "Springsteen's New Jersey songbook was instrumental" to his "believing that the Garden State was a fit subject and setting" for his Frank Bascombe novels. He simply avoided direct reference for fear of undermining his own art.[2] This didn't worry Bobbie Ann Mason with *In Country,* or contributors to the story collections inspired by his songs (*Trouble in the Heartland,* edited by Joe Clifford), or by a single song (*Meeting Across the River*, edited by Jessica Kay and Richard J. Brewer), or by an album (Tennessee Jones's *Nebraska*-inspired *Deliver Me from Nowhere*).[3] Springsteen is himself indebted to classic and contemporary American writing. He describes "films and writers and novels" as "primary influences" (TAD 198). A musical "traditionalist," he's equally part of the writing continuum.

As with many artists, the interaction between solitude and companionship has to do with Springsteen's experiences and innate disposition. Anthony Storr writes of "the emotional significance" of what goes on in an individual's mind when alone, and of "the central place occupied by the imagination in those capable of creative achievement." Not least because Springsteen's art oscillates between solitude and the communal, he's become, in Storr's terms, an "attachment figure" people feel they "can rely on even though the person concerned is not actually present." In a given situation, individuals ask of such figures what they would do (be they a public figure or a deity, or simply absent). For Storr, this amounts to "relying upon someone who, although not there in reality, has been incorporated into an individual's imaginative world as someone to turn to in a dilemma."[4] In the case of artists, the work provides sustenance by exuding an apparent sincerity born of the communal impulse within the experience of solitude. For Storr, success can be intimately related to "emotional scars." Activity designed as "compensation for deprivation" becomes "a rewarding way of life" that proves "as valid as any other, and more interesting than most." Often the artists themselves have developed "imaginative capacities as a compensation for the absence of, or severance of, intimate relationships with parents." Creativity takes on a "healing function." Our drive to understand and connect is also "a hunger for integration and unity within." ("Everybody," Storr may as well be saying, "has a hungry heart.") This is the intersection between lonesomeness and community, and between solitary creation and a paradoxical loss of self that is lessened by sharing that creation with others.[5] Connected, no doubt, with his early sense of isolation, Springsteen has referred to relationships as "the bonds that keep you from slipping into the abyss of self-destruction" (TAD 176). But like many artists, he's turned these feelings into something of social value. In *The Varieties of Religious Experience*, William James writes of how the "mystical states" involved in artistic activity can transport the individual "from tenseness, self-responsibility, and worry, to equanimity, receptivity, and peace."[6] A disposition toward solitude, oscillating with a need to connect, explains Springsteen's intense assertion of his symbiotic relationship with his audience. "I had to infuse the music with my own hopes and fears," he's said. "If you don't do that, your characters ring hollow" (S 69). Introspection leads to connection. For Springsteen, "this conversation," helped by the E Street Band as "the living manifestation of the community I write about," has ensured his continued desire to write, record, and perform (TAD 197).

In this, Springsteen is a fellow traveler with a wide range of American literary figures. Various sources, including the 2014 *New York Times Review* interview, testify to his intellectual interests.[7] He's read plenty of literature, and not just American. But while you don't read *The Brothers Karamazov, Anna Karenina,* and *Love in the Time of Cholera* without them affecting you, it may be conversely true that, as a product of American culture, he need not have read Emerson, William James, and so forth to absorb their worldview. Through such reading, his main discovery may have been not new ideas so much as a realization that others have asked similar questions. When Emerson advises that we speak our "latent conviction, and it shall be the universal sense," he reminds us that we learn from observation.[8] Like many independent thinkers, Springsteen took time to master not only his craft but also some self-understanding. Therapy led him to see more of how he really was. Solitude resulting in self-discovery and contemplation of others has long been an American activity. Frederick Douglass learned to read and write. Nathaniel Hawthorne entered shadowy worlds. Herman Melville set out to sea. Henry David Thoreau sought the woods by Walden Pond to build a cabin. Emily Dickinson escaped patriarchal dictates by descending into her cerebral labyrinth to "hit a World at every turn." Walt Whitman sang from the rooftops, and Mark Twain wrote of life on the Mississippi, away from the conventions and cruelties of shore. To contribute "productively to a community," writes Kevin Lewis, individuals have often "taken strength from their obligatory solitariness."[9] Working for hours alone, artists exemplify this. What follows, therefore, may illuminate Springsteen's relationship with what I've termed "classic solitudes" in American writing.

Reading *Born to Run* I found myself thinking of *The Autobiography of Frederick Douglass, an American Slave* (1845). For all their obvious differences in shape, size, and substance, the autobiographies share certain themes. One of these is empowerment through expression. As far as the dominant culture is concerned, and in some ways within African American culture, Douglass is an outsider looking in. He's born not just into physical slavery but also into the likelihood of growing up ignorant, and therefore mentally enslaved. In seeking a way out he must balance cultural identification with objectivity. He comes to realize, in maturity and freedom, that "to make a contented slave, it is necessary to make a thoughtless one," or, perhaps more accurately, to ensure an uneducated one.[10] If individuals acquire an education they acquire broader perspectives. They then empower themselves and are able to empower others. In childhood Douglass has "a want of information" about who he is. He's lost his mother, knows only that his father is white, and has no knowledge of the historical context of his position. His master, who may be his father, deems even basic enquiries by a slave to be "improper and impertinent, and evidence of a restless spirit."[11] Douglass experiences mental and physical trauma from childhood on, not least with the "cursing, raving, cutting and slashing" of the overseer, Mr. Severe. But he also learns from observing and listening. He sees the ambivalence of the slaves' attitudes toward those with power. "The Great House Farm," he explains, is "associated in their minds with greatness."[12] He sees how they express themselves and understands that expression shapes reality.

Douglass's story is also, in particular, associated with *artistic* expression, including music. Hearing his people's songs, he acquires, in sentiments later echoed in W. E. B. Du Bois's *Souls of Black Folk* (1903), James Baldwin's *The Fire Next Time* (1963) and Toni Morrison's *Jazz* (1993), an understanding of its ironic edge: obvious to those who know, unrecognized by those who don't. African Americans' "greatest gift" to the nation, writes Du Bois, suggests that a slave's life was "joyous," when in fact it's the music of "an unhappy people." "White Americans," writes Baldwin, "seem to feel that happy songs are *happy* and sad songs are *sad*," and don't "understand the depths out of which such an ironic tenacity comes." "Laughter is serious," writes Morrison. "More complicated, more serious than tears."[13] "Into all their songs," writes Douglass, the slaves weave "something of the Great House Farm," but he appreciates, as the masters may not, "the deep meaning of these rude and apparently incoherent songs." For all the spirited nature of the sounds, they express "the prayer and complaint of souls boiling over with the bitterest anguish," testifying against injustice and yearning for deliverance. Where Du Bois will describe himself as "within the veil," Douglass is "within the circle," and so able to see and hear differently from "those without." But he finds an art form—writing—that provides a way out of the circle and, to an extent, into the master's world.[14]

This basic pattern is the root of Springsteen's appeal, too. His version of "the Great House Farm," is a Mansion on a Hill. At first it's beyond attainment, but in the end he owns it, even while staying true to the people whose lives he makes use of in his art. Alain Locke, a student of William James's writing and the most notable African American pragmatist, describes the pattern in terms applicable to individuals regardless of race. In "The Ethics of Culture," he explains how such individuals educate themselves into becoming people who, having worked matters out internally, are eventually able to pass their self-taught knowledge onto others. "Culture," he writes—meaning self-cultivation in the deepest sense—"proceeds from personality to personality." It can't be taught, only learnt. But its appeal," he argues, is that it's the "self-administered part" of a person's education, representing one's "personal index of absorption." "As faulty as is the tendency to externalize culture," he goes on, "there is still greater error in over-intellectualizing it." Rather, such individuals cultivate themselves through experience. They start with their own lives and those of people they know. Only then can they look outward and appeal to those beyond this. "True culture," therefore, "must begin with self-culture." For this reason initially such individuals start out in solitude, for "in the pursuit of culture one must detach oneself from the crowd." The "pardonable concentration upon self-cultivation" allows for "spiritual capital" to accumulate. For Locke, this "must have been the essential meaning of Socrates's favourite dictum—'know thyself'—that to know, one must be a developed personality. The capacity for deep understanding is proportionate to the degree of self-knowledge, and by finding and expressing one's true self, one somehow discovers the common denominator of the universe."[15]

What Douglass and Springsteen share is the voice of a person who, brought up among entrapped people, finds freedom through knowledge of self, others, and context, combined with a skill that enables transformation. The solitary being, through force of will, must journey alone to a position that allows for a return to the community to teach what they've learned. Their writing—as with Du Bois's, Baldwin's and Morrison's—is what Russian critic Mikhail Bakhtin would call "double-voiced." It speaks of the two worlds, of double selves, and addresses different recipients, with a literal meaning and an ironic meaning, a surface exuberance and an inner complexity. Such writers are expert manipulators of tone, leading to wide appeal even if not all recipients quite understand the contents of the artwork. This is precisely why the phrase "Born in the U.S.A." came to be famously misinterpreted by George F. Will as "a grand, cheerful affirmation." All this conservative columnist heard was the upbeat sound and surface sentiment, when, as Eric Alterman puts it, the song is characteristic of an album featuring one "thrilling rave-up about a miserable human being" after another. Springsteen puts his debt to the blues succinctly in a 1996 interview. "I heard tremendous depth and sadness in the voice of the singer singing 'Saturday Night at the Movies,'" he explains, "and a sense of how the world truly was, not how it was being explained to me." He knew that rock music "should also be fun," but often, as noted, that fun would mask desperation.[16]

Further into Douglass's autobiography these resemblances strengthen. Douglass acquires the Word. Not unlike Springsteen's discovery of music and songwriting, Douglass recognizes articulation as "the pathway from slavery to freedom." "With high hope, and a fixed purpose, at whatever cost of trouble," he learns to read.[17] The more he reads, the more he detests his "enslavers." Fearful of being used by them, he needs another power, and so finally succeeds "in learning to write."[18] From here, he teaches others, tapping into their own wish to learn. His passion becomes to pass on to them his "life-giving determination."[19] While there are degrees of enslavement and violence, you needn't be a slave, or descended from slaves, to identify with disempowerment. Few contemporary readers have experienced life in a Siberian gulag, but experience of rigid control, whether in the army, in prison, or at boarding school, enables you to identify on some level with Aleksandr Solzhenitsyn's *One Day in the Life of Ivan Denisovich*, whose story of humdrum deprivation ends with the devastating reminder that "there were three thousand six hundred and fifty-three days like that in his stretch."[20] Few contemporary readers have experienced or witnessed the kind of extreme violence meted out to slaves in the antebellum south, but experience of violence, whether within a family, an institution, or society at large, and not least that perpetrated by an adult to a child, enables you to respond to Douglass's descriptions. Art, however haphazardly and inconsistently, cultivates the empathic impulse— and music, suggests Kathleen Higgins in *The Music of Our Lives*, at least as much as any other form.[21]

Both Douglass and Springsteen set up an opposition between facility and hostility. The combination helps shape their self-acquired vision. The parentless Douglass portrays his master and mistress as parent-figures. Think about Springsteen's evident relationship with his father and mother in the following passage from Douglass, and the similarities are striking. "What he most dreaded, that I most desired. What he most loved, that I most hated. That which to him was a great evil, to be carefully shunned, was to me a great good, to be diligently sought." In sum, writes Douglass, "I owe almost as much to the bitter opposition of my master, as to the kindly aid of my mistress. I acknowledge the benefits of both." Springsteen's mother may have bought him his first guitar, but without his father to kick against, his subject matter would have been drastically curtailed. Both men's life trajectories result from positive and negative forces. We are, as Montaigne reminds us, "double in ourselves."[22]

R ed and black make me think of not only Stendhal's novel and *Nebraska* but also *The Scarlet Letter*. All are dark works with a streak of brightness, like a red dawn or dusk through storm clouds or silhouetted trees. Rereading *The Scarlet Letter* with Springsteen in mind, I noticed that Nathaniel Hawthorne is as conscious of his Puritan ancestry as Springsteen is of his Catholic upbringing. He makes clear in the "Custom-House" preface that to write is to rebel. There were two unpopular things in the Springsteen household in his late teens: Bruce and his "goddam guitar."[23] Had the youth read Hawthorne's preface, no less than Douglass's autobiography, he'd have found solace. The relationship of art, not least music, to damnation, has a long history. "No aim, that I have ever cherished, would they recognize as laudable," writes Hawthorne. "No success of mine—if my life, beyond its domestic scope, had ever been brightened by success—would they deem otherwise than worthless, if not positively disgraceful. 'What is he?' murmurs one gray shadow of my forefathers to the other. 'A writer of story-books! What kind of business in life,—what mode of glorifying God, or being serviceable to mankind in his day and generation,—may that be? Why, the degenerate fellow might as well have been a fiddler!'"[24] This time it's less Springsteen's "restless spirit" against economic hardship that comes to mind than Springsteen's rebelliousness against Catholicism. As Hawthorne implies, writing and musicianship are akin. "'What is he?' mutter the nuns, 'a mumbling strummer!'" Dreams of dark forests permeate Springsteen's oeuvre, from "My Father's House" to "Downbound Train," just as they do Hawthorne's, not only in *The Scarlet Letter* but in, say, the allegorical story of "Young Goodman Brown," whose nightmarish forest excursions represent a permanent psychological scar. In such ways, Hawthorne's art illuminates Springsteen's like a lantern on a lonesome trail away from family and social expectations into the perceived wilderness of the "outsider art."

If the preface of *The Scarlet Letter* indicates Hawthorne's ambivalence toward his cultural upbringing, his story is of another near-solitary being, Hester Prynne, ostracized for childbirth outside marriage. Forced to wear a scarlet "A" on her tunic, signaling "Adulteress," she and her daughter, Pearl, are exiled to the dark woodland on the edge of town. Although Pearl eventually escapes this gloomy community, Hester herself, though for a while suffering the kind of ignominy Springsteen dramatizes in "Streets of Philadelphia"—very much a *Scarlet Letter* tale—not only outlives the community's "scorn" and wins its respect and even "reverence," but also opts to stay there. "Here had been her sin; here, her sorrow, and here was yet to be her penitence." People visit her with "all their sorrows and perplexities" and beseech "her counsel."[25] If there's a kind of parallel between Hester's choice and Springsteen's recognition that his subject matter and his community are primarily the Jersey Shore, it's also true that, as Jim Cullen shows in detail, part of him retains something of that Catholic upbringing and those cultural expectations.[26] He can't escape his cultural any more than his genetic make-up. "Let them scorn me as they will," writes Hawthorne of the Puritans, "strong traits of their nature have intertwined themselves with mine."[27] "Brainwashed as a child with Catholicism" (TAD 412), Springsteen admits that, while he doesn't "buy into all the dogmatic aspects" (TAD 165), "once you're a Catholic, you're always a Catholic" (TAD 412). Growing up in the immediate vicinity of the Catholic church, "with the priest's rectory, the nuns' convent, the St. Rose of Lima church and grammar school all just a football's toss away" (BTR 5), and experiencing the violence of a nun getting a "beefy enforcer" to give him a "smack across the face" may have estranged him from his "religion for good," but even those who remain "physically untouched" evidently find that Catholicism has seeped into their bones. As he grew older, Springsteen admits, he "came to ruefully and bemusedly understand" himself to be "still on the team" (BTR 16–17). As for genetics, despite Springsteen's fights with his father, he's always been aware, as he writes in "Independence Day," that they were "just too much of the same kind," or, in "Adam Raised a Cain," that "the same hot blood" ran in their veins.

So, too, might there be a partial explanation for the darker moments of his life in terms of a residual guilt. It's startling to finish Hawthorne's novel with Springsteen in mind and contemplate those final lines, depicting Hester's gravestone. On it is carved an inscription the somber nature of which is "relieved only by one ever-glowing point of light gloomier than the shadow": "ON A FIELD, SABLE, THE LETTER A, GULES."[28] Like this red letter on a black background, the novel is a shadowy tale in lurid red. No doubt it's coincidental that Springsteen's darkest, most guilt-ridden, most depressive album, wrought in solitude in his bedroom on "a four-track Japanese Tascam 144 cassette recorder" as he tried to come to terms with the meaning of his life and art after initial success, is his red and black album, *Nebraska* (BTR 299). With its stories of guilt with or without redemption, its doomed sinners, and *Twilight Zone* figures, the album is smeared with fear and self-hatred. "State Trooper," "Open All Night," and "Atlantic City" are gloomy stories of souls in purgatory. The link between "My Father's House" and Springsteen's visits to a psychiatrist to ask why he habitually drove nights by that childhood home on Randolph Street, and so by the church on the corner, is more than a twice-told tale. *The Scarlet Letter,* then, along with other Hawthorne material, has a family resemblance to Springsteen's work. He's a Hester figure himself, an adolescent outcast, a "freak," "on the outside looking in," dumped in a garbage can, unable to graduate, an acned youth ousted from college, yet turning his scarlet letter into the substance of his redemption. Like Hester, he outlived being labeled (in his case "Blinky" as well as "Saddie"), and used the very source of the "scorn" to bring upon himself, through his Art and Actions, Adulation and Awe, a truly American tale.[29] Maybe red on black is the color combination not just of the gothic romance but of rock and roll, from the cover of *Nebraska* to the field sable and red Gretsch guitar of the Cochran memorial in my hometown.

Melancholy solitude is no less evident in Herman Melville. In *Moby-Dick,* Ishmael starts out alone and morbidly depressed. Impecunious and beset by "a damp, drizzly November" in his soul that causes him to pause "before coffin warehouses" and follow along behind funerals, he opts to "see the watery part of the world." His "substitute for pistol and ball" is to "quietly take to the ship."[30] Time for a breakaway: the eternal urge of youth to escape. That town might be Freehold, or Verrières in the Franche-Comté, which Julien Sorel must escape in *The Red and the Black,* or Joe Gargery's place in *Great Expectations,* or Emma Rouault's father's farm in *Madame Bovary,* or the homestead where Yevgeny Bazarov's parents live in *Fathers and Sons,* or Hannibal, Missouri, in *Huckleberry Finn,* or Oak Park, Illinois, for Hemingway, or the English Northeast of the Animals in "It's My Life" and "We Gotta Get Out of This Place," or Dartford, Essex, "somewhere to get out of" for Keith Richards and Mick Jagger, or any number of small dots on the map of Europe, America, and wherever else.[31] In doing so, along the Nantucket boardwalk, Ishmael finds interracial companionship with Queequeg and then a crew of misfits. The Pequod pulls away from the Eastern Seaboard crewed by hunters of invisible game, born, as it were, to sail.

Springsteen said of *Moby-Dick*, which he'd recently finished when asked about his reading in 2014, that though it scared him off "for a long time" he in fact "found it to be a beautiful boy's adventure story."[32] The Pequod contains a band of searchers. Picture Federici, Weinberg, Clemons, and Tallent joining Van Zandt in crewman garb. The elusive quarry, the white whale, is metaphorically a pursuit of meaning. On board, Ishmael, the "cautious man," as Dave Marsh calls Springsteen, encounters his twin and opposite. Where Ishmael weaves back and forth reflecting and commenting on the chase, another solitary figure, Captain Ahab, single-mindedly pursues his prey.[33] Ishmael is no less "a seeker" than Ahab, but of "truth, experience, reflection of the world as it is," as he sings his "blues away" (TAD 400). The monomaniacal captain, in contrast, is hell bent on pursuit. He'll stop at nothing in his mad hunt for the "ungraspable phantom of life."[34] Set apart in the studio, month after month, the Boss will stop at nothing in his mad pursuit of unattainable perfection that, in Springsteen's analogy of his ambition while making *Born to Run,* was like trying "to shoot for the moon" (TAD 222). Faith in your vision is the only fuel. "Stay true to the dreams of your youth," runs a sentiment close to Melville's heart.[35] Like Melville, Springsteen knows that "true places" are never "down on any map."[36] Hence the complexity of the search: the next song, story, performance, trip, or book. Of course, *Moby-Dick* is much more than an "adventure story." Springsteen issues a warning that "you will learn more about whales than you have ever wished to know."[37] Perhaps he was thinking of the passage where Melville lists creatures ranging from "the Bottle-Nose Whale" through to "the Quog Whale; the Blue Whale &c" before stating that he will now leave his "cetological System standing thus unfinished, even as the great Cathedral of Cologne was left, with the crane still standing upon the top of the uncompleted tower." Yet, Springsteen can't be oblivious to his own Melvillian pursuit. "God keep me from ever completing anything," proclaims Melville. "This whole book is but a draught—nay, but the draught of a draught."[38] The tortuous search for perfection with the *Born to Run* album testifies to Springsteen's capacity for obsessiveness. As much to the point is the pragmatist nature of this: fallibility, process, pursuit.

A disciple of Emerson, Henry Thoreau absented himself from Concord, Massachusetts, to conduct an experiment in simple living. As he writes in *Walden: or, Life in the Woods,* he lived "a mile from any neighbor" in a cabin he built near Walden Pond, and earned his living by manual labor. The shore of a Massachusetts pond in the mid-nineteenth century may differ significantly from the Jersey Shore, but his reasons are familiar. Another young man alienated from his hometown, Thoreau asks why his fellow citizens should "begin digging their graves as soon as they are born." "The mass of men," he states, "lead lives of quiet desperation." In contrast, he's determined to live life on his own terms. "What old people say you cannot do, you try and find that you can," he writes. "Old deeds for old people, and new deeds for new."[39] His writing anticipates the young Springsteen's tensions with his father, the "one-man minefield," and with the older generation of that blue-collar community (BTR 356). Seeing trapped lives, the young Springsteen would have found his feelings echoed in Thoreau's opinion that "the old have no very important advice to give the young, their own experience has been so partial, and their lives have been such miserable failures, for private reasons, as they must believe." Thoreau claims that he's "yet to hear the first syllable of valuable or even earnest advice from my seniors."[40] He believes that he must become intellectually self-reliant. Springsteen had to do much the same; to make from his solitude a sturdy construct; to find a path out of the trap that those around him fell into; to see that it's not necessarily an individual's fault—the result of "private reasons"—but may have a wider context related to social and economic forces. In doing that, he would cast his eyes back to his society and write songs like "Factory" and "Independence Day."

Why, he asks in such songs, do people become the living dead? How is it that they end up living desperate lives? "If I am the guy in 'Born to Run,'" out there, away from society, he said to himself, "where is everybody?" He "began to question from that moment on the values and the ideas" set out on *Born to Run*. Out of this contemplation came *Darkness, The River,* and *Nebraska.* "You just get out there and you turn around and you come back because that's just the beginning." As he goes on to explain, "It's like that great scene in *The Last Picture Show* where the guy hits the brakes and turns around."[41] Both Thoreau and Springsteen escape society, turn back, and assess. "Where I Lived, and What I Lived For," Thoreau titles a chapter. Springsteen, too, shows an acute interest in creating a life purpose. Both strive to fulfill their human potential by confronting issues that those around them have no time for. To ask "what you can do with your life" and to use your observations to enable others to "experience their own inner vitality" is a version of Thoreau's evangelical zeal to alert his contemporaries to life's possibilities (TAD 256). Far from proposing "to write an ode to dejection," Thoreau intends "to brag as lustily as chanticleer in the morning, standing on his roost," if only to wake his neighbors up. "To be awake is to be alive," he asserts. "Is there anybody *alive* out there?" shouts Springsteen into the crowd. "We must learn to reawaken and keep ourselves awake," writes Thoreau. "I know of no more encouraging fact than the unquestionable ability of man to elevate his life by a conscious endeavor."[42]

In the end such writers look inward in order, through artistic expression or through action, to find the communal out of the solitary. Thoreau speaks directly to us as "you" just as Springsteen looks "into the faces" of the crowd each night. "I look straight at you," he's said, "and I see you looking straight back" (SOS 366). Thoreau's findings sound like a gloss on the singer's career. "I learned this, at least, from my experiment," he writes, "that if one advances confidently in the direction of his dreams, and endeavors to live the life which he has imagined, he will meet with a success unexpected in common hours." In particular, "solitude will not be solitude." Like many young people of such dispositions, Springsteen initially created a "fortress of solitude" (BTR 392). Thoreau's take on it is that, "if you have built castles in the air, your work need not be lost; that is where they should be. Now put the foundations under them."[43] The foundations of castles in the air—in the publications, recordings, performances, images, and memories that artists provide—take the form of art, and art enhances lives. Art in its broadest sense is communion often born of a need to express and therefore share feelings of solitude. It thus relates to human companionship. In youth, Springsteen wanted to know "if love is real." He found the answer. As any parent knows, and as he eventually articulated, "children are the 'living proof' of our belief in one another, that love is real. They are faith and hope transformed into flesh and blood" (S 218).

Reportedly identifying during a period of his life with Ethan Edwards, the John Wayne character in John Ford's *The Searchers*, Springsteen often refers to his protagonists as "searching" (TAD 143 and 185). The solitary figures in *Nebraska* search for family, connection, or community. Much discussion of this album centers on Springsteen's empathy for criminals, but the songs also focus on family and personal memories and, as he put it to Gilmore, with the "tone" of his childhood.[44] No Springsteen songs and no Emily Dickinson poems are bleaker, when it comes to the sense of exile we experience from our own childhood, than

"My Father's House" and Poem 609. Indeed, Springsteen might as well have modeled his song on the poem. "I Years had been from Home," begins Dickinson, "And now before the Door / I dared not enter, lest a Face / I never saw before / Stare stolid into mine / And ask my Business there—." Envisaging a stranger answering the door, she replies that her "Business" was "a Life I left / Was such remaining there?"

> I leaned upon the Awe—
> I lingered with Before—
> The Second like an Ocean rolled
> And broke against my ear—

The speaker hesitates. Reflecting on how time has passed, she's terrified of what she might find. She laughs "a crumbling laugh" that she "could fear a door," and fits her hand to the latch "with trembling care." But nerves fail her and she flees "gasping from the house." The strange phrases create an unsettling tone. We at once understand the temptation to return yet are warned that to do so will bring heartache. To borrow the title of a Thomas Wolfe novel, you can't go home again.

"My Father's House" has a similar troubling theme. Both poem and song are about a solitary being whose lonesomeness has as much to do with time as with space. *Nebraska* grew in particular out of Springsteen's memories of the timeless feel of his grandparents' house on Randolph Street, with its living room dominated by the photograph of his father's sister, Virginia, dead aged five, struck by that truck in 1927. Given that several stories "came directly" out of his family experience, he often opts to write "from a child's viewpoint" (S 138). The quality of fearfulness suggests that Dickinson, too, is writing of a childhood memory. Springsteen was interested in "the thin line between stability and that moment when time stops and everything goes black," and "wanted the music to feel like a waking dream" (S 138–39). Both depict a common nightmare. Springsteen's speaker dreams that he (or she) is a child trying to get home through a forest before night. The wind rustles in the trees. "Ghostly voices" rise from the fields. Scratched by "branches and brambles," clothes torn, the child breaks into a clearing and there shines the father's house. Falling into the father's arms, the speaker wakes from the dream and drives to the house. But the occupant is a stranger behind a door chain. Her apologetic response is that "no one by that name lives here anymore." The song ends with the speaker contemplating the father's house.

"Hard and bright it stands like a beacon" in the night, "calling and calling so cold and alone / Shining 'cross this dark highway where our sins lie unatoned."

To become an adult is to understand that if you do try to return home, which means to return to the past, you'll haunt a location that's no longer yours. Perhaps not least because of the trauma of migration and distance, it's a recognizably American theme. In *Death of a Salesman,* for example, Arthur Miller has Linda Loman tell Biff, away for months between infrequent visits to his parents, that he's such a child, failing to realize that one day he'll find strangers there. Dickinson's speaker desists from turning that latch and daren't even knock. Springsteen's finds the door opened by an unknown woman. We carry with us images of places from our past, and to go back is invariably to discover that the life and people we left have vanished. As Springsteen attests in "Independence Day," "different people" fill the empty spaces. Much of what we've known has been "swept away." Dickinson and Springsteen express the existential lonesomeness of human experience. "I like to get on the bus after the show and ride all night," Springsteen said in 1980. "I don't like *staying.*"[45] Born to run as we think we are, only in our dreams can we return to our origins. A flight of fancy might allow us to imagine that the girl in Dickinson's poem anticipates the ghost of little Virginia Springsteen, forever five years old, and living on as a photograph forming the centerpiece of the room on Randolph Street. "I Years had been from Home," she tells us, too frightened to enter in case the owners ask her business there. "My Business but a Life I left / Was such remaining there?"

It's because our self-identity is dependent upon accumulation of memory that the notion of an afterlife has power. Springsteen addresses this in such songs as "Souls of the Departed," "We Are Alive," and the intriguing "County Fair," written, he explains on the lyric page of *The Essential Bruce Springsteen,* "shortly after the *Nebraska* album." Dickinson's most famous meditation on the theme is Poem 712, "Because I could not stop for Death—" the shock of which rests not merely in the leisurely way that kindly Death drives the speaker by carriage past a school and fields and on, as the sun sets, to her grave, but with the actual time frame the final stanza alerts us to.

> Since then—'tis Centuries—and yet
> Feels shorter than the Day
> I first surmised the Horses' heads
> Were toward Eternity—

What seemed like a life that would last forever is now long gone. Springsteen administers a similar shock in "County Fair." Described by June Skinner Sawyers as "a wistful piece of nostalgia," it depicts the anticipation, experience, and memory of such events.[46] Unlike in "We Are Alive," where the speakers are a chorus, those in Dickinson's poem and in "County Fair" seem utterly alone. At first we think both poem and song are about the present, but it dawns on us, as each unfolds, that they're about the past. "Summer comes around," muses Springsteen's speaker. They "stretch a banner across Main Street," and "you feel something happen in the air." We see the lights being set up, viewed from Carol's house on Telegraph Hill, yet Carol herself is strangely absent from the middle section, and is only named again in the final verse. Whether colloquial metaphor or literal, the middle verses refer to "Daddy" speaking directly to his "little girl." Two-thirds through, the tone darkens. The band playing are "James Young and the Immortal Ones." Since no one remains young or is immortal, we realize that this is a memory. It gets late, but before heading back for town they let the "fortune wheel spin." The speaker cajoles the operator to tell him "what's waiting out there." Seeking the car, he kisses his companion, who then morphs back into Carol by the final verse. Back home he and Carol sit outside and listen to the radio. He leans back, stares "at the stars" and wishes he'd "never have to let this moment go."

As Sawyers notes, the melody "lingers long after the song stops." "Rather than repeating the catchy chorus," Springsteen "defies expectations and pulls back, ending the song on an uncertain note." Reviewing the details, we find that the song's "leisurely pace" has misled us.[47] Childhood excitement gives way to young romance; anticipation of new beginnings mingles with anticipation of endings. Moments dissolve as we grasp at them. Carousel horses may go round but the horses' heads pulling the carriage of time are toward eternity. Then again, another possibility occurs. What if we've misread the timescale? What if objections to Springsteen's "infantilization of women" would be entirely misplaced here?[48] The disconcerting element of the song is that the listener is never Carol. She is referred to in the third person at the start and end. In between, he's speaking to someone else. This might be a substitute for Carol, or it might be that the "little girl" is all he has left to remind him of her. Where the girl brags of not being scared at the top of the rollercoaster, and of winning "one of these stuffed bears," there's an invitation to see her as an actual child and the man as her actual father. What if the memory of taking his daughter to the county fair triggers another memory of when he and her mother were young and in love? What if Carol has left him or died? Our options are (1) that Springsteen is a clumsy songwriter or (2) that the song toys with our perception of time. Such subtlety has precedent. Dave Marsh notes that in "Reason to Believe" it takes a while "to see that what passes in the instant" is in fact a "lifetime, that the baby dunked in the water and the old man flung back into the earth are the same person."[49] The man in "County Fair" is regretting a lost relationship and the illusion that allows us to squander time. The autobiography confirms that this idea haunts Springsteen. "The price I paid for the time lost was just that," he writes. "Time lost is gone for good" (BTR 311). "County Fair," in the manner of "Reason to Believe," thus provides a narrative jolt similar to "Because I could not stop for Death—." Both speakers turn out to be looking back, in deepest solitude, on times they took for granted. Carpe diem! Robert Coles cites William Carlos Williams saying that "art gets a second life—the first in the life of the creator, the second in the life of the person who hears or sees what the creator has sent along, with her paintbrush, with her fountain pen or typewriter, with her voice, signing or speaking." Through its very ambiguities, "County Fair" invites such a "second life."[50]

Fellow travelers in "lonesome Glee" (Poem 774), Dickinson and Springsteen recognize, above all, that, for all the joy of creativity, for all the communion it offers, we are in the end solitary beings. They therefore see fame—being "known" by multiple others—as an ephemeral, illusory phenomenon. Dickinson wrote to Thomas Wentworth Higginson that if she sought fame she'd never find it but if it sought her she could not escape it.[51] Springsteen's song about Elvis Presley, "Johnny Bye-Bye," adapted from Chuck Berry's "Bye Bye Johnny," is his pithiest statement of his wariness of fame. The song starts out with an image of a mother and son. She puts him on a Greyhound with his guitar "on a one-way ticket to the promised land." News of Elvis's death comes on the radio. In another example of the fast-forward mode, suddenly it's his funeral, with his coffin in a white Cadillac and a woman crying by the roadside. In the final verse we learn that they found him drugged up and "slumped against a drain." The song closes with the title and the refrain, "you didn't have to die." Dickinson might have appreciated the song. "Fame is a fickle food / Upon a shifting plate," she writes in Poem 1659. "Men eat of it and die."

* * *

he summer always makes me want to pick up *Leaves of Grass* for a while and sit on the front porch," Springsteen has said. "I come away happier." As an altogether more expansive writer than Dickinson—a "louder" writer, one might say—Walt Whitman speaks to another side of Springsteen. They both shout their "barbaric yawp" from on high. Yet for all his poetical crowd surfing, Whitman's persona is still set apart from the audience he claims to belong to. In his insistence that he can speak with us across the decades he resembles a wandering ghost, haunting the places he used to inhabit.[52] Springsteen's most Whitmanesque offering, in this sense, is most obviously "Land of Hope and Dreams," a song about community even as it champions inner worlds. But no less in tune with Whitman is the melancholy flipside to this, that sad and soaring song, "The Promise."

As Sawyers explains, "Land of Hope and Dreams" grows out of an "old African-American spiritual 'This Train (Is Bound for Glory).'" First recorded in 1925, it's been performed by numerous artists, including Woody Guthrie, Big Bill Broonzy, Pete Seeger, Johnny Cash, Bob Marley, and the Indigo Girls. Guthrie's memoir, *Bound for Glory,* makes ironic reference to it. Springsteen places the phrase on Jimmy the Saint's car in "Lost in the Flood." In more general terms, his version draws on "gospel songs about the Promised Land" that date back to the nineteenth century. But it also subverts the original religious message. "This Train (Is Bound for Glory)" emphasizes that "if you ride you must be holy." "Liars," "gamblers," "midnight ramblers," "jokers," "cigarette smokers" and other such rabble are unwelcome.[53] Springsteen, in contrast, wanted his "refrain to be inclusive" (S 296). Theoretically it's all aboard the rock-and-roll flyer. As Ernie Sandonato showed in his 2012 symposium presentation, the train is Springsteen's oeuvre and the passengers his characters.[54] It thunders through sunlit fields carrying "saints and sinners," "losers and winners," "whores and gamblers," "fools and kings." Whatever you have faith in, it "will be rewarded." "*No one* will be turned away," Sawyers assumes. "Brother Bruce's expansive universe is big enough to hold anyone who wants to join him."[55]

Whether Springsteen, any more than Whitman, is so all-inclusive, however, seems contestable. "Hope and dreams" is a seductive phrase, but one person or group's hopes and dreams, whether or not the intentions are malevolent, can have devastating consequences for other people. "Land of Hope and Dreams" is not the same as Elvis singing "American Trilogy" in Las Vegas, where, as Greil Marcus puts it, his "YES," his "grandest fantasy of freedom," is "finally a counterfeit freedom," because "it takes place in a world that for all its openness (Everybody Welcome!) is aesthetically closed, where nothing is left to be mastered, where there is only more to accept."[56] Springsteen's song doesn't at all state that "anyone" can hop aboard, and he's not himself without judgment. Aside from his assessment of Reagan's appropriation of "Born in the U.S.A.," and the "public service announcements" that punctuated the *Magic* tour during the second Bush administration, there's the story of "Oliver North's infamous secretary and fellow document shredder, Fawn Hall," sending word that "she and her date, Rob Lowe, would like to come back stage and introduce themselves." Springsteen's curt response would suggest that not everyone is welcome on his railroad. Eric Alterman's reference to this comes after quoting Springsteen telling an audience, "Pat Robertson can kiss my ass." He, too, might find it hard to acquire a ticket. Years later Springsteen tells a crowd, "Don't vote for that fucking Bush, no matter what!" Given that Springsteen has called Donald Trump "a flagrant, toxic narcissist" with "no sense of decency and no sense of responsibility about him," it seems unlikely that he'd get aboard.[57] Aside from the question of whether all Americans are welcome, regardless of religious or political views, or degree of sanctimony, mendacity, or criminality, there should also be some doubt about, for instance, psychopaths, malevolent dictators from Vlad the Impaler through Pol Pot into the present, and the architects of the Final Solution.

In "Paradise," Springsteen does contemplate the mind of a suicide bomber, but neither his art nor Whitman's speak of inclusivity. He may write that he wants his refrain "to be inclusive" of "everybody," but there's no reference to "everybody" in the lyrics (S 296). "Trust the art and be suspicious of the artist," we recall him echoing Lawrence (TAD 314). Whitman's version of the sentiment in "Song of Myself" is to give "the sign of democracy," accepting "nothing which all cannot have their counterpart of on the same terms." "Through me many long dumb voices," he writes, from "prisoners and slaves" through the "despised" and "forbidden."[58] But the absences speak for themselves. There's no mention of governors, rulers, the rich, the powerful. Similarly "Land of Hope and Dreams" emphasizes the downtrodden rather than the successful and, although Springsteen refers to kings, in an American context that might just mean that rogue in *Huckleberry Finn*, or the fan-anointed Frank or Elvis, since the fiction of hereditary "royalty" has no place in a republic.

In assessing hopes and dreams, Springsteen's song might still seem overly optimistic, portraying inner worlds as benevolent. This tendency, in Louis Menand's words, to assume that everyone's "wants and beliefs" will lead them to act positively toward themselves and others, is one of pragmatism's "deficiencies as a school of thought." It's not enough to say, "faith will be rewarded." As Joyce Carol Oates puts it, "men and women will die for the sake of beliefs we know to be delusional (i.e., other people's religions)."[59] Then again, despite the vividness of those great wheels rolling through sunlit fields, the train is only a metaphor. As Colin Burrow puts it, "metaphors don't carry guns" and "people rather than words kill people." Positively or negatively, they "influence how people think about their relationships" to others; the Nazis exploited this by inter-splicing newsreels about Jews with footage of scurrying rats.[60] But this only illustrates Rorty's point that "any philosophical view is a tool which can be used by many different hands." The first step toward a better world is to believe that it's possible. As for what "better" might mean, we live in a world of specifics, not abstractions. Context is all.

Whitman and Springsteen both expound the belief that art can change and even save lives. They're concerned with how inner worlds shape outer realities. Our metaphors—the art of our language—shape our thoughts. This belief is tied to the conviction that, in James Baldwin's words, each of us is "responsible to life" as the "small beacon" between "the terrifying darkness from which we come and to which we shall return," and must "negotiate this passage as nobly as possible, for the sake of those who are coming after us." The trick, he urged, is "to say 'yes' to life."[61] We have a choice. "From a pragmatic viewpoint," writes William James, "the difference between living against a background of foreignness and one of intimacy means the difference between a general habit of wariness and one of trust." If we're materialistic we'll be suspicious, "cautious, tense, on guard. If spiritualistic, we may give way, embrace, and keep no ultimate fear."[62] Springsteen's version of this is that "you have to remain interested in life and in the way the world's moving" (TAD 417).

To cite an updated expression of pragmatism, what Giles Gunn calls "pragmatism with a vengeance," Richard Rorty's perspective (as Gunn explains) is that the language we use is contingent. Truth, therefore, is not "a reality beyond language" but exists only "in the relations among our sentences." Hence, language is less a medium of "representation or expression" than "an instrument of redescription." To accept this premise is to see the self as "linguistically constructed." From that, it follows that "cultural change has a lot more to do with alterations in language than with revolutions in belief." Thus, for the Rortian pragmatist, language "is more like a set of tools for performing a task than a medium for getting something straight." If we accept this, then "the question is no longer how to secure agreement between one's language and something that stands beyond it, such as fact, truth or reality—'the world offers no criteria for comparing alternative metaphors'—but how to get over one way of talking and acquire the habit of another."[63] Change your metaphors, change your vocabulary, and you can change minds. Nothing is guaranteed but if, in Rorty's words, "discursive practices go all the way down to the bottom of our minds and hearts," this allows us to think of individual minds being "capable of ever more novel, ever richer, forms of human happiness."[64] Whitman and Springsteen share with Dewey, Rorty, and other pragmatists this emphasis on language as our primary art form. Whitman decides to describe his poetic self not merely as a man but as something far more encompassing. He wills his art to be greater than the individual artist. Springsteen holds up his guitar, without which he would, like the rest of us, be his actual, diminished, fallible, vulnerable, stumbling clown of a self. The language of music, lyrics included, can make us all something more. "Talk about a dream / Try to make it real."

Of course, there's a burden to this, too, and Springsteen articulates it a long-buried song from the *Darkness* era, finally resurrected, decades later, as the title track of *The Promise*. The speaker of "The Promise" is in a band "looking for that million-dollar sound." He bunks off his nightshift to lose himself in movies, following "that dream just like those guys do way up on the screen." But when the promises are broken he cashes in some of his dreams, sells the Challenger he's built, and spills his secrets. By this stage in the song many a listener thinks of the lawsuits of the time between Springsteen and his first manager, Mike Appel. ("I don't write songs about lawsuits," Springsteen retorted, and the song stayed unreleased for over thirty years.)[65] But more importantly the song is about the dream of being an artist and the struggle to retain the belief that art matters in a world where economics predominates. "This is my life," Springsteen told a hearing, and as the song goes: "Every day it just gets harder to live this dream I'm believing in."[66] As with Whitman, the speaker's emotions are directed outward. He feels responsible for "the broken spirits of all the other ones who lost." In contrast to "Land of Hope and Dreams," he focuses on how wrong it can go: how against "fortune" always stands "that other thing" that "never feels that far away." The speaker is losing touch with what has given his life meaning. But part of that loss and pain is about more than himself as an individual. Both songs have a vivid image of wheels moving. In "Land of Hope and Dreams" it's the big wheels rolling through fields. In "The Promise" it's "the tires rushing by in the rain." The first image is of exhilaration. The travelers are bound for the metaphorical sunshine their dark past must accede to. The second image is of a man whose faith is faltering. Since he built it himself, the car he's sold is really a crafted vision, a body of work. He's trudging the rain-soaked roadside. On his road to nowhere, the wheels "rushing by" cover him in filthy spray.

The moment in the song that brings Springsteen closest to Whitman focuses not on self-pity but on social responsibility. We make best use of our inner selves by looking outward. The promise within us must become a promise to others, especially "the broken spirits" who gain sustenance from the artist's conviction. Success, he writes, brought "a sense of accountability to the people I'd grown up alongside of" (S 65). He knew himself to be an anomaly. Others around him had seen hopes and dreams slip away. "The promise" is a promise the speaker has felt within, has made to himself and then makes to those he grew up with, and to his audience. "Your ticket is your handshake," as he puts it in the Austin address (SOS 394). But it also suggests the promise unfulfilled in many individuals. "The whole thing of the wasted life," he's said, "was very powerful to me" (TAD 308). Promise anticipated, promise fulfilled, promise kept, promise betrayed, promise wasted. The theme of the promise binds the nineteenth-century poet and the contemporary songwriter on precisely this point: the promise the writer makes to us has to do with his reminder of the promise within us. The artist is a catalyst.

Springsteen, no less than Whitman, articulates the intimate message of spiritual sustenance through words that speak of shared experience. We return to his songs as we return to Whitman. "If you want me again look for me under your boot-soles," writes Whitman, for the artist, by way of the art, stops somewhere, waiting for us. The final lines of "Song of Myself" are a vision of how a voice can transcend time and place. The intimacy of a voice from another time or place can change and shape a life here and now. In this mutual belief, Whitman and Springsteen show themselves to be comrades in art, neither one above the other. Bruce Springsteen, Whitman might have proclaimed, a kosmos, of New Jersey the son, "Turbulent, fleshy, sensual, eating, drinking and breeding. / No sentimentalist, no stander above men and women or apart from them, / No more modest than immodest."[67] At the very least, he would surely have approved of one of his successors as, in the words of Robert Coles, "a poet singing" with "the people listening."

* * *

rnest Hemingway notes in *Green Hills of Africa* that "all modern American literature" derives from *Huckleberry Finn*. F. Scott Fitzgerald in turn writes that Mark Twain was the first American writer to look back across the continent rather than to project westward with European precedent in mind.[68] Greil Marcus links Huck with Ahab in that, though Ahab is obsessive while Huck seeks peace of mind, both will choose damnation over compromise. He sees "the obsessiveness and the wish for peace of mind" as "cornerstones" of rock music to be found "together more often than not." For, he later adds, the link between great rock careers is "volcanic ambition." "It is that bit of Ahab burning beneath the Huck Finn rags of 'Freewheelin'' Bob Dylan, the arrogance of a country boy like Elvis sailing into Hollywood, ready for whatever kind of success America had to offer."[69] All this would seem true enough of Springsteen. His art exhibits "obsessiveness," but there's also that milder, ruminative side, a lonesomeness that expresses itself not in stormy rage but a yearning to become emotionally becalmed. To find it, no less than to fulfill obsessive dreams, requires both companionship and solitude.

The word "lonesome" crops up often in Twain's novel, but Huck, while a good companion, ultimately chooses to be alone. Only when beyond social constrictions can he reflect and grow, in a way that Tom Sawyer never can. "Learning, thinking, innovation, and maintaining contact with one's own inner world," Anthony Storr explains, "are all facilitated by solitude." Moreover, to grow must involve a sense of incompleteness. "The process of remedying incompleteness" is such that many of us experience "adaptation through maladaptation." For Storr, "the hunger of imagination, the desire and pursuit of the whole, take origin from the realization that something is missing."[70] Springsteen makes a similar point when he speaks of those who "take their own thoughts and formulate them in some fashion" that channels dysfunction into "something positive and creative." Art derives then from a "need to sort yourself out" (SOS 270). Both echo Alain Locke. It's not that merely rock and roll is the "outsider art," but that art—including the art of self-cultivation—is, in many cases, an outsider activity. Yet it's also true that the *Born to Run* album cover features Springsteen leaning on Clarence Clemons, a twentieth-century version of Huck and Jim. Huck's relationship with Jim is essential to his growth, and his moment of revelation is about Jim even while it necessarily occurs in solitude, just as he'll end the novel alone. Anguishing over whether to betray his friend or to lie to save him from recapture, he writes a note revealing Jim's whereabouts to his owner, Miss Watson.

But something gnaws at him. In Storr's terms, "something is missing." He knows the "right" thing to do in this slave society, but his recognition of Jim, not only as a human being but also as an actual and surrogate father, won't allow such betrayal. "All right then," he says, "I'll *go* to hell" and destroys the note.[71] Too young to understand that society is wrong, he must work through these dilemmas alone, without Tom telling him what to think and without Jim's or anyone else's presence to distract him. Lighting out for Indian Territory, he's probably aiming for what is now Oklahoma. Springsteen will resurrect the motherless Huck by way of Rainey Williams, who leaves his presumably dying mother behind in "Black Cowboys," and travels alone toward that very same state.

Both *Huckleberry Finn* and "Black Cowboys" are about loyalty and self-reliance. Twain makes no mention of Huck's mother, Springsteen none of Rainey's father. Each has to deal with a single self-destructive parent whom they must escape. Rainey's mother tries to raise him but also provides the tools for his departure, both by stimulating his imagination and by hiding the money that funds his journey. "What does it mean to be a friend to somebody?" asks Springsteen in an interview. What indeed does it mean to be a good parent, or someone's child? In contrast to the drunkard, Pap, Jim shows what it means to be the former, teaching Huck, too, about the responsibility of child to parent. Huck works out that he must act according to innate feelings of justice regardless of society's judgment. Stuck with Aunt Polly's attempts to "sivilize" him he feels, as Lewis writes, "so lonesome" he "could die."[72] Post-Elvis, we hear "Heartbreak Hotel" in this. Maybe we can also imagine Jim's influence as the equivalent of Clemons's saxophone in Springsteen's music—the soft, mellow, gentle, sometimes urgent sound of a voice and presence that shows Huck how to feel, and that it's okay to do so. Rainey is equally alone and must make his own perilous decisions, but he, in turn, is haunted by the idea of the black cowboys, imaginary companions whom he will never find but for whose spirits he searches. The bones in his mother's chest become the bone of the desert as he approaches Oklahoma, starting point of *The Grapes of Wrath*, the state Cochran's parents were from, and once known as the Territory. Thus a contemplation of classic solitudes in light of Springsteen's music leads to a contemplation of his work in terms of contemporary solitudes.[73]

One writes against one's solitude and against the solitude of others.
—EDUARDO GALEANO, *Days and Nights of Love and War*

3

CONTEMPORARY SOLITUDES

For Uruguayan journalist and novelist Eduardo Galeano the motivation to write is a need to communicate and so commune, to denounce the sources of pain, and to share the sources of happiness. Writing is ultimately adversarial both to the solitude the writer feels and the solitude the writer witnesses or intuits in others.[1] Kevin Lewis's twentieth-century "inheritors of Whitman's and Dickinson's lonesome" include Robert Frost, Wallace Stevens, and Theodore Roethke. One might also think of the Beats, of southern writers Carson McCullers with *The Heart Is a Lonely Hunter* and Anne Tyler with *Dinner at the Homesick Restaurant*, of Toni Morrison's depiction of the isolation caused by trauma and grief in *Beloved*, and of novelists Springsteen refers to, not least Cormac McCarthy.[2] Solitude abounds in American twentieth- and twenty-first-century writing, and similarities of preoccupation and tone are palpable among writers contemporary with Springsteen. But there's another aspect of Galeano's sentiments that interests me. Galeano was an activist, author of *Open Veins of Latin America: Five Centuries of the Pillage of a Continent* (1973) and the *Memory of Fire* trilogy, completed in the 1980s. His key word is "against," and his key phrase is "against the solitude of others." In contemplating contemporary American writing in light of Springsteen, the following comments on a fellow Catholic, Walker Percy, and a fellow commentator on the Jersey Shore, Richard Ford, might complement what others have written. But I will also focus on two writers who use their art on behalf of those whose solitude is linked with injustice: Richard Wright and Joyce Carol Oates.

Where Galeano uses the word "against," for James Baldwin "to write is to attack." Both have politics and religion in their sights. Baldwin asserts that our human solitariness is precisely why we should abandon the primitive posturing of much of the human past, including the "totems, taboos, crosses, blood sacrifices, steeples, mosques, races, armies, flags, nations," and other paraphernalia of cultural and religious tribalism.[3] Galeano is equally uncompromising about the Catholic Church. Wright's *Native Son,* with its emphasis on how fear and isolation can lead to criminality and to the solitude of a death row cell, connects up one of Springsteen's concerns, the class (and race) skewed phenomenon of incarceration and the death penalty. Oates is a prolific writer of novels, stories, essays, poetry, and even plays, but one short story, "High Lonesome," allows a comparison with Springsteen. By way of their mutual admiration for Flannery O'Connor, Oates has parallels with Springsteen in being brought up in a blue-collar, Catholic household, being a long-time New Jersey residency, and sharing not a little related subject matter. Contemporary American writing is itself, of course, part of American art in more general terms, including American film, an obvious influence on Springsteen in such movies as *The Grapes of Wrath, The Searchers, The Night of the Hunter,* and *The Last Picture Show.*

Comparisons between Springsteen and Percy, Ford, and O'Connor have been made before. June Skinner Sawyers and Michael Kobre each discuss Springsteen in terms of Percy. Sawyers's focus is on *The Moviegoer.* Kobre considers Percy's novels with regard to *Working on a Dream.* David Gellman discusses Springsteen's and Ford's mutual "use of Western landscapes and Independence Day metaphors," not least in terms of Ford's novel of that title which, as he told Elinor Ann Walker in 1997, comes as much from Springsteen's song as all the other possible sources. Of the several excellent discussions of O'Connor, particularly noteworthy is Irwin Streight on the "O'Connoresque characters" of *Nebraska,* Springsteen's specific use of the word "meanness" in the title song—an echo of the end of her story "A Good Man Is Hard to Find," which he in turn uses as a song title—and the authors' mutual Catholicism.[4] Perhaps what I suggest here will add to that broader discussion. With regard to Wright and Oates, it may also take it in new directions.[5]

* * *

Whatever the arguments over Robert Coles's version, Walker Percy is not such an unlikely Springsteen conversationalist. Kieran Quinlan writes illuminatingly on Percy in a book subtitled *The Last Catholic Novelist.* When Springsteen played "If I Was the Priest" at his audition with John Hammond, Hammond's response was, "Were you brought up by nuns?" "Of course," Springsteen replied.[6] For Quinlan, Percy's Catholicism defined him as a novelist. Springsteen and Percy are, however, mirror images; Percy converted to the faith in the 1940s after surviving tuberculosis, whereas Springsteen was born into Catholicism and, while its residue remains, evidently rejected it as a belief. What he retains, however, is his fascination with Catholic culture and spiritual matters. The most revealing place to discover why Percy would admire Springsteen is in his essays. As Sawyers shows, and as is evident from Springsteen's discussion of them with the novelist's nephew, Will Percy, they express "a way of thinking that echoes Springsteen's own thoughts."[7] Once again, solitude is to the fore. Percy's essay collection is titled *The Message in the Bottle,* while another work of nonfiction, a spoof on self-help books, is called *Lost in the Cosmos.* Both writers are engaged in a deeply personal, intellectual, and emotional quest. In his letter to Springsteen, Percy expresses interest in the singer's "spiritual journey." Springsteen's eventual reply to Percy's widow states that "the loss and search for faith and meaning" has been "at the core" of his work most of his "adult life."[8]

As a Catholic convert in a secular age, Percy was very different from Springsteen, yet this also creates their shared sense of being outsiders. He has an essay titled "How to Be an American Novelist in Spite of Being Southern and Catholic." In Quinlan's words, his "embattled stance" is built on being "at odds with the 'wisdom' of the age." Quinlan feels that staunch religiosity compromised Percy's art but that he's still "one of the few contemporary novelists who has made a difference in the lives of many readers."[9] Like Springsteen, he's not least influential because he conveys conviction. It's equally true that the roots of both men's art involve dealing with trauma. Percy, writes Quinlan, was "a depressive" with an "acknowledged need to use the medium of fiction to come to terms with the suicides in his family," not least his father's.[10] Given Springsteen's equally intense need to understand his early years, however much their work entertains it also asks what nineteenth-century Russian thinkers referred to as *proklatye voprosy*—"the accursed questions."[11] No wonder both writers name Dostoevsky, Chekhov, and Tolstoy among their reading. To use Percy's phrase in "From Facts to Fiction," both address "what it means to be a man living in the world who must die."[12]

Quinlan refers to a 1950 *Partisan Review* edition of essays published under the title "Religion and the Intellectuals." "Assuming that in the past religions nourished certain vital human values," asks the preface, "can these values now be maintained without a widespread belief in the supernatural?" No, states Percy. "With the passing of the cosmological myths and the fading of Christianity as a guarantor of the identity of the self," he writes, "the self becomes dislocated." "Imprisoned by its own freedom," it roams the Cosmos like "a space-bound ghost."[13] Springsteen echoes Percy in depicting alienated beings seeking reasons to believe. Such songs as "State Trooper" and "Radio Nowhere" depict his own "space-bound" wanderers. The end of "State Trooper" encapsulates the existential dread of an untethered life facing cosmic nothingness: "Hey somebody out there, listen to my last prayer / Hi ho silver-o deliver me from nowhere." Two decades later, the "Radio Nowhere" driver is still "spinnin' 'round a dead dial," the sounds "bouncing off a satellite," as he seeks to drown out the silence of the universe.

William James writes of pragmatism that it offers nothing new. These concerns are ancient, from Pascal's infinite silences, to Frost's "Desert Places," to the notion that art alone might suffice, in Virginia Woolf's words, as "the one dependable thing in a world of strife, ruin, chaos."[14] Percy, like Pascal, opts for a religious answer. But it's perfectly possible from a pragmatist perspective to reject the supernatural yet affirm life: to believe, in Richard Rorty's words, that religion and philosophy, both of which assume a truth beyond the human, are "relatively primitive" ideas and that "the human imagination" is our "only source of redemption."[15] Whether or not, as Percy's friend Shelby Foote notes, "art is by definition a product of doubt," Percy and Springsteen use art, in Quinlan's phrase on Percy, to "express" or "discover" ideas and therefore "reality." "Our doubt is our passion," writes Henry James, "and our passion is our task. The rest is the madness of art." As Springsteen said early in his career, "some people pray, some people play music."[16] Percy the Catholic convert and Springsteen the lapsed Catholic both convey an understanding that a sense of being an outsider fuels a concern to assert purpose in life. Regardless of a reader's religious persuasion, notes John Hardy, this Catholic novelist presents "the essential drama of the search for faith." However secular Springsteen's music may be, he shares with Percy just such a drama.[17]

* * *

What Springsteen might get from Richard Ford is as interesting as what Ford acknowledges getting from Springsteen. The most pertinent work is the first Frank Bascombe novel, *The Sportswriter* (1986), which resurrected Ford's career under the influence of Springsteen's music. In 1985 Ford wrote of how Springsteen left him thinking that this was rock and roll "of a somewhat higher order." In 1997, he told Elinor Ann Walker how he'd specifically quelled his desire to reference Springsteen directly in *The Sportswriter* for fear it would "gobble up" his scene, and suggest he "was poaching."[18] This novel was my introduction to Ford many years ago. It's instructive to reread it, imagining Ford listening to Springsteen and Springsteen reading Ford. The novelist, who like his protagonist, Frank Bascombe, is approaching middle age, asks questions common to individuals entering that phase, taking stock of where he's been and where he's going. To do this can amount to what Erik Erikson calls a "Crisis of Generativity." What is the net result of life thus far? Albert Camus refers to the dawning awareness that we're on a curve we must see through to the end.[19] Faced with our own mortality, what should we do? What matters?

Like most of us, Frank has compromised. He's foregone literary ambition for security and writes for a magazine. Sportswriting teaches you "that there are no transcendent themes in life," he rationalizes. "In all cases things are here and they're over, and that has to be enough." Sport has wider resonance as an absorbing activity. Camus, who played in goal for a university soccer team (Racing Universitaire Algerios), has a character in *The Fall* say that he's "never been really sincere and enthusiastic" except on stage while in the army, and "in sports." "In both cases there was a rule of the game, which was not serious but which we enjoyed taking as if it were." You live in the now. You concentrate on your performance. The sportswriter and sports fan can live vicariously in this same illusory yet consuming drama. To be a sportswriter, Frank observes, you need "a willingness to watch something very similar over and over again, then be able to write about it." What you shouldn't expect is for the athlete to be an interesting person. "Athletes at the height of their powers," he muses, "make literalness into a mystery all its own simply by becoming absorbed in what they're doing."[20]

Imagining Springsteen reading this, it's natural to see sport as standing for things music-related. Camus's linking of sport and theater as serious games finds its echo in Springsteen's Austin comments about the seriousness or otherwise of rock music. "Be able to keep two completely contradictory ideas alive and well inside your heart and head at all times," he says, treating rock and roll "like it's all we have" while also remembering that that's all it is (SOS 398). When absorbed in the moment, rational discussion becomes irrelevant. The young Springsteen's retort to Robert Hilburn that there's no answer so no point in asking, might have been an athlete's to a sportswriter. It challenges the assumption that the activity requires commentary. As entertaining illusions, sport and "the dream world of popular music" have clear kinship. Ford's metaphor points to intertwined ways of being; you can act and/or you can reflect upon the action. You can write and/ or you can perform. You can perform and/or you can watch and reflect. You can ruminate alone and/or you can converse. Ford and Springsteen write about such options. Indeed, when the young Springsteen made this comment, he's likely to have had performance in mind. Only later in his career will he point out that his job combines both the "reflective" experience of writing, and the "physical experience" of performing (TAD 139). The autobiography testifies that these two activities, not unlike sport, are a complex interplay of thought, word, and action.

Having lost his son to illness, and his wife in the wake of their grief, Frank describes his struggles for meaning and intimacy. Writers "need to belong," he says. "Only for real writers, unfortunately, their club is a club with just one member." To assuage isolation he seeks romantic adventures. What could be "more mysterious," he asks, than "the exhilaration of a new arrival"? But, since such comments preclude the possibility of long-term emotional intimacy, they accentuate our awareness of his solitary nature.[21] His mental state echoes Springsteen's mid-career lyrics and interviews, more recently expanded upon in Born to Run. After his time as "a serial monogamist" and a "short shot at being Casanova," only as he was getting older—in his case his mid-thirties—did he recognize his need to find a way out of these kinds of patterns (BTR 330–31). "Why did I only feel good on the road?" he asked himself (TAD 157). "Once out of the touring context, and out of the context of my work," he says, "I felt lost." Music had provided a meaning that he'd grasped with "religious intensity" (TAD 159). But he'd muddled the distinction between narrative and life itself. "I had become a master manipulator," he admits. "I avoided closeness." He could afford to do this because he had the band and the work. "When I hit the stage, it was just the opposite. I would throw myself forward, but it was okay because it was brief." After all, as Frank would have it, "what could be better" than "the exhilaration of a new arrival"? Hence, says Springsteen, "I went out in '85 and talked a lot about community, but I wasn't part of any community" (TAD 161). Therapy eventually meant that he "crashed into" himself and saw that his "speciality" was keeping distance so that if he "lost something, it wouldn't hurt that much" (TAD 164).[22]

Emotional maturity, as Frank Bascombe finds out, can arrive a long time after physical maturity. "Sometimes we do not really become adults until we suffer a good wacking loss," he reflects, "and our lives in a sense catch up with us and wash over us like a wave." He's found a path that suits him up to a point, but understands, now—well past Camus's curve—that he's as involved as everyone else in "The Race To The Tomb." He's "fighting the battle with age; discovering how to think of the future in realistic terms." He and a fellow sportswriter "were both stuck like kids who had reached the end of what they know they know." Disorientated by the passing years, he says that "sometimes I can even forget my own age and the year I'm living in, and think I'm twenty, a kid starting new in the world—a greener, confused by life at its beginning."[23] But the truth must be faced. "We Play at Paste—," writes Dickinson in Poem 320, "Till qualified, for Pearl—." Springsteen, in turn, has long been conscious of how you might resolve matters in such a way as to function at one age, but have to readjust for a later phase. The aging boys still "racing in the street" are akin to Ford's characters in having "reached the end of what they know they know." Springsteen saw that song, he's said, as a depiction of the speaker in Brian Wilson's "Don't Worry, Baby" ten years on (TAD 403). He was "always interested" in developing his music to suit the concerns of the different ages he reached. His "usefulness as a thirty-eight-year-old," he realized, would differ from his "usefulness as a twenty-seven-year-old."[24] It's not that an isolationist urge will dissolve but that you accommodate it rather than let it dominate. "Isolation is a big part of the American character," he's said. "Everyone wakes up on one of those mornings when you just feel like you want to walk away and start brand new" (TAD 250). The mature adult, to use F. Scott Fitzgerald's definition of "a first-rate intelligence," holds "two opposed ideas in the mind at the same time": in this case the need to balance solitude and companionship. Ford's novels and Springsteen's later lyrics dramatize this.[25]

Frank's view that "New Jersey is the purest loneliness of all" reminds us that Ford and Springsteen share physical as well as mental territory. In a novel saturated with melancholy, the Jersey Shore reflects Frank's "stranded" life. "New Jersey's like the back of an old radio," he tells us. Newark has a "spiritless skyline." At least in New Jersey, he muses, "illusion will never be your adversary." But out of this, he seeks a glimmer of energy and purpose. Asking similar questions, Ford and Springsteen articulate similar answers. "Maturity," thinks Frank, is recognizing what's "bad or peculiar in life" but "going ahead with the best of things."[26] Having put so many people in cars, we recall Springsteen saying, he has "to figure out a place for them to go." One answer is to pass on your hard-earned wisdom to others. Frank does this in his compassion for the sullen would-be police cadet, Cade Arcenault, brother of his short-term girlfriend, Vicki, as well as for the Springsteen-inspired carhop Debra Spanelis, and the suicidal Walter Luckett, a fellow divorcee whose life has gone off the road. He can't do much about older folk who, as in that *River* outtake on *The Ties That Bind*, "piss their lives away," spending the rest of their days "down in Whitetown." But with younger people, he retains hope. He gives the objectionable Cade the benefit of the doubt, and wishes the best for Debra. "I'm getting older," she says. "I don't wanna piss away my whole life."[27] To use Springsteen's versions, she doesn't want to work forever at the car wash "where all it ever does is rain." In pragmatist terms, that she's even thinking of it is the first step toward actually bettering her lot.

Ford and Springsteen also implicitly find the answer through work, which needn't be the same as employment. Vicki's father, Wade, a one-time engineer, has had to move "down in rank" and sits out his days at a turnpike tollbooth, but his self-worth comes from working on his car. He ascends the stairs from the basement happy, his devils in the dungeon.[28] "I always come back to the same thing," says Springsteen. "It's about work—the work, working, working" (TAD 277). "There's people that get a chance to do the kind of work that changes the world, and make things really different. And there's the kind that just keeps the world from falling apart" (TAD 121). While he "never knew anybody who was unhappy with their job and was happy with their life," he acknowledges that some find "a sense of purpose" elsewhere (TAD 122). You can soup up your car and race in the street, even if in the longer term not all such activities prove sufficient. What matters too, of course, is perspective: taking your work rather than yourself seriously, as Springsteen intimates in his Austin keynote, or as Nietzsche puts it, "he who is a teacher from the very heart takes all things seriously only with reference to his students—even himself."[29] Ford and Springsteen concur that humorous self-deprecation is essential. Ford is wry about his own career by way of Frank's limited literary success. A reviewer of *Blue Autumn* describes "Mr. Bascombe" as "a writer who could turn out to be interesting." He begins to fail when his "literary career" and his "talents for it were succumbing to gross seriousness."[30] In attesting that Ford's novels "nail the Jersey Shore perfectly,"

Springsteen notes in an aside that they are "poignant and hilarious" and cites *The Lay of the Land* as the last book to make him laugh. His own self-deprecation is perennial. "I never got into being discouraged because I never got into hoping" is his Bascombesque explanation of his youth (TAD 20).

The lesson is that solitude can be dealt with once you see, in Frank's words, that "anyone could be almost anyone else in most ways." Work, looking outward, and accepting the mutual experience of solitude, turn out to link. Friendship's truest measure, he decides, is "the amount of precious time you'll squander on someone else's calamities." Work, then, amounts to focus. When Dewey writes of "intellectual work to be done," it's about becoming "an organ" for resolving "social and moral strifes."[31] Frank, in pragmatist fashion, decides that sportswriting is merely "a *way* of going about things rather than things you actually do or know."[32] His final thoughts bear comparison with Springsteen's that "the writer's job" is to "collect and create" memories that help artist and recipient "experience their own vitality." In Frank's version of this revelation of the wonder of being, memories of youthful ardor come back like "a feeling of wind on your cheeks and your arms, of being released, let loose, of being the light-floater." Since this "is not how it has been for a long time, you want, this time, to make it last, this glistening one moment, this cool air, this new living, so that you can preserve a feeling of it, inasmuch as when it comes again it may just be too late."[33]

I f solitude is part of ordinary life, it's all the more part of the lives of those who end up on the outside of society altogether: those deemed beyond redemption, convicted of crimes of such dimension that they are incarcerated and in some cases condemned to death. The tradition of scrutinizing the death penalty by dramatizing the mind-set of the condemned reaches back into literary history. The condemned Claudio states in anguish in *Measure for Measure* that "the weariest and most loathed worldly life that age, ache, penury or imprisonment can lay on nature is a paradise to what we fear of death." Raskolnikov in *Crime and Punishment*, on a spiritual death row in believing himself damned, wants "to live, no matter how!" Stendhal, Thomas Hardy, Mark Twain, and many others have also written about it. In "Reflections on the Guillotine," Albert Camus focuses on the inhumanity of the death penalty and on its dubious consequences in terms of its effect on witnesses and criminals alike. In *Darkness at Noon*, Arthur Koestler depicts the solitary pain of an ex-commissar of the people, N. S. Rubashov, whose life he describes as "a synthesis of the lives of a number of men who were victims of the so-called Moscow Trials." As soon as officials of the People's Commissariat of the Interior arrest Rubashov, he realizes that he will stay in an isolation cell until execution. Not unlike Camus's novel of the same period, *The Outsider* (1942), *Darkness at Noon* follows the prisoner's thoughts as he faces execution. George Orwell, in "A Hanging," provides a ghastly first-hand description of capital punishment, from the response of a dog that strays into the proceedings to the way the prisoner steps "aside to avoid a puddle on the path" to the gallows. Implicit in this is both the psychological effect on those who live under threat of execution and those who, directly or indirectly, witness or condone it. The dog cannot reflect with the eloquence of Orwell, but its reaction is no less telling. At the sight of the corpse it retreats to stand among the weeds in the corner of the yard, "looking timorously" at those responsible.[34]

Particularly pertinent to Springsteen is Richard Wright, who entwines the issues of class and race. *Native Son* owes something to Camus's novel, which itself owes something to *The Red and the Black*. Julien Sorel's cold logic in his death cell ("What shall I be left with," he asks, "if I despise myself?") informs Bigger Thomas's contradictory assertions. "I don't want to die," he exclaims, yet his "will to kill" includes a desire to consume himself.[35] Both writers, like Camus, have their protagonist contemplate his life in the face of execution. Convicted to die despite failing to kill Madame de Rênal, Julien refuses to try to save himself and abuses the bourgeoisie who are "outraged" in the face of "a peasant who has rebelled against his lowly lot."[36] This points unerringly at one of the functions, for Camus, of the death penalty: its use as an instrument of ruling class "retaliation" and "intimidation."[37] *Native Son* offers a bleak depiction not only of what it means to feel you are "black and at the bottom of the world" in a society where capital punishment is a ready weapon of control, but also of how that combination of socially engineered low self-worth and desperate economic conditions can fuel a psychology of hatred and fear that results in violence. Moreover, violence against others can be matched by a desire for oblivion, and perversely render the death penalty a way out of a cordoned-off existence.

Native Son vibrates with the words "dread," "scared" and "fear." For Bigger Thomas "hate and fear" are rarely separate emotions.[38] But the most important aspect of his psychology is the way committing crime affects him. Mary's "accidental murder" leaves him sensing "a possible order and meaning in his relations with the people around him." Accepting "moral guilt and responsibility for the murder," he feels "free for the first time in his life."[39] He realizes that white society has not merely "resolved to put him to death" but intends "to make his death mean more than a mere punishment." He knows, moreover, that this has as much to do with its view of him "as a figment of that black world" it's "anxious to keep under control" as with his actual behavior.[40] As his Marxist lawyer, Max, sums up, Bigger's "entire attitude toward life is a *crime!* The hate and fear which we have inspired in him, woven by our civilization into the very structure of his consciousness, into his blood and bones, into the hourly functioning of his personality, have become the justification of his existence."[41] Michelle Alexander, in *The New Jim Crow*, echoes that sentiment in the twenty-first century. "Practically from cradle to grave," she writes, "black males in urban ghettos are treated like current or future criminals."[42] Only violence leaves Bigger feeling self-determined, since "*he* had done this," and so brought about "the most meaningful thing that had ever happened to him."[43] Such feelings go some way to explaining how, in Alexander's words on our own times, "gangsta" culture enables young black men to put on "a show—a spectacle—that romanticizes and glorifies their criminalization." All such activities have their "roots in the struggle for a positive identity among outcasts."[44]

Springsteen may know *The Red and the Black, Native Son,* or Camus or Koestler, but he certainly knows the equivalent musical depictions of injustice—from the incarceration songs in Harry Smith's *Anthology of American Folk Music,* such as the Carter family's "John Hardy was a Desperate Little Man" and Blind Lemon Jefferson's "Prison Cell Blues," through Robert Johnson's "Hellhound on My Trail" to John Fogerty's "Fortunate Son"—and he continues the concerns with "systematic racial injustice" (S 298). Being "quite a student," his teachers include Dostoevsky and Orwell. The victim of a mock execution, Dostoevsky is unique among these writers in being able to testify first-hand what it feels like to expect imminent capital punishment, while Orwell not only witnessed killings during his time in Burma but was also shot through the neck during the Spanish Civil War.[45] Springsteen's serious interest in violence and social oppression goes back to *Darkness on the Edge of Town,* and more tangentially *Born to Run,* and his interest in the death penalty at least to *Nebraska,* in the title song and "Johnny 99." It's reprised with "Dead Man Walkin'," written for the soundtrack of Tim Robbins's 1993 film based on Sister Helen Prejean's account of comforting death-row inmates in the Louisiana State Penitentiary, Angola, and described by criminal lawyer Abbe Smith as "one of best songs ever written about being on death row."[46]

In 1967, when Springsteen was starting out, a national moratorium on the death penalty came into effect. Only in 1972 did the Supreme Court strike down all statutes in the country, and only in 1979 did a state, Florida, perform an involuntary execution (the 1977 Utah execution of Springsteen critic Mikal Gilmore's brother, Gary, being voluntary). The fact is that what American citizens have faced in the past, they still face in terms of poverty, dispossession, and the temptation of criminality. Alexander's concerns are shared by the national organization, Black Lives Matter, and by contemporary commentators.[47] "Hardly to our credit," Joyce Carol Oates introduces a collection of inmates' writing, "the United States locks up nearly 25 percent of the world's prison population, while having only 5 percent of the world's overall population. Or, in other terms, the United States incarcerates more than 2.2 million individuals, a far higher rate per capita than any other nation."[48] Alexander reminds us just how much of an increase this has been—"from around 300,000 to more than two million" in "less than thirty years," and with "drug convictions accounting for the majority of the increase."[49] In the face of these figures, the questions Stendhal, Koestler, Camus, Orwell, and Wright raised, Springsteen still raises: how does it feel to have no choice, to be isolated and invisible? How different are those sentenced for crimes from fellow citizens? Alexander addresses head-on the fact that "racial indifference" prevents understanding, as does the fiction that "a vast gulf exists between 'criminals' and those of us who have never served time in prison."[50] For Abbe Smith, Springsteen's identification "with the common criminal" and songs "about the damaged, the dispossessed, the poor, the prisoner" provide a significant public service. Writing in 2005, Smith anticipates Alexander, detailing how, "since the 1970s, when mandatory sentencing swept the United States," "more than two million people" have been locked up, and "more than 5.6 million" have been "in prison or have served time." "Thirteen million," he writes, have been "convicted of a felony," which amounts to 7 percent of the population. "If all these people were placed on an island together," he notes, "that island would have a population larger than many countries, including Sweden, Bolivia, Senegal, Greece, or Somalia."[51] We live, he explains, in "a very punitive time," and "most people want to lock up all criminals and throw away the key." This is why he's impressed that "Springsteen tells stories about people who have committed crime from their perspective, unflinchingly and without judgment."[52]

"You're laying claim to that character's experience and you're trying to do right by it," Springsteen has said. "You're taking the risk of singing in that voice."

But "the writer's job" is to "imagine the world and others' lives in a way that respects them."[53] Although inspired by the film *Badlands*, loosely based on the murderous road trip of Charles Starkweather and Caril Fugate between December 1957 and January 1958, Springsteen's narrator in "Nebraska" is his own creation. He gives him a sensitivity the original source may not have possessed. What is clear, however, is that the speaker, like Starkweather, fulfills Camus's delineation of the psychology of the condemned. "For centuries," he writes, "the death penalty, often accompanied by barbarous refinements, has been trying to hold crime in check; yet crime persists." This is because the forces warring within us are never "in a state of equilibrium." "For capital punishment to be really intimidating," Camus explains, human nature "would have to be stable and serene as the law itself." The fact that it's not explains why "the murderer, most of the time, feels innocent when he kills," and "acquits himself before he is judged," at the very least "excused by circumstances."[54] Springsteen's "Nebraska" narrator tells the judge that he can't apologise and that, "at least for a little while," he and his girl "had us some fun." Alternately respectful and sardonic, he asks that she be sitting on his lap when they release the current. As for what he did, he has no explanation other than that "meanness in this world." We can take this to be a confession about his nature or a condemnation of the world that's shaped him. But he's full of self-justification, as are killers and oppressors the world over, inside or outside government.

In "Johnny 99," influenced by a Smith anthology song, Julius Daniels's 1927 recording, "Ninety-Nine Year Blues," Springsteen takes a different tack. This time we view the protagonist from outside. Ralph is not a criminal on the scale of Starkweather, though like Gary Gilmore he pleads for execution. He's lost his job and in a drunken stupor has shot a night clerk. Whether the victim dies is unclear, but Ralph hasn't calculated to kill. He's desperate and threatening suicide. Unlike the protagonist in "Nebraska," his explanation is extensive. Losing his job has meant mortgage problems. The bank is repossessing his house. He doesn't claim innocence, only justification, and that he'd "be better off dead." The song is silent on race but clearly about a man driven to extremes by a loss of all that might provide esteem or lawful self-determination. Years later, Springsteen will write "Youngstown," in response to reading *Journey to Nowhere*, a book in the tradition of James Agee and Walker Evans's documentation of impoverished families during the Great Depression, *Let Us Now Praise Famous Men*. Dale Maharidge's text and Michael Williamson's photographs haunted him. He knew these people were similar to the kind he grew up with. Having worked as a scarfer in a steel mill, now closed down, the "Youngstown" speaker, with no one to address except the Jeannette blast furnace, states that when he dies he wants nothing to do with heaven. He "would not do heaven's work well," and prays the devil come and take him "to the fiery furnaces of hell." Ralph, in asking to be executed rather than given the eternity of life in prison, hopes for the same.

"Dead Man Walkin'" calls to mind the end of *Native Son*. It's the speaker's last night. He'll "rise in the morning," his "fate decided." He once had the ordinary things others have, but "between our dreams and actions lies this world." He'll probably die by lethal injection. Like Bigger, his victims haunt him, but forgiveness is beyond seeking. His sins are all he possesses. We leave him, as with Bigger, in the silence of his cell with a night of dreams ahead. In detail and sentiment it takes us beyond those earlier songs. The man's drugged state when he killed rings true. "Almost all the killings here in St. Thomas," writes Prejean of the New Orleans housing project for poor black residents where she working when asked to befriend a death-row inmate, "seem to erupt from the explosive mixture of dead-end futures, drugs, and guns."[55] Compared with Springsteen's earlier songs, "Dead Man Walkin'" is a deeper version of the horror that a consciousness is about to vanish. These men have destroyed minds and therefore worlds. But for opponents of the death penalty that realization only adds to its obscenity. Bigger and Springsteen's speaker echo Camus's observation that "every criminal acquits himself before he is judged." Feeling free of fear when he kills, Bigger refuses "the consolations of religion," instead finding self-recognition.[56] The condemned man clings to his criminality, not unlike Alexander's explanation of gangsta culture. When we look at twenty-first-century society, with its forms of enslavement, its brutalities, the actions of desperate people, and the vindictiveness of some individuals and governments, we might feel that, for all life's joys, all the advances and forms of intercultural understanding that do exist, the past and present are not so far apart. Springsteen, among other writers, is a witness to that, and not least to the solitude of those who—whether perpetrators, victims, or both—fall outside, and remain there.

I n contrast to the mutual admiration between Springsteen and both Percy and Ford, and his praise for another New Jerseyan, Philip Roth, Springsteen and Joyce Carol Oates might appear to inhabit different artistic universes.[57] In fact, in their Catholic and blue-collar roots, New Jersey residence, interest in the criminal justice system, fascination with Flannery O'Connor, and artistic drive, they have much in common. Oates also happens to be friends with Ford. *High Lonesome: New and Selected Stories 1966–2006* is dedicated to the novelist and his wife, Kristina. Princeton seems a world away from the Jersey Shore, but Oates is, in Henry Louis Gates Jr.'s words, "a daemon from the lower depths." Born during the Great Depression, she grew up in in Millersport, near Lockport on the Erie Canal. In biographer Greg Johnson's phrase, her parents' "toilsome lives" permeate her work. As with Springsteen, family circumstances led them to live with grandparents. In the 1990s I visited Frederic and Carolina Oates in their small house on Transit Road. Through the living-room window glowed a giant Exxon sign. "The traffic never stops," Frederic told me. "We used to live in the country and now we live in town, yet we haven't moved." "*Where did the country go?*" cry the travelers in Oates's "Dreaming America," as they speed down the highway past *Sunoco, Texaco,* and *Gulf* signs. "*Where did the country go?—ask the strangers. / The teenagers never ask.*"[58]

Like Springsteen, Oates grew up in a nominally Catholic household and, when her maternal grandfather died in 1950, she and her brother were made to attend regular mass with their parents. Her rejection of religion informs her writing. Violence, too, is integral to her background. Her paternal great-grandfather beat his wife in a jealous rage and shot himself. Her maternal great-grandfather was murdered in a tavern brawl. As products of blue-collar Catholicism, Oates and Springsteen share an interest in Flannery O'Connor's grotesque southern gothic characters. Noting that Oates's "Catholic background and work-centered, puritanical temperament" resembles O'Connor's, "another outwardly quiet person whose fictions were typically resolved through acts of violence," Johnson points out that, unlike O'Connor, she "repudiated Catholicism and adopted a non-judgmental stance toward her fictional characters." Long resigned to the view that "the world has no meaning," she notes instead that the world has "many individual and alarming and graspable meanings," and that the human "adventure" is to seek them out.[59] But while her hostility to religion is beyond retraction, her interest in Catholicism as a cultural repository of images mirrors Springsteen's.

"I don't think most people comprehend how onerous 'religion' can become when it's shoved down a child's or a young person's throat week after week; what resentment builds up. The more imaginative you are, the more rebellious—the more restless and miserable," she's said. "I think people have been brainwashed through the centuries." "The churches, particularly the Catholic Church, are patriarchal organizations that have been invested with power for the sake of the people in power, who happen to be men. It breeds corruption." Her disdain for the Church is evident in her public statements and private journals. In a 1993 essay she produced a newspaper article on the "mysterious cruelty" of inventing "despair as a sin," noting scathingly that the Church, "as the self-appointed voice of God on earth," somehow seemed to think that it had the right to dictate that an individual could not be allowed to fall into such a state. Corresponding with a priest, she explained that she "could not comprehend" how, "knowing what we do of the earth's evolution, and the universe, and mankind's penchant for fantasizing all manner of gods to guarantee 'immortality' as well as to punish enemies and to justify earthly imperialism, an intelligent man or woman could be 'religious,' let alone Catholic." A journal entry of 20 March 1976 expresses her fury at a group of cardinals who proclaimed abortion unacceptable "even to save the life of a mother—since it was possible, they said, that the fetus could be male." Such "brutal diminishment of woman" exemplified for her "the stupidity of these 'great' religions."[60]

Yet ambivalence existed early in the face of her parents' faith. As late as 1960, they were against her marriage because her fiancé had lapsed. She herself was not beyond slipping off to mass alone, even if, as she claims in her autobiography, this was for her parents' sake.[61] O'Connor, too, remained important despite the southern writer's religiosity. Letters to college friends in the late 1950s and early 1960s were evidently "peppered with references to O'Connor's new stories as they appeared." On the publication of *The Violent Bear It Away* in 1960, Oates wrote to the author and received a brief reply. When O'Connor died, Oates told Granville Hicks that, beyond "literary affinities," she'd "always felt" a "closeness," possibly because she intuited that O'Connor "was a very lonely person."[62] In sharing O'Connor's predilection for depicting criminals, Oates's impulse, like Springsteen's, is to find common ground with them. An extreme example is her novel *Zombie*, based on cannibal psychopath Jeffrey Dahmer. *The Rise of Life on Earth*, in turn, deals with a female psychopath. For Oates, like the rest of us even the psychopath is an artist of sorts—shaping obsessions. But other novels and stories deal in milder form with solitude, and, as in the story of a working-class female academic, *Marya, A Life*, with the price you pay for obsessive ambition.

A glance at "A Good Man Is Hard to Find" underlines O'Connor's role as the artistic link between Springsteen and Oates, not least in its focus on inexplicable violence. It depicts a grandmother, parents, son and daughter, and family cat traveling from Georgia to Florida. When they detour to find a plantation mansion remembered by the grandmother, the cat escapes its box, causing the car to roll into a ditch. A psychopath named "The Misfit" finds them. Recognized from the papers by the grandmother, he and his companions slaughter the entire family. The story is shocking for more than just the violence. The detour was pointless; the grandmother realizes too late that the mansion is not in Georgia but in Tennessee. The children, thrilled to be in a real accident, are shot along with the adults. The Misfit picks up the cat at the end and says, "It's no real pleasure in life." The only ray of light (given O'Connor's faith) is the conversation about Jesus between the Misfit and the grandmother, and her gesture of compassion, even as this leads him to recoil and shoot her.[63]

Compare a Springsteen song and an Oates story, and the resemblance sharpens. "From Small Things (Big Things One Day Come)" and the title story of *High Lonesome* are about violent crime involving family. Dramatic confirmation that we don't really know a close friend or relative constitutes an ultimate sense of isolation. Common as violence is in southern gothic, from Edgar Allan Poe to O'Connor, it's also a staple of country music as is, in Cecelia Tichi's words in her book about such music—also titled *High Lonesome*—"the primacy of story."[64] "From Small Things" owes something to all this. Springsteen recorded it in two takes in 1979, gave it to Dave Edmunds, and only released it on the bonus CD of *The Essential Bruce Springsteen*. Told in the third person to the sound of Springsteen's driving Gretsch "country gentleman" guitar, the song's thrumming energy camouflages a curious tale. The protagonist leaves high school to serve hamburgers. Her only direct phrase, in letters to her mother, is that "from small things, mama, big things one day come." At first she's suggesting that the most menial job might lead to bettering herself. But the phrase changes meaning through the song. She marries a customer named Johnny, and they have a son and daughter. Years pass. She grows restless. Love proves fleeting. She runs off to Tampa with a new man and writes the same phrase home to her mother. Perhaps she now means that flirtation led to a grand passion, or maybe she considers life with her lover an improvement on housewifery. Then suddenly, shockingly, she's shot her lover dead. Arrested and asked why she did it, she states that she "couldn't stand the way he drove." The song ends with the husband looking after the children and praying for her parole. Either he's an incurable optimist or the murder therefore took place between 1967 and 1972, before Florida reintroduced the death penalty to America. Regardless, the final chorus belongs to Johnny or the singer, and with new meaning. The original love has produced offspring who must continue through life with their mother's actions in their rearview mirror.

In "High Lonesome," Oates covers ideas and people of the kind we see in O'Connor and Springsteen, not least in terms of family, the law, violence, and isolation. Narrator Daryl McCracken tells of the suicide of Pop Olaffson, his grandmother's widower, when Daryl was fifteen. Pop spent summer nights "making this high lonesome sound" with his banjo, "a crock of hard cider at his feet all the hours that he'd sit out there on the porch so it didn't matter how alone he was." Not long after Pop's death, Daryl's older cousin Drake, a deputy sheriff, had been killed and his gun and badge taken. It transpires that Pop, "lonesome for something he hasn't been getting for thirty years," had propositioned an undercover policewoman. Drake does nothing to help and later ignores the family, "like Drake stabbed us in the back, Mom says." Pop's shame is such that he shoots himself. A week after a cursory appearance at the funeral, Drake cold-shoulders Daryl in a bar. Daryl subsequently turns up at Drake's apartment and smashes his cousin's skull with Pop's claw hammer. Over the twitching body he makes "this high sharp lonesome sound." Twenty years later, suffering from insomnia, he goes to his garage and handles the badge and gun, filled with "this lonesome feeling I'd make a song of, if I knew how."[65]

Both Springsteen's song and Oates's story are about crimes arising from frustrated lives, and the repercussions of those crimes. Oates has more room to explain. With the song, we're left asking what happened, who is to blame, why she gave up married life, whether she was born bad or driven insane by a suffocating marriage. In the uncertainty of her motives, she's akin, in fact, to Cathy Trask, described problematically by Steinbeck as "a monster" in *East of Eden*, but rewritten by Oates as Clara Dawes in *A Garden of Earthly Delights*. Do we take Springsteen's protagonist literally when she states that she killed her lover because of the way he drove? Maybe we do, in the gothic country tradition. "I shot a man in Reno," sings Johnny Cash, "just to watch him die." Springsteen's song, though, is uncommonly subtle. While the lines she writes home imply that the murder is the big result of successive small events involving a build up of feelings, at the same time the big things that come from small are the children. The title hints at the ephemeral emotions of sexual love as the nub of the problem. She presumably falls in and out of love twice, and with large consequences each time. There's no more explanation for her actions than for those in "Nebraska." From small things big things one day come, but what those small things are needn't be clear even to the criminal. As José Saramago notes, "it is well known that the human mind often makes decisions for reasons it clearly does not know, presumably because it does so having traveled the paths of the mind at such speed that, afterwards, it cannot recognize those paths, let alone find them again."[66] Perhaps this is sometimes truer to life than the literary convention of the actual and revealed motive. In contrast, it's clear why Daryl kills Drake, but that's because we hear the story from Daryl's viewpoint. Seen from the outside, by family or townsfolk, the murder might seem just as motiveless. But the themes are similar. Indeed, "High Lonesome" might equally be viewed as an inverse "Highway Patrolman," with the phrase "nothing feels better than blood on blood" taking on deeper, darker meaning.

Just as Springsteen's song and Oates's story are indicative of similar preoccupations, so are their remarks about their artistic impetus. In his biography, *Bruce,* Peter Ames Carlin notes Springsteen saying that he always felt that he had to "get it out now, on this record," because "there may be no tomorrow," and yet, if he succeeded, in Carlin's words, "he was already damned for having become famous. If this record failed, he'd be damned for being forgotten. He was simply *damned,*" a "suspicion," Carlin ponders, that may come "easily to Catholics." He records Springsteen admitting to an "obsession with the idea of sin" and acknowledging, in Springsteen's words, a tendency to be "obsessive-compulsive."[67] Another driven writer, Oates spent years exploring her artistic impulses. "Your struggle with your buried self, or selves, yields your art," she writes. "These emotions fuel your writing." Questioned about her upbringing, she's said, "all childhoods are partly obscured by pockets of amnesia, as by patches of fog. Perhaps it is best so?"[68] Whatever the catalysts, she refers in *(Woman) Writer* to "two general theories about the genesis of 'art.'" One is that "it originates in play; in experiment, improvisation, fantasy." The other is that "it originates out of the artist's conviction that he or she is born damned; and must struggle through life to achieve redemption." In the deeply enigmatic "Bishop Danced," Springsteen combines these two ideas. When I hear the lines "Indian screams / With fire on their fingertips" and "feathers made of moonbeams," while Papa gets "a switch stick" and is "pumping little Bill," I envisage a child using fantasy to protect himself from physical violence.

Resorting to the imagination to deal with guilt-inducing punishment is not uncommon in Catholic writers. One thinks of the poet W. S. Di Piero describing "writing as a life-sustaining answer," and work as "the chief way of suffering redemption."[69] Such individuals turn to art as a savior. They grow obsessively productive. Carlin writes of how Springsteen would put art at the center of his life at the expense of much else. "The perpetual romancing of the muse, and the constant (if self-generated) pressure to make his work more and more powerful," he surmises, locked Springsteen's focus. Everything had to "fit in around the edges of a life dominated by its own internal visions, machinations, and riddles." In turn, Oates writes of her own obsessive personality. "The primitive force fields that generate 'theme' (or obsession)—are clearly given," she writes. It's "inevitable" that, "driven by passion," writers "'vampirize' their own experiences." Springsteen admits to being haunted by the lives of his parents. Oates defines her art as a "pursuit of 'hauntedness.'" "Writing is not merely the record of having lived but an aspect of living itself," she explains, and "there are those to whom living is a preparation for writing." "The composing of fiction," she states, is not "an escape from experience; it is experience." Or, as Springsteen once said, "the record is my life," and elsewhere of "Born to Run," "that song is me."[70]

Such a shared perspective between these two culturally Catholic writers marks both as exponents of what Gunn calls "pragmatism with a vengeance." Like Springsteen, Oates is suspicious of our fascination with artists over art. In fact, she's sceptical of the notion of a unified self at all. If for Springsteen problematic identity is the more evident from his being an "attachment figure" for millions, for Oates it's from her being a high-profile "(woman) writer." "Subject matter," she writes, is "culture-determined, not gender-determined. And the imagination, in itself genderless, allows us all things. Where can personal identity, let alone personality, reside, in so neuter a phenomenon as *words?*" Rather, "the very rhythms and cadences of language speak to selves—fluidity, movement, ever-unfolding revelations." "Two faces have I," echoes Springsteen in "Two Faces" on *Tunnel of Love*, an album that includes "Brilliant Disguise," which he calls its "center." "You drop one mask and find another behind it," he expands, "until you begin to doubt your own feelings about who you are" (S 191). As their imagined dialogue goes, Oates responds, "it might be argued that most human beings, writers or not, are in disguise as their outward selves; and that their truest and most valuable selves are interior." "Writing about yourself is a funny business," muses Springsteen toward the end of *Born to Run*. Ultimately it's just "the story you've chosen from the events of your life." Noble as that promise is "to show the reader his mind" (BTR 501), he may as well proclaim himself president of Pluto. Being "from a board-walk town where almost everything is tinged with a bit of fraud," he knows this (BTR xi).[71]

Their shared worldview on the subject of art, identity, sin, and redemption may be culturally Catholic, and may stem from an American outlook, but it's also deeply connected with their working-class origins. To avoid damnation is more about damnation in *this* life. If Springsteen hadn't learned to write songs, he'd have been working "the fiery furnaces of hell," walking an empty house "looking for someone to blame," trudging through factory gates with death in his eyes, thinking "someone's gonna get hurt tonight." If Oates hadn't won a scholarship to Syracuse and, with that voice in her head saying "*I can't fail, I must succeed,*" gone on to produce numerous novels, stories, poems, essays, and plays, she'd never have become a professor, National Book Award winner, and Nobel nom-inee.[72] Both turned to telling stories, and while their subject matter is broad, both return often to class issues and the struggle to rise from poverty to distin-guished achievement. They share a commitment to depicting what Oates calls "the great American adventure" of "social ascension," for "only the writer who has risen economically in America," she writes, "can understand the fascinating, ever-dramatic, class war in its infinite variety." Such writers, in Gates's words on Oates, see the bruises in American society and "press, *hard.*"[73]

But at the heart of Oates's writing, as with Springsteen's, is that sense of iso-lation: a shared preoccupation with the country's vastness and the individual's smallness. Though an easterner, Oates has spoken of her fascination with places like Montana, with "the sound of the wind whining across the plains" and "the loneliness made palpable as the palm of your hand," even as she's intrigued by the "less populated places" of the Jersey Shore. "America is my home," she writes, "the place of my soul." Such sentiments call to mind songs like "Dry Lightning" and Springsteen's motorcycle trips out to the desert in Southern California and Arizona, traveling "a thousand miles, two thousand miles, where nobody recog-nizes you" (SOS 215). When Springsteen's "moods descended between tours," writes Carlin, he sought "refuge in a desert hotel in Arizona, where he'd spend days or weeks by himself strumming his guitar, scribbling in his ever-present notebooks, and contemplating the emptiness on the horizon." Such people, pos-sessing a combination of intense imagination, intelligence, and will power, try to balance the pragmatism that drives them to be useful with the self-containment that drives them to light out for the Territory. "My exterior life, as it might be called," writes Oates, "is in exact balance to my sometimes rapacious inner life; as the height of a tree is said to be balanced by its root system beneath the ground. Otherwise, the tree would be blown over, or wither away and die." Such has ever been, perhaps, the way of the artist, and an explanation of the prevalence of solitude in American writing.[74]

O thers have written and Springsteen has spoken about the influence of film where, again, solitude is so often the watchword. From *The Grapes of Wrath, The Searchers,* and *The Night of the Hunter* to *Badlands* and *The Last Picture Show,* such movies invariably deal with that tension between the feeling of or need for it and that search for community. When Tom tells Ma Joad he'll be there in spirit wherever there's injustice, that tension is brought into focus. He's leaving yet asserting connection. For Ethan Edwards in *The Searchers* home is a fragile place and he's soon back on the road in search of his brother's surviving daughter after the Comanche attack. He'd rather travel alone but tolerates companionship and then, having rescued the niece, is still on the outside looking in.[75] In *The Night of the Hunter* Robert Mitchum's serial-killing preacher, Harry Powell, with Love and Hate tattooed on his knuckles, is a solitary figure silhouetted against the evening sky as he tracks two children for money they've hidden. Springsteen alludes to director Charles Laughton's "decayed fable" by way of Bill Horton's knuckles, in "Cautious Man" (BTR 298). Tattooed as they are with Love and Fear, the latter word draws us back to that crucial element of criminality, the emotion that afflicts Bigger Thomas. In another 1950s classic, *High Noon,* Gary Cooper's Marshall Will Kane is the quintessential strong, silent, isolated hero. When Springsteen's song takes over at the end of *The Wrestler,* he's doing for Mickey Rourke's character, Randy "The Ram" Robinson, what Tex Ritter's "Do Not Forsake Me, Oh My Darlin'" does for Marshall Kane, articulating for the inarticulate hero. As Cecelia Tichi notes, such songs "become a soundtrack of the hero's mind," "an audio version of the psyche."[76] Meanwhile, Sonny Crawford, Timothy Bottoms's character in *The Last Picture Show,* intends to escape his tumbleweed Texan town but, as Springsteen observes, turns around and comes back. Such films resonated in Springsteen's struggle between contradictory impulses. In *Rebel without a Cause,* Jim Stark, played by James Dean, arrives at his latest high school having failed to fit in elsewhere. In trouble again, he escapes with two other outsiders to a deserted mansion in a doomed attempt to form a new family. In *On the Waterfront*, Marlon Brando's character, Terry Malloy, struggles between his role in the community and his desire to be alone with only his racing pigeons.

Likewise with American painting, the most obvious examples of solitude are those of Edward Hopper, which, writes Robert Coles, "lend themselves especially well to the viewer's inclinations—in the tradition of Rorschach cards."[77] But I also think of Andrew Wyeth's watercolors; George Segal's sculptures; the photo-realism of Ralph Goings, Robert Bechtle, and Richard Estes; the surreal photo-paintings of Fran Forman; and of numerous other evocations of the fact that, as Gertrude Stein puts it, "In the United States there is more space where nobody is than where anybody is." If we include photography, we might think, too, of Springsteen's album designs, and not least the photographs on *The Promise*.[78] To ponder solitude in American writing—and by extension American art in general—in light of Springsteen's work is to see it as part of a cultural continuity. He mines seams found in classic as well as contemporary American writing, and not merely writing, and not merely American. Varied though these examples are, he absorbs diverse influences, and something in his work links with them all. If music and movies were his early points of reference, since, skipping "most of college," he "didn't begin reading seriously" until his late twenties, once he began he was soon reading voraciously, from some of the writers discussed through to James M. Cain, John Cheever, Sherwood Anderson, and Jim Thompson, as well as writers beyond America and plenty of nonfiction. To return to near where we began, with Hawthorne, Hester Prynne, and usefulness, people feel that they can turn to Springsteen's music for solace and remedy. Out of the gloom comes a brilliant light. In facing his own failings and sorrows, as well as embracing the communal by way of his band, he finds the universal sense. From solitude, then, I now turn to the unutterable upside of Springsteen's work, even if its brightness might render the darker side of his work all the darker: the E Street Band in live performance.

I think onstage is about as carefree as I get, that's when things
switch off and you're just living.
—SPRINGSTEEN, INTERVIEW, 2006

The stadium crammed full of spectators for a Sunday match,
and the theater, which I loved with unequalled intensity,
are the only place in the world where I feel innocent.
—ALBERT CAMUS, *The Fall*

4

OF TIME AND *THE RIVER*

t's a rainy December morning. I turn the ignition. The car thunders into life.
Headlights blaze the driveway. I scroll the music. This is the first time I'll hear
the Agora Ballroom, Cleveland, show of 9 August 1978. I haven't looked at the
set list. I want the surprise of a "live" show. August 1978 was nine months before I first flew to America and two years before I registered Springsteen beyond
"Born to Run." Out of Chippenham I drive down Rowden Hill on the A4 toward
Cochran's memorial. Traffic lights explode in droplets between the wipers. The
rain on the glass roof echoes the downpour that battered the Capitol Airways
plane hurtling across the tarmac in June 1979 for the first of my five flights to
reach Stony Lake, Michigan, to work as a camp counselor. The plane refueled at
Gander Airport in Newfoundland, and I switched flights in New York for Chicago
before a hop via Milwaukee to Muskegon. That extended entry to America is as
vivid as this rainy December morning. "The future ain't any damned thing," said
the young Springsteen (TAD 68). Well, time and place, past and present are about
to coincide in it.

First up, a radio voice-over: *This is Danny Sanders welcoming you to a live net-
work broadcast of tonight's concert featuring Bruce Springsteen and the E Street Band.
The stations carrying tonight's broadcast are WABX Detroit, WDVE Pittsburgh, WEBN
Cincinnati, WLVQ Columbus, WXRT Chicago, KSHE St. Louis, KQRS Minneapolis,*

and your originating station tonight is WMMS Cleveland. . . . And you can hear the crowd building up. . . . Boy, Bruce is gonna knock 'em dead. . . .

Shouts and whistles. Instruments tuning.

"Good evening, and welcome to the WMMS Tenth anniversary concert," says the emcee, Kid Leo. "Round for round and pound for pound, there ain't no finer band around. Bruce Springsteen and the E Street Band!"

"Woh!" says Springsteen. "Gimme some lights! He must have memorized that at home. I know you did! Cleveland, How're you doin'? Are you ready to shake them summertime blues?"

A heavy drumbeat, strumming E chords: "Are you smilin'? I wanna tell ya. . . . Well, I'm gonna raise a fuss, I'm gonna raise a holler about a-workin' all summer just to try to earn a dollar. Sometimes I'm thinkin,' I gotta get a date."

"No dice, son," intones Clemons, "'Cos you gotta work late."

"Sometimes I wonder what I'm a gonna do, but there ain't no cure for the summertime blues."

The traffic slows, a constellation of red, white, and orange fractures and sparkles on the windshield. The black chunk of Cochran's memorial plaque slants to my right against the rain, the depiction of his red Gretsch guitar and the inscription lit up by the car behind. We move forward. The memorial recedes. Rudy's Bridge comes into view, its gothic foliage black against the streetlights.

Whenever I drive under the bridge, I imagine the accident. I first found the details in newspaper archives of the Chippenham town library. Nowadays they're online. It's almost midnight on Easter Saturday, 16 April 1960. "Three Steps to Heaven" is number one on the UK charts. Cochran and Gene Vincent are passengers in a Ford Consul on a deserted stretch of the A4 rushing them from their concert at the Bristol Hippodrome to London to fly home. Both feature in the 1956 rock-and-roll film *The Girl Can't Help It*. The screen-on-screen Cochran (on color TV within the movie) remains to this day, forever in the midst of his "weird, brilliant, Elvis-in-a-straightjacket performance of 'Twenty Flight Rock.'" But half a decade later—and now over half a century ago—the real human being proves to be as mortal as the rest of us.[1] The car skids. The back end hits a lamppost. The stroke of midnight, a witness tells *The Wiltshire Times*, brings "a screeching of brakes," "a whistling noise," then *bang!* Rear "completely wrecked," the Consul steams, half on the curb, half on the road. Springsteen's "Wreck on the Highway" superimposes itself on the scene. There's blood and glass everywhere. As the rain tumbles "hard and cold," I see "a young man lying by the side of the road." Contrary to the entry in *The Encyclopedia of Rock Stars*, Cochran hasn't been thrown through the windshield but through a rear door. He lies near Vincent on the grass verge. Further down the road, business manager Pat Thompkins crawls to Cochran's girlfriend, cowriter of "Somethin' Else" Sharon Sheeley, who kneels among photos and sheet music. Cochran's Gretsch is a flat-topped island in a stream of oil. People rush out with blankets and cushions. Blue and red lights flash against the darkness like the end of *Rebel without a Cause*. An ambulance takes the victims to Greenways Hospital. Easter Sunday morning they're transferred to St. Martin's in Bath. Vincent has a broken collarbone and ribs and further damage to a leg already crippled in a motorcycle smash. Sheeley has a broken back and pelvis. Thompkins and driver George Martin are unhurt. That afternoon, Cochran succumbs to multiple head wounds and hemorrhages. Six thousand miles away in California, police knock on his parents' door. In the words of "Three Steps to Heaven": "And as life travels on, and things do go wrong." He was twenty-one years old.[2]

The curse of the American popular musician: all those road or air crashes, killing Buddy Holly, the Big Bopper, Ritchie Valens, Patsy Cline, Otis Redding, Duane Allman, Ronnie Van Zandt, Jim Croce, Harry Chapin, John Denver, and the rest, and all that self-destruction, from Hank to Charlie to John to Elvis to Janis to Jimi to Kurt. "Now some may wanna die young, man / Young and gloriously / Get it straight now, mister / Hey buddy that ain't me," sings Springsteen on "All That Heaven Will Allow," just as he addresses Presley indirectly in such songs as "Johnny Bye-Bye" ("You didn't have to die"), "Pink Cadillac," and (with the reference to "that long black limousine") "Walk Like a Man." In *Born to Run* he denounces "the rock death cult." "The exit in a blaze of glory is bullshit" (BTR 214). "Leaving a beautiful corpse" means nothing but heartache for family and friends, but for the young there's romance in the artist's untimely demise, from Christopher Marlowe to John Keats, James Dean to Marilyn Monroe (BTR 213). Moreover, for many non-Americans growing up in the 1960s and 1970s, America was an imagined world. Alive or dead, its stars framed the firmament. America beckoned. My dreams were adolescent. I'd hang out in the parking lot of Arnold's with Ritchie, Ralph Malph, and Fonzie, and wear a white T-shirt under a short-sleeved checked shirt. I'd cruise for girls down Main Street with Paul LeMat and Harrison Ford in *American Graffiti*, and sit on a car with Richard Dreyfuss to watch a rerun of JFK's assassination. I'd give old Holden Caulfield a buzz and meet up in the goddamned Wicker Bar of the Seton Hotel to shoot the shit about *The Great Gatsby*, for Chrissake. Then I'd light out for the Territory ahead of the rest.

My sense of American geography was equally naive. My fixation with Alaska hazily related to a late-night viewing of a Patricia Moraz film, *Les Indiens Sont Encore Loin*—"The Indians Are Still Far Away"—in which Isabelle Huppert, later to star in *Heaven's Gate*, plays a girl in Switzerland searching for what Thomas Mann evidently called "the unattainable place of inexpressible happiness" (a phrase I've yet to find in Mann). Obsessed with the lost lives of Native Americans, she's found dead in snowy woodland far from home. Perhaps I too felt something of that adolescent despair. But Alaska also sounded like a world of promise. A land of stupendous bears and caribou padding through snow, streams pulsing with salmon, it seemed to hold all the mystery I'd never find in Chippenham. Not that I was too particular. Hawaii would do. I'd seen Elvis in *Blue Hawaii* and knew what to expect. I worked two jobs, fifteen hours a day, saving for my breakaway. I wasn't really cleaning urinals. The trade winds of my imagination had swept me nine thousand miles across the Atlantic, the American continent, and the Pacific to Technicolor islands concocted by James Michener and populated by girls with nā lei around their necks. I wasn't sweeping floors. I was flying into a sunset over the extinct volcano of Diamond Head to jam with Jimi at the foot of Haleakalā. So when, one spring day, a letter arrived from Camp Miniwanca granting me a summer job, I accepted with the intention of visiting both Alaska and Hawaii. Headlines splashed news about a radioactive leak at Three Mile Island, but nothing would intervene. I was bound for the Promised Land in pursuit of happiness. Within weeks, torrential rain clattered the portholes and swept across the runway. I was nobody, invisible, irrelevant, in need of adventure. "Go west, young man," said an elderly gentleman named Horace Greeley in the aisle seat. "Go west and grow up with the country." Airborne, the plane shuddered between rain clouds and burst through cumulous castles into a sun-filled sky.

Meanwhile, nearly forty years later, but listening to the noise in the Agora Ballroom, Cleveland, back in 1978, I drive on through the rain into Bath. The car contains thousands of people, along with Springsteen and the band, and we're having a great time. When I lament the multitude of concerts I never saw I keep in mind the Faulknerian view that there is no *was*.[3] "The past is never the past," echoes Springsteen. "It is always present" (TAD 357). More than that, not only can past and present intermingle in our minds, but so too, in a very real sense when we talk of recorded music and performance and memory, *then* can be *now* and *there* can be *here*. The footage of young Springsteen and the band performing "Rosalita" on 8 July 1978 in Phoenix, Arizona, is physically part of the present. The same goes for such recordings as Boston in 1973; Philadelphia and London in 1975; Cleveland, Passaic, Atlanta, and San Francisco in 1978; Tempe in 1980; New York in 2000; Barcelona in 2003; Dublin with the Sessions Band in 2006; and London in 2009 and 2013. In a different way, it's true, too, for the concerts I've attended—including the first and last, London in 1981 and Paris in 2016. *Of Time and the River* is the title of a Thomas Wolfe novel, but it could stand for my journey through Springsteen in performance, from the 1980–81 *River* tour—or World Tour as my baseball shirt describes it—to the *River* tour of 2016. My discussion of Springsteen live is, among other things, about that sense that what matters is *now*.

M y journeys to and from work along the A4—the Cochran Road, as nobody else calls it—continue through the winter, and involve numerous live performances. The one I play most often is the San Francisco concert at Winterland, 15 December 1978. The memory of that first transatlantic adventure mingles with the warm interior of my weather-battered automobile. Through that winter's rain and snow, in the car I'm part of a community. Peopled by ghosts of voices from long ago, it builds through music into a life force. I'm on the road through the dark morning into Bath in the twenty-first century, and enjoying a far-off evening forty years earlier. On the third disc, deejay Norm Winer of the Bay Area's KSAN-FM sums up the event. He thanks those who've made it possible, namechecking the other FM stations broadcasting the show, in Seattle, Portland, and other cities of the Northwest. When Springsteen says that "the radio can still feel like it's a magical device," he goes on to explain that "it's something you can hear in your room" and can feel "incredibly personal," even while it's "being disseminated over the airwaves" across "thousands and thousands of miles" (TAD 267). But perhaps a recording of a radio show provides an even greater magic in being a portal back in time to that moment of spontaneous immediacy, placing us in twentieth-century San Francisco, in the crowd, at the back, in the middle, at the front, on the stage, behind the microphone. I'm Max Weinberg on drums, Clarence Clemons on sax, Danny Federici on organ, Roy Bittan on piano, Steve Van Zandt on guitar, Garry Tallent on bass, and finally Springsteen himself. Even as Winer tries to corral the evening once more, the band again breaks loose, three hours in, with "Raise Your Hand." Driving back and forth between Chippenham and Bath, I'm no longer part of the Wiltshire-Somerset commute, I'm with those radio audiences in cities and towns and hamlets spread out across the American night, as if seen from space, on a continent that, back in 1978, I'm soon to discover.

The grandeur and lonesomeness of the landmass, with all those people, and spaces between, was brought home to me on those inaugural flights. I'd read *Of Time and the River* and was now reading *You Can't Go Home Again,* a prescient choice for an eighteen-year-old discovering a new continent. The long dead Wolfe, through the alchemy of the written word, told me about the land far below, seen from a sky with barely a cloud over North America. "Go seeker, if you will, throughout the land," Wolfe urged, "and you will find us burning in the night." My odyssey between 1979 and 1985, from eighteen to twenty-four, criss-crossing the United States, began with Wolfe exclaiming: "Behold the gem-strung towns and cities of the good, green East, flung like star-dust through the field of night. That spreading constellation to the north is called Chicago, and that giant wink that blazes in the moon is the pendant lake that it is built upon." I craned my neck to see behind us through the porthole. "There's Boston," he continued, "ringed with the bracelet of its shining little towns." "Here, southward and a little to the west, and yet still coasted to the sea, is our intensest ray, the splintered firmament of the towered island of Manhattan. Round about her, sown thick as grain, is the glitter of a hundred towns and cities. The long chain of lights there is the necklace of Long Island and the Jersey shore." The "Jersey shore" (no capital "S" for Wolfe)—what strange seaboard might that be? Wolfe's sense of the promise of America captures the exhilaration of casting my eyes down across the country that night. "Observe the whole of it," he urged, "survey it as you might survey a field. Make it your garden, seeker, or your backyard patch. Be at ease with it. It's your oyster—yours to open if you will." I took Wolfe literally. Seeker, I thought. Ah yes, I must seek out life and meaning. I must go in search of America. "It's your pasture now," he affirmed, "and it's not so big—only three thousand miles from east to west, only two thousand miles from north to south—but all between, where ten thousand points of light prick out the cities, towns and villages, there, seeker, you will find us burning in the night."[4]

Driving through the rainy December morning, I think back to when, pre-Springsteen and pre-arrival, the United States existed for me only on the radio and TV and in films. The dry cocoon of the car against the wet dark is akin to the comfort of the radio-as-community. As Danny Sanders on the Cleveland broadcast cites each station, the sounds I hear are so far away in time and place that they might as well belong to the Voyager II spacecraft, or the spooky sounds of the Philae lander descending from the Rosetta spacecraft to bounce and balance precariously on the comet 67P/Churyumov-Gerasimenko. But the past is alive in the performance. Recall and survey live concerts, and you confront a kaleidoscope of images and sounds drawn from audio and visual recordings and memory. To reprise Borges's observation in "A New Refutation of Time," in certain respects, if not in terms of our own aging, time "is a delusion" in that the past doesn't exist, the future doesn't exist and the present moment disintegrates even as it occurs.[5] To reflect on a show is to enjoy an illusory power over time. Actually or mentally, we can rewind, select a scene, freeze-frame, re-watch. However fragmented, the hours of the concert are on a continuous loop. First-hand experience is part of this but also another class of memory. It can never be captured on YouTube or packaged recording. To be at a show is to be in the moment, but it passes into memory. Examine a memory, and it begins to dissolve. Memories of being at performances are the most elusive and precious, but I'll start with concerts I witnessed in the 1980s and the twenty-first century—which is to say, in youth and in middle age—and from there, as befits Whitman's notion that "it avails not, time nor place," move from 1973 to the present by way of recorded concerts, whether visual or merely aural, to meditate on their nature.[6]

These are full-band concerts. Only too late for this book did I see a solo performance. Robert Hilburn asserts that not having seen a *Tom Joad* show is to have missed among "the most stirring" of Springsteen's career. Gene Santoro is more equivocal, describing the audience as "respectful, quiet, supportive, a bit baffled, hanging in there for the Boss but not always quite sure why."[7] Either way, I missed them and, Springsteen reminds me again, that "time lost is gone for good." But, if there are similarities between all Springsteen concerts, glued together by his personality whether in a stadium or, in 2017 in the wake of the autobiography, the intimacy of the 960-seat Walter Kerr Theatre on Broadway, even those I attended could hardly have felt more different from one another. This was only partly because of where I was in the venue. It also had to do with the contrast between the Springsteen of 1981, 1985, and the twenty-first century. At the first concert, I had a third-row seat, with 12,000 people behind me, at what Dave Marsh refers to as "crumbling Wembley Arena."[8] In the second show I was in the Carrier Dome in Syracuse, New York, on the final date of the first American leg of the *Born in the U.S.A.* tour. With around 36,000 of the 38,000 people there in front of me, and the band like ants before the giant U.S. flag, high up and far back in the mezzanine, worse than what Dale Maharidge calls "the nosebleed seats," I'd "got me a nice little place in the stars."[9] In the first two new-millennium shows, I repeated the pattern, only in reverse. In Cardiff in 2008 my family and I might as well have been in the parking lot, so in Coventry in 2013 we queued all day and got our "Golden Circle" wristbands in the first few hundred. The resulting experience led directly to this book, and to the most memorable of them all, the first of two shows in Paris in 2016.

To coin a phrase that will make sense shortly, *we'll get that one for you later.* First off was Wembley Arena, where it all began. I still have my ticket for a 4 April 1981 concert that never took place. Springsteen instead arrived in June. We used the same tickets on the later date. The momentous fact, lost on me until the show began, was that my Block A, Row 3, Seat 9 ticket was right in front of where Clarence Clemons would tower above us. I don't recall the band coming on but can nowadays Google the details. I can therefore verify that this was the only night at Wembley Arena that Springsteen played "Backstreets." The reason he did is because, according to my young self, I asked him to. This was the original *River* tour, but he opened with "Prove It All Night." A few songs in and the stage silhouetted him against blue light. He sang Woody Guthrie's "This Land Is Your Land" followed by "The River." The hush between songs gave me the opportunity to call out. People echoed. We went quiet for "The River," then tried again. Springsteen came forward, looked me in the eye, perhaps a little peeved, and said, "We'll get that one for you later."

This was, on one level, a trivial event. Unlikely as he is to remember it, if he did it would probably be as an example of how irritating young fans can be. But who knows what stays in a person's head? Springsteen later said that the tour was "tremendously exciting" and gave the band "confidence." "I can remember coming home in the end," he recalled, "and everyone feeling it was one of the best experiences of our whole lives."[10] As for my memory, the resulting cheer ran through me like an electric pulse. Why do such things matter? A single sentence can change a life. Relieved of my need to receive a response, I flew through the rest of the concert. When eventually Bittan's piano built then mellowed into the story of the singer and Terry one summer, sleeping in a beach house, "getting wasted in the heat," we were no longer at Wembley Arena, we were on the Jersey Shore, on the beach, on the backstreets. Clarence gazed down, tapping a tambourine, his face sometimes wooden as a cigar store Indian, other times breaking into a life-devouring grin. But, however I recall it—and now, as I write, I see an actual beach house, that tiny bungalow of 7½ West End Court and the backstreets of West Long Branch—the night is decades gone. No doubt we left the steaming arena and, ears ringing, sloped intoxicated into the rainy London streets.

That same month I saw Dylan, whose music also had an effect on my adolescence, though not in a good way, since I'd listen to it before parties then attend them so detached, cynical, and cool that I froze myself out of any kind of social interaction. Dylan's appeal, I see now, had very much to do with an adolescent mind-set that he fostered in me. I still listen to Dylan, and am aware of the story of Springsteen first hearing "Like a Rolling Stone."[11] Perhaps "Born to Run" and "The Rising" will be remembered for as long in different ways, but Springsteen has never had a song with the mind-bending lyrics of "Mr. Tambourine Man" or the profile of "The Times They Are A-Changin'." Dylan's impact had to do with his incisive commentary on a cultural wave. "A seismic gap had opened up between generations," writes Springsteen in Born to Run, "and you suddenly felt orphaned, abandoned amid the flow of history, your compass spinning, internally homeless" (BTR 167). In this sense, lonesomeness has a specific historical and cultural context for the generation who came of age in the 1960s. Also, the remarkable, hypnotic unity of tone of, say, Blood on the Tracks, Planet Waves, or Modern Times would seem hard to match. But I was struck on recently hearing "Positively 4th Street" at the nastiness of lyrics that allude to empathy. If for just one moment you could be in my shoes, sings Dylan, you'd know "what a drag it is to see you." Even "Like a Rolling Stone" has an aggression unimaginable in Springsteen's work. For all Springsteen's songs of betrayal, there's nothing to compare with such sentiments from singer to listener. Indeed, it's rather how Dylan behaved that night. As Mikal Gilmore implies, his relative reticence toward his audience is a mirror image of Springsteen's warmth toward his. ("I'm not gonna give it all—I'm not Judy Garland, who's gonna die on stage in front of a thousand clowns," Gilmore cites him saying. "People come up to me on the street all the time, acting like I'm some long lost brother—like they know me," he cites him saying another time. "Well, I'm not their brother, and I think I can prove that.")[12] It didn't help that I was in the gallery, and half behind a pillar, but Dylan wore shades, barely moved, sang songs I'd never heard, said, "Some folk want to hear the old songs. Seems to me like some folk want to live in the past," and then, grudgingly it felt from behind my pillar, played "Like a Rolling Stone," raising the guitar head to signal an emotional high point. How did it feel? This particular clown became that rolling stone and left before the end. Dylan had shut me out, I felt in my unforgiving youth, while Springsteen had welcomed me in. He'd even bothered to speak to me.

That's not to say that all was crisp and even in my relationship with Springsteen live, even if the next encounter was that snow-caked January night in upstate New York. From an upper tier it was possible to see that somewhere down below and far away was Springsteen—or maybe Sylvester Stallone, it was hard to tell—in a bandana and cut-off jean jacket with Old Glory behind him. Between us thousands of people waved little flags as he straight-strummed through "Born in the U.S.A." Springsteen had suddenly become mainstream popular. He now addressed a whole new swathe of people. Many who appreciated Springsteen before 1984 would agree with Eric Alterman's description of what this felt like. Here, now was "an individualist speaking through the voice of a corporate-dominated delivery system, an artist who employed an essentially conservative set of symbols to deliver a message of personal liberation and communal responsibility." Springsteen concerts were now "huge events," and "the members of the invisible church of Springsteen felt themselves being shunted aside." Here, now were "millions of loudmouthed parvenus," with many earlier listeners high in the stands of a stadium, recalling like Alterman their first time, in a venue a twentieth of the size. "Tickets were harder to come by, Springsteen was more difficult to see," and the size of the shows meant that he was "forced to sacrifice virtually all the subtlety and spontaneity his performances once offered."[13] Miles back in the stadium, and not born in the U.S.A., I felt uninvolved. That was the first song. I recall nothing more of the concert other than the way that actual distance led me to suspect a distance in Springsteen himself. Back in England, I got engaged and began my academic career. New albums were still events, but *Tunnel of Love* doesn't have the exhilaration and defiance that had attracted me. The record spoke of the opposite of my own life. I couldn't relate to the songs or respond to the synthetic sound. Moving onward and inward, Springsteen seemed to be giving up on his band and part of his fan base. I now appreciate *Tunnel of Love* as a deepening of his art that I wasn't ready for. *Human Touch* and *Lucky Town* coincided with parenthood, and these were truly "Better Days," but it was a plateau. There were songs I enjoyed. "With Every Wish" was a sober reminder that not all goes well, and I played "I Wish I Were Blind" through the blossoming spring, but Alterman is right about the clichés, not least the cloying bluebird's song of love.[14] I didn't wish I were blind, and wouldn't have for any lost love—too high a price, surely?—and the rest of *Human Touch* left me indifferent. On *Lucky Town,* I could relate to songs like "If I Should Fall Behind" and "Living Proof," and to the preoccupations of parenthood, but Springsteen's influence was receding, only to return in the new century.

Time notwithstanding, the second of the series of twenty-first-century shows I saw reignited my interest. The 2008 concert at Cardiff's Millennium Stadium reminded me of the Syracuse one if only because we were so distant that virtually all we could see of the band was on the big screens. It centered on *Magic,* though Springsteen opened it with a solo of "From Small Things (Big Things One Day Come)." It had that blend of the political and personal that has come to characterize Springsteen live. He made his "public service announcement" about the Bush administration's "eight years of mismanagement," and told a story about Federici, who had died of melanoma. But to the naked eye the band were dots in colored lights. Down on the floor, figures wandered to and fro with beer. We even walked around the half-empty seats to the back of the back to see if the experience was any better. We corrected the error four years later. For the *Wrecking Ball* tour we bought standing-only tickets for the Ricoh Stadium, Coventry, arriving at dawn for the mosh pit. By now Clemons, as he would put it, had turned "the corner," met up with Federici, and they weren't coming back.[15] Meanwhile, the night before had brought the news that James Gandolfini, Tony in *The Sopranos,* had died. Steve Van Zandt, who starred with him in the show, missed subsequent dates. Springsteen began with a solo of "Tom Joad," before the full band came on for "Long Walk Home." The set included a full rendition of *Born to Run,* with "Tenth Avenue Freeze-Out" as a tribute to Clemons and dedicated to Gandolfini. There was no jumping on the speakers or piano anymore; no sliding across the stage on his knees; no Clarence to pose with, his place taken by his nephew, Jake, only months old when the band had played that Wembley Arena date. Was it then or during another song that Springsteen came forward, during his hammy routine of pointing, à la Iggy Pop, at individual members of the crowd, and seemed to point at me? Perhaps he spotted my black T-shirt with "Nebraska" in red. Or perhaps I imagined the whole thing, but still. Are you looking at me? I thought. Let's say he was looking at me. As they moved toward the end and "American Land," the whole band except Weinberg came forward, Springsteen slapping and shaking hands, smiling. Joy, I recalled from 1981. Exhilaration, the promise fulfilled. "I still believe in its power," Springsteen said of music to Michael Hann in 2016. "I believe in my ability to transfer its power to you. That's never changed. One of the things our band was very good at communicating was that sense of joy."[16]

Driving home, I thought of a Wallace Stevens poem, "The Idea of Order at Key West." Describing listening to a singer with the sea behind her, it's about how a musical performance can intoxicate, transforming and heightening perception.

> It was her voice that made
> The sky acutest at its vanishing.
> She measured to the hour its solitude.
> She was the single artificer of the world
> In which she sang. And when she sang, the sea,
> Whatever self it had, became the self
> That was her song, for she was the maker. Then we,
> As we beheld her striding there alone,
> Knew that there never was a world for her
> Except the one she sang and, singing, made.

The speaker asks his companion why, as they turned for home, the lights of the fishing boats at anchor "mastered the night and portioned out the sea, / Fixing emblazoned zones and fiery poles, / Arranging, deepening, enchanting night." Kathleen Higgins writes of "music's psychophysiological power to influence the listener's outlook." The music had indeed altered not just my perceptions both mental and physical. "The dynamism of music," she argues, "reminds us of our own dynamism." It can help us achieve more. Nor was it a fleeting effect. Just as that 1981 show was the starting gun for my personal life race, so Coventry, more than three decades later, after days of tingling energy, brought a sense of renewal, and the decision to distill this phenomenon of Springsteen's ability to harness music's power and present it to us to rediscover our own vitality. It would lead, in time, to Paris 2016, the second *River* tour, and a completion of the circle.[17]

B ut I'll get that strange event—the strangeness of the first of two shows—for you later. Moving for now from my own experience of live shows to recordings of them, I should explain that, like others, I'm not including *Bruce Springsteen and the E Street Band: Live/1975–85*. The first official attempt to capture live performances as a recording failed as a whole, even though it contains enjoyable anecdotes and stirring performances. "In a sense, it was the most ambitious effort of his career," writes Mikal Gilmore, "but also the least satisfying and least consequential. It didn't play with the sort of revelatory effect of his best shows or earlier albums and it didn't capture a mass audience in the same way either." Rob Kirkpatrick writes that in hindsight "Springsteen's boxed set stands very much as a record (*record* in the sense of *document*) of the *Born in the U.S.A.* era." It offers "next to nothing in the way of performances from the early years" and only one from before 1978 ("Thunder Road" from 1975). Moreover, "performances from different years and venues" are "mixed with audience noise fading one into the next in an attempt to re-create a single concert experience."[18] The overall result is deadening. There's no sense of a whole concert's momentum, of the band adapting to audience mood, just songs out of context. Springsteen makes much of participation, with a cascade of interaction, progression, and contingency that uplifts performers and audience.[19] "You have to keep it present and living," he's said, not allow it to "get embalmed." The effect of cutting and splicing live songs was precisely to embalm them in their own time and space. Marc Eliot calls it "Bruce's musical coffin."[20] It's hard to erase Simon Frith's image of "boxes piled high by the cash desks" to capitalize on what Jim Farber, reviewing the video anthology of 1989, describes as Springsteen's "super-duper stardom." As Frith goes on to say, while the supposedly "truth-to-life" nature of the set involves it lasting about as long as a show, the overall, distinctly postmodernist effect is of a "false event." This leads Frith to his view that Springsteen merely "represents 'authenticity,'" and to his statement: "If Bruce Springsteen didn't exist, American rock critics would have had to invent him." While Springsteen's admirers don't like to think that his "authenticity" is more an idea than an actuality, in the 1980s he was indeed facing, and would continue to face, "the fate of the individual artist under capitalism."[21] But fortunately we have much more than that document. We can't save "time in a bottle," to use Jim Croce's song title. Nevertheless, if it's not, as David Pattie ponders, a paradox to imagine "authenticity through the medium of performance," we can at least savor the "authenticity" bottled and labeled in a range of live shows.[22]

The recorded performances between 1973 and 1978 reveal shifts from laidback entertainment to urgent drama. The change has to do with personnel but above all with Springsteen's persona. The Boston radio recording of 9 January 1973 provides a glimpse of Springsteen at the start of his album career. It begins with a mellow Duke Ellington instrumental. After joking about the band as relatives, with Clemons as his brother, and the band as available for "Bar Mitzvahs and stuff" (technically that should be Bar Mitzvot, but he's Catholic), he offers a surreal preamble about the wordplay in "Bishop Danced," rolling out a collage of images centering on the story of a boy who suffers beatings by his father and retreats into his imagination. For all the rage he witnessed in his secular childhood, the ghosts of that Catholic upbringing intensify it. "What's going on here?" the interviewer asks. "I don't know," says Springsteen. The next song, "Wild Billy's Circus Story," he describes as a "behind the scenes adventure story." Years later, he would talk about the Clyde Beatty–Cole Brothers Circus that came to Freehold, and of how the things a child notices "aren't the things you're meant to notice" (TAD 369). This image of a passing circus, with its inner drama of oddballs and curiosities, is a mainstay of Springsteen's career. The circus world is not unlike the "outsider" world of rock and roll (SOS 388). Misfits set up tent and entertain for a while, providing theater by exposing themselves to physical and emotional risk. "Oh God save the human cannonball," prays the little boy.[23] The 1973 Philadelphia show continues the mellow mood. Only with "Spirit in the Night" do we get something less low key, even if the energy merges with melancholy. A succession of easeful songs with muted drums includes a jazzy "Does This Bus Stop at 82nd Street?" and funky versions of "Tokyo" and "Thundercrack." There's no hint that Springsteen will write "Born to Run," let alone any anticipation of the angst of 1978.

By the time of Philadelphia, 5 February 1975, Roy Bittan has replaced David Sancious on piano. "Incident on 57th Street" leads into to Harold Dorman's "Mountain of Love" and the drum-led, driving rhythm that ushers in Springsteen as rock star. Part of the band's texture of this period is the oscillation between jazz and rock. "Born to Run" precedes an elongated "E Street Shuffle" to tell the story of how the Big Man joins the band. Springsteen is a raconteur, reassuring the audience that this is an act and that, when he bellows his angst-ridden lines, there's no need to call for the psychiatrist yet. Yet after "Wings for Wheels"—"Thunder Road" before Springsteen found the song's title—such reassurance gets drowned out as "She's the One" segues into "Backstreets." As in the Atlanta concert of 30 September 1978, Springsteen launches into a frenzy of bitter words in an early sign of soul baring. This is the beginning of the shouted vocal. He reaches into the silt, dredging catharsis. It's easy to understand why this mesmerizes the audience. If, heightened to melodrama, it owes more than a little to the latter stages of Van Morrison's "Madame George," there's no more of the laconic here: a primal beat is exorcising demons.

Perhaps it's all an act, a psychological version of the cult of illusory or actual bodily harm some rock performers undergo in the name of their art: Alice

Cooper being mock-guillotined, Iggy Pop lacerating himself with glass. As Steve Waksman notes, such artists play "on their own victimization, punishment, even death." It's beyond disentanglement as to whether, to use Philip Auslander's theory of three layers of performance, this is "the real person," "the performance persona," or "the character." Perhaps, as Paul Nelson suggests, it's akin to method acting, with the effort making real and projected emotion almost indistinguishable.[24] But Springsteen, that September night as on innumerable other nights, steers it back to clear showmanship. The concert ends in celebration, with Springsteen hamming it up in pursuit of a hamburger during Chuck Berry's "Back in the U.S.A." He's found the three-hour theatrical journey that will bring fame. It's only rock and roll after all, to be treated as seriously as death but also as entertainment. Like *A Midsummer Night's Dream*, it's not to be worried over. "If we shadows have offended," Puck explains, "think but this and all is mended, that you have but slumb'red here while these visions did appear." The show ends with the equivalent of Shakespeare's return to strong rhythm and obvious rhyme. Order is restored, awkward questions forgotten. Springsteen and the band are just performers. They're Shakespeare's "rude mechanicals," Bottom and Co., putting on a play. Don't go home thinking there's any more to it.[25]

To see as opposed to just hear a 1975 concert is another thing again. Sound lasts better than fashion. Springsteen refers to "the sartorial horror" of the E Street 1980s. "The band had never looked and dressed so bad," he writes (BTR 326). Take another look at 1975, Bruce. Mike Appel evidently had the Hammersmith Odeon show filmed with no special arrangements for visual broadcast—merely Marc Brickman's usual lighting. For Appel, Brickman's understanding of "color, drama, positioning," transformed the shows.[26] But with that one, at least, the lighting comes across as crude and dated; its 1970s emphasis on alternating primary colors is a reminder of yesteryear. Remnants of the laconic Springsteen remain. When the lights come up after a Springsteen piano solo of "Thunder Road," the band appears with Weinberg wearing a shoulder-strap undershirt (possibly one of what New Jersey native Fred Schruers means by "guinea-T's" or "Newarkys" as worn by "Newarkylanders," the Joe Greasers who filled Joe Colleges with contempt and fear). In contrast, Clemons and Van Zandt in wide lapels and fedoras resemble pimps from *Kojak*.[27] Springsteen wanders around in loose shirt and wooly hat like a straggly street urchin. As for the shape of the concert, "Born to Run" is dropped in without fanfare as just another song. "The deliberate peaks and valleys" that characterize later performances are there, but it's not a mammoth show, and there's nothing on the level of the drama that, evident in the Philadelphia concert, would in time come into its own.[28]

Move on three years to 1978, and the emotional risk of Springsteen's music takes center stage. Between islands of excitement the tone darkens, reflecting his self-professed tendency to "drift into that other thing" and produce "a lot of desperate fun" (TAD 162). When he says, years after these performances, that the greatest rock-and-rollers "are desperate men," he knows what he's talking about (TAD 373). Whatever the demons, it's almost too clear that he needed to "make something" of them (TAD 372). Aspects of the 1978 shows resemble public psychotherapy. Discussing creativity and depression, Storr describes writing as "a form of therapy" requiring no "therapist other than the sufferer himself." Listeners to the shows of that year might beg to differ. Storr does go on to say that, while "the initial response to depression is to turn inward," "once a work is completed it can be shared with others." But the need for this material to be acted out in public is palpable. Whether this is the "real" person, performance persona, or a character, if uttered by a street-corner tramp, or if Springsteen's career had collapsed, it would be painful to hear. The Springsteen of these 1978 shows is the human cannonball: thrilling to witness, dangerous to be. No wonder those April 1981 dates were put back to June due to his being "physically and mentally exhausted."[29] In "Wild Billy's Circus Story," circus boy "dances like a monkey on barbed wire." If this song has shades of the Beatles' "Being for the Benefit of Mr. Kite!" there's a personal dimension absent from Lennon's composition. Just as in "The Last Carnival," Springsteen sings, after Federici's death, of an end to "dancing together on the high wire," so too in "Wild Billy's Circus Story" there's a sense of the toll exacted on the performer who puts his soul (and body, judging from Ben-Gay and liniment references, and candid details in Born to Run) on the line for the crowd's vicarious pleasure.[30]

From the outset, the Cleveland show of 9 August 1978, which I first heard passing Cochran's memorial, reflects a new, political dimension. "Badlands" follows "Summertime Blues," and a mélange of the heavy songs from Darkness follows "Spirit in the Night." As in other shows, that Bo Diddley beat morphs "Fade Away" into "Gloria" into "She's the One." This is musical pragmatism. The sound, he implies—by showing how Holly, Morrison, and he all use the Bo Diddley beat—belongs to no one. Acknowledging himself as part of a continuum, Springsteen explains elsewhere how he learned the guitar at a time when local guitarists would sit in a circle on the beach. Later in the interview he reprises the idea. Dylan, he said, first gave him a "map of America" that "felt real and true." Through music he found Sinatra, James Brown, and singers in between. "I want to be part of that story," he said, "part of that circle on the beach" (TAD 341). From that communal sound onward in the concert, in a pattern Springsteen periodically maintains to this day with songs such as "American Land," the downbeat middle of the show gives way to the upbeat ending. The Cleveland concert concludes with "Twist and Shout," the first song Springsteen learned, and so again nods to his fandom preceding his role as performer.

By the time of Winterland the sense of urgency is unmistakable, from the vocal intensity, squealing guitars, heavy rhythm, to the counted-in songs. Despite "Santa Claus Is Coming to Town," a darkness dominates not altogether having to do with the album of the moment. Springsteen speaks more seriously. He dedicates the album's eponymous song to Ron Kovic, having read his memoir, *Born on the Fourth of July*. His tone, here the rage of the disabled Vietnam veteran, is barely recognizable from 1973. He's now contemplating others' perspectives. In "Factory," he honors his father, listening to it back home on the radio. He prefaces it with a memory of him tinkering with the car "to get it started so he could go to work," a story the emotions of which are more common in literature than rock. The observations recall, for instance, those of another working-class writer, D. H. Lawrence, in his evocation of his father's morning habits prior to going down a coal mine in Victorian times. When Springsteen writes in *Born to Run* of the "kerosene stove in the living room" that was all they had for heating, and of how all their cooking was "done on a coal stove in the kitchen," we're very much in Lawrence territory (BTR 9–10). Brought up in Eastwood, in the English Midlands, he produced in *Sons and Lovers* (1913) a novel of family life in which his father, known only as Morel, slides from "bullying indifference" to such a diminished sense of assurance that he becomes "more or less a husk." Turning to drink, abusing Paul Morel's mother, he's emotionally "shut out from all family affairs." But on the morning after a particularly ugly incident, when he forces Paul's mother into the cold night, Lawrence describes this man with tenderness, making his predawn breakfast prior to his day down the pit. Sitting by the fire "on a little stool with his back to the warm chimney-piece, his food on the fender, his cup on the hearth," reading "last night's newspaper—what he could of it— spelling it over laboriously," we can imagine Morel happy, just as Camus imagines Sisyphus happy during the time between rolling the boulder up the hill and starting over.[31]

Lawrence has father-son demons to exorcise through that first novel, and Springsteen in *Darkness* performs a similar ceremony. Both men's stories are of growing up as (in Springsteen's words) "gentle," "sensitive" children in a poor household with a father's soul in tatters (TAD 215). If "lack of work creates a loss of self," it's equally true, as he's also said, that unhappiness at work leads to an unhappy life. Both grew up in a house where the mother remained "steadfast" but the boy "picked up a lot of the fallout." When the father lacks that self-worth, Springsteen continues, it creates "tremendous emotional turmoil" all around (TAD 415). "Work was the surround that absorbed them every morning and restored them to us at day's end, a little transfigured by dust or grease, their hands smelling of borax, their breath a little sour with beer or whiskey," writes W. S. Di Piero of his South Philadelphia childhood. "None ever seemed happy or expectant, as if the work, the need and the duty of it, was a mineral substance they wore like a coat. It impressed on me, before anything else, that work was never a lightness and gaiety, but something gravid, earthborn and earthbound. The departures were built on ritual morning preparations: the clatter of cups on saucers, the gurgle of coffee perking, the familiar (and threatening) cadence of feet down the stairs." "Fool with the rigors of habit and you became your own bad luck," reflects Di Piero, contemplating his childhood ignorance of "the daily humiliations" many of this generation suffered. For all their "sharp intelligence," "formal education wasn't available to them and many had to make their way as unskilled laborers. They seemed not so much beaten or embarrassed by their work, of whatever kind, as numbed to a silence their children could hardly pierce." I think of Springsteen's lines to his mother in "The Wish": "If pa's eyes were windows into a world so deadly and true / You couldn't stop me from looking but you kept me from crawlin' through."[32]

The content of the songs and shows involved Springsteen dealing with this material on two levels. On one level, it has a deep, emotional core. On another level, he was dealing externally not with the thing itself but with the emotions. "You're not trying to re-create the experience," he's said, "you're trying to re-create the emotions and the things that went into the action being taken" (TAD 206). At the same time, he sought in his own experience the wider contexts. He said of his father in 2012, at a press conference in Paris: "So, I kind of lost him, and I think a lot of the anger that surfaced in my music from day one comes out of that particular scene. And as I got older, I looked toward not just the psychological reasons in our house, but the social forces that played upon our home and made life more difficult. And that led me into a lot of the writing that I've done" (TAD 415). While not articulated by Springsteen in 1978 or perhaps really understood by his audience of the moment, this accounts for much of the emotional power of these shows. The son will not live the stunted life of the father. Intent on portraying, with compassion as well as anger, the world of dead-end jobs and wasted lives, he's building new dreams and actualities out of the materials at hand. When Lawrence describes his father trying to read the newspaper, and "spelling it over laboriously," we know that the father lacks the tools that empower the son: reading and writing. The son is articulate, and the power of the word is his way out. In Springsteen's case the key line here, from "Thunder Road," is that he's got this guitar and he's "learned how to make it talk." As he says in an interview, "I picked up the guitar because I wanted to speak to you" (TAD 242).

In pragmatist terms, to articulate a situation is to start to transcend it. If you master language, you can describe or re-describe a scenario. To articulate a future is to create the possibility that it will happen. There's another element to this. The son will work, but rather than drawing him down to hell the work will lead to transcendence: not emptiness but epiphany. To return to Di Piero, coming "from a culture of working-class Southern European Catholics," he "was bred to believe that work is, in conscience and in fact, the curse of the fall from grace, and that the curse determines and defines one's life. Adam fell, brought himself *down,* bound to earth: existence is the struggle to rise from the earth of work that compacts life in habit." Di Piero therefore talks of poetry as "a dutiful adversarial engagement with the object world," and "the task of writing" as "a life-sustaining answer." The gravity and weight of work on the adults he witnessed led him in childhood "to infuse their weightedness with some ethereal element. Lightened, lifted, they could be stopped and held in mind. The bricklayer on his scaffold is reshaping the sky." Work had to be "an ascendency." "Caliban is enslaved, but Ariel does the important work." There is much of this in *The Rising* as well as in Springsteen's performance work ethic, in wearing his father's work clothes on stage, in the heavy boots, the dripping sweat, panting lungs, and bulging veins, the trudge around the microphone when performing the later "Shackled and Drawn." "One night I had a dream," writes Springsteen in *Born to Run.* "I'm onstage in full flight, the night is burning and my dad, long dead, sits quietly in an aisle seat in the audience." Then the son is kneeling beside the father, and together they watch the man onstage. "I touch his forearm and say to my dad, who for so many years sat paralysed by depression, 'Look, Dad, look . . . that guy onstage . . . that's you . . . that's how I see you'" (BTR 414).[33]

Back at this Winterland show, in San Francisco in 1978, Springsteen follows "Factory" with "The Promised Land." Life doesn't have to begin and end with alienated labor. He tells Elvis Costello in 2009 that Van Zandt one day announced his approval of a comment, made by a go-go dancer on *Shindig*, that rock and roll "creates an energy that pushes you toward the future." It's "a developmental force," concurs Springsteen. It's about living with "the ever present now" but it also anticipates "tomorrow." Hence, he says, Elvis Presley "presaged a certain type of modern citizen more than a decade away. Gender lines dropped, racial lines dropped. He crossed all those boundaries." A rock-and-roll song is "for tomorrow too because what I see isn't here now. But I have some sort of faith that it can exist" (TAD 382). How do we get there? As William James advocated, we open ourselves to life—this is what crowd surfing is about; as Elias Canetti writes, "as soon as a man has surrendered himself to the crowd, he ceases to fear its touch"—and, believing the future into being, we work to achieve our goals.[34] Seen in this light, the psychological undercurrent of the Winterland sequence of songs becomes all the more compelling. "Prove It All Night" succeeds "The Promised Land." Dead-end entrapment gives way to a vision of something better. Springsteen's concerts take place at night. After sunset a magical world provides escape from the working life. Our lives reflect back at us as in a hall of mirrors. "Prove It All Night" is one of several Springsteen songs taking place at dusk or night or dawn, in the darkness or semi-darkness, on the edge of town, beneath the covers, in the margins. These are the spaces where the outsiders dwell, the nobodies, the invisible. Introducing the song, he says that he was told when he went to bed as a child that as long as he said his prayers everything would be fine. You find, in fact, he laughs sardonically, that you must "prove it all night, prove it every night," then launches into a guitar solo. The song plays out over nearly thirteen minutes, with the lengthy solo providing a barrier between daily life and the world of the song. "Racing in the Street" follows, dedicated to "everyone back home in Asbury Park," and returns us to the small-town setting that begins the sequence.

With hindsight, Auslander's theory of performance layers notwithstanding, the self-abuse Springsteen later admitted was a part of these concerts becomes very apparent.[35] The rendition, for example, of "Point Blank" is more menacing than the *River* version. A soft voice turns to bullying. The way he utters "point blank" implies murder. Phrases like "the pretty lies that they sell," and "how fast you learned" suggest a pimp threatening a prostitute. A "false move" and "the lights go out." The voice is cruelly intimate. The urgent whisper of "out" is grimly repeated. "Fade Away" with the same rhythm segues into "She's the One" with Springsteen's voice an elongated shout, sometimes a screech. "Without your love," he sings alarmingly, "I might as well die." Part way through, talking to Clemons about stopping by the girl's house, he sounds like a stalker. "I drive by her house real late. I see two silhouettes in the window shade. That's when I get mad," he says, "like Al Capone . . . like Popeye. . . ." The comic undercutting loosens the tension. "She gets me so mad that I just wanna . . . I just gotta . . . I just *don't know*. . . ." The audience cheers, but the levity is precarious. "Backstreets" brings us back to something shockingly bleak. On this performance it's about rather more than a melancholy yearning for lost friendship. "I hated you when you went away," is a plaintive cry that Springsteen lingers on in concert. Muttered confession becomes a shout, like a drunken tirade, as if the speaker seizes the girl and hisses into her face. She is silent, cornered. "It's good to see you back again," he slurs. The monologue becomes manic. "I remember way back then that you promised you'd never leave without me . . . and you lied, didn't you? You lied, little girl, you lied," he repeats, "so now you come back and I want to know why," repeated four times, and the shout: "and I want to know just what makes you think it's so easy"—and then, repeated over and over, "to stop": a frenzied killing.

The exhausted voice brings us again to "hiding on the backstreets" and safer ground. The tirade appears at other shows, but here in particular, heard rather than seen, it's a troubling performance. The final heartfelt howl suggests someone struggling out of sleep paralysis or awakening from a trance. We can't worry for him now, but in retrospect it has a quality perhaps beyond hearing at the time.[36] Once again, the party atmosphere returns. It's all been a dream and will soon be dawn. But even here it's as if there's a struggle to awaken. "Somebody stop me," cries Springsteen, "before . . . I . . . hurt myself." The drumroll ends the song, but up comes the chorus of "Bruce, Bruce," and an insistent clapping. "Are you talking to me?" is followed by a silence as if after a thunderclap and then, as disturbingly as anything heard that evening (unless, following Auslander, you buy the idea that this is merely the performance persona, which I don't), the muttered words, "I think I'm going to throw up." And off it goes again, not unlike Duke Ellington at Newport in 1956, higher and higher, faster and faster, defying inevitable descent.

Finally, in this sequence, I think of the 5 November 1980 *River* tour show in Tempe, Arizona, included in the *Ties that Bind* collection. This is one of the last and best live visual recordings of the era on which Springsteen's reputation was built. It's also scant months before our rendezvous at the Wembley Arena concert that was put back to the end of the European *River* tour. It's startlingly different and better than Hammersmith in 1975. With Marc Brickman's lighting, as Appel suggests, the performance does this time take on "dramatic dimensions" that raise "the entire show to new visual, musical, and emotional heights."[37] But there's also now a sophisticated architecture. The chiaroscuro of the lighting matches the contrasts in the performance. "The peaks and valleys" are beautifully carved. After the jagged drama of "Born to Run" through to "Out in the Street," "The River" takes us down into a dark, quiet valley, and the same happens with an opening sequence to "I Wanna Marry You," and later the intensity of "Drive All Night." When eventually the lights come up with the Detroit Medley, I'm of two minds. One of these is of the recorded moment. Springsteen is thirty-one. I'm a teenager caught up in the energy and emotional drama. But the other is the living room and TV screen. I'm aware that this is taking place in a time when certain things that do now exist weren't even dreamt of, either in personal terms for Springsteen and his audience or in terms of the songs and albums he would produce. Above all, career-wise it was before *Born in the U.S.A.*, mainstream acceptance, hit singles, and Bossmania, before he became dissuaded about the idea that "those big coliseums ain't where it's supposed to be," or, put more succinctly, "better bring your binocs" (SOS 34). In that first phase, 1978–81 was surely the wave crest, and I was lucky to see him before a great deal changed: when, happily for the audience if not in all ways for the man himself, his art was the center of his life. "Sometimes when I'm playing," he told Dave DiMartino in 1980, before trailing off and refocusing his response, "life just ain't that good, you know? And it just ain't. And it may never ever be. But that doesn't make those emotions not real. Because they are real and they happen. And that stuff happens onstage a lot, when people sing some of the songs it's like a community thing that happens that don't happen in the street" (TAD 104). If the Springsteen of this era felt most at home on stage, if he couldn't stop, why was that? "Playing a show brings a tremendous amount of euphoria," he told David Kemp just prior to the publication of *Born to Run*, "and the danger of it is, there's always that moment, comes every night, where you think, Hey, man, I'm gonna live forever! And then you come off stage, and the main thing you realize is, 'Well, *that's* over.' Mortality sets back in." It's clear now, if it wasn't before the autobiography, that he felt there was nothing beyond the show but his own heartbeat against the lonesome silence of the night.[38]

In the 1990s Springsteen came to realize that there's more to life than rock and roll. In *Bruce,* Carlin quotes him musing on his writing. As early as 1977 he'd been interested in how he might bring "adult concerns" into his music "without losing its vitality." Far from thinking that "the future ain't any damned thing," as the years passed he began to focus on the fact that he and his audience were aging. It plainly matters to Springsteen that his music and lyrics brighten lives, not least those whose existence tends otherwise to be relentlessly dark. Carlin asserts what Springsteen has often confirmed since, that he's "committed to the idea that music, particularly his music, really does have the power to change lives." If this wasn't obvious early in his career, it became so sometime after *Born to Run,* helped by viewing *The Grapes of Wrath,* and later distilled in the title of *The Ghost of Tom Joad.* "Something in that picture," he's said, has "resonated" through subsequent work. He realized not just who he was but what he could do with that fact. What matters, he decided, is the galvanizing effect on others. Carlin describes tour director George Travis making sure "that every new crew member, or a down-in-the-dumps veteran, walks with him to the back of the arena in midshow." He explains that between them and Springsteen "stand *x* thousand people," of whom "a small but important segment will go home with something that will be with them their entire lives." That, he reminds them, is "what makes their job, no matter what it is, important."[39]

I've pondered the role performance plays in Springsteen's "real job" (TAD 256). When he reunited the band in 1995, and then consolidated that reunion at the end of the century, something must have brought him back to a renewed sense of how important that role is. The pragmatist thrives on work that's productive for the individual and the community. Surveying or recalling Springsteen's concerts in the new millennium, from *Live in New York City,* recorded in 2000, through *Live in Barcelona,* and the *Live in Dublin* show with the Sessions Band, to *London Calling: Live in Hyde Park* and beyond, as well as my experiences in Cardiff, Coventry, and Paris, means facing the gallop of time. The reuniting of the E Street Band, recorded in the 1996 *Blood Brothers* documentary, came toward the end of the twentieth century. Perhaps the fin de siècle, as well as the death of his father in 1998, sharpened Springsteen's focus. The events of 9/11 must only have added to the sense of urgency about using as best he could the time that "heaven will allow." Settled domestically, and with some sort of work and personal life behind you, the question becomes: what else am I here for? *Live in New York City* is most notable for its political edge, especially with "Youngstown," "Murder Incorporated," and "American Skin (41 Shots)," offset by the entertainment of Springsteen's quasi-evangelical fervor. There's humor in his impersonation of a gospel preacher of rock and roll—at the second Paris show of 2016 he "married" a couple as "Mr. and Mrs. Rock and Roll"—but there's also something serious about why the band plays, as he is recorded as saying on *Live in New York City,* "night after night after night." During the course of his New York gospel spiel that intertwines such songs as Al Green's "Take Me to the River" and Curtis Mayfield's "It's All Right," he tells the story of coming through the woods to the other side, of needing a band and an audience. This is a serious joke having to do with the E Street Band being "purpose-based." The New York show's purpose is spelled out in a way that those early shows were not.

Nine/eleven followed months afterward, along with that often-recorded comment from a Sea Bright local to Springsteen that he was needed. The *Live in Barcelona* DVD preserves a *Rising* show. Caryn Rose points out differences between the New York and Barcelona crowds. Perhaps this had more to do with timing than a cultural divide.[40] In 2002 the band and audience, European including, would have felt renewed purpose. That need for emotional uplift had never been greater. When Springsteen sings "Prove It All Night" it really does come across as a promise to the audience since "there's nothing else that we can do." *Live in Dublin* is as exuberant as New York and Barcelona. That Springsteen chose in the years following 9/11 to go back to American roots also relates to this sense of community and continuity. He's always used earlier music but, once he brought these folk songs back into a large public domain, first with *We Shall Overcome* and then intermingled live with his own music, another aspect of the pragmatist impulse became clear. They include songs of sorrow ("Mrs. McGrath"), of teamwork ("Erie Canal"), and of struggle and triumph, from "Eyes on the Prize" to "O Mary, Don't You Weep" to "Jacob's Ladder," that express an impulse toward solidarity informed by historical perspective. That this renaissance could extend well into the twenty-first century, with the huge crowds at the open-air events in Hyde Park, Glastonbury, and elsewhere, testifies, moreover, to the pertinence of his approach.[41] Exhilarating as the later concerts are, and interesting as they are as quasi-spiritual, quasi-political events, they also illustrate damage limitation against the tsunami of time; the future will belong to the next generation in the audience. While rarely mere exercises in nostalgia, their poignancy lies in our awareness less that the singer may never see Sandy again—we assume he hasn't seen her for decades—than that we may not see him again in person, or some other member of the band. In 2008, Federici is the ghost of the show. In 2013 Clemons, barely mobile by 2008, is a giant photograph on the back screen for "Tenth Avenue Freeze-Out." The celebration of *now* is still the focus. The *then* remains, but as electricity on screen, all the more poignant as the century advances.

Yet life has a way of confounding expectations. Not all its patterns are of our own creation. In 2016 in Paris strange things happen. By this time, I'm researching the book. With my wife, Nicki, I'm traveling to the show because to comment on American writing is part of my job. Given the burden of such work, it's with heavy hearts that we pack our bags, drive to Folkestone and onto Eurostar to roll beneath the Channel to France, plunge through the fields of Flanders, zip around the Périphérique to stay near Fontainebleau in preparation for the shows of 11 and 13 July. Since I've been aiming to get fitter and leaner now that we're not that young any more, I accompany Nicki to the line for the Fosse mid-afternoon (despite her attempts to disown me) in my 1980–81 World Tour baseball shirt, which fits again after thirty-five years. Time loops in on itself. *The River* tour has returned. What chance that Springsteen and I might make contact again, just as we did when I was twenty and he was in his thirties? No chance, of course. There will be up to thirty thousand people there, and my ticket is the cheapest available. Still, I'm open to possibilities. The crowd becomes individuals. In the line we meet Gary Foodim of Washington, DC; Pat and Rachel from Quebec; and, inside the AccorHotels Arena, Giles Withers, who owns a shoe shop in Wells, near Bath, a single father for whom traveling to watch Springsteen is his "thing"; and Valerie, a white-haired, jolly lady from Orleans. Valerie is celebrating her sixty-sixth birthday at the show, alone except for a few thousand others. Rachel is anxious and pregnant. We meet her and Pat because we talk to Gary when Pat goes off to search for her, assuming she's fallen asleep from jet lag. He only knows Pat through Springsteen and has yet to meet Rachel. But he'll be traveling with them to Rome after Wednesday for a performance at il Circo Massimo, the Circus Maximus. We promise Pat to look out for her while he goes off to search. She turns up breathless with worry a short while later and, between grateful gulps of our water, explains that she got lost.

I expect nothing special of the show, but serendipity has long been a companion. We get into the second section of standing area, with the numbers 357 and 358 felt-tipped on the back of our hands, and find ourselves right by a gangway. During "Hungry Heart" and then again, without his guitar, during "I'm a Rocker," around comes Springsteen. This second time, by whim or happenstance, or maybe some osmosis connected with my need to shape a narrative, he stops by us. This, I realize, will be the moment of contact that rounds things off. Bruce approaches. There's a swamping, joyful, cacophonic hysteria, a current of energy carrying us forward and an undertow swirling us back. A red balloon bobbles among the placards and waving arms. I think, now, of all those dreams I used to have of meeting him: the one where he knocks on the door, a giant of a man, and asks if he can set up and play with his band for our family in our humble living room; the one where he calls off sick and asks me to go on for him—much like his dream of substituting for Mick Jagger at Convention Hall (BTR 67), except that I can barely play guitar, can't sing, don't know all the words, have twenty thousand or more expecting *him*, and am truly "an imposter who expects to be asked for his stage pass," even as the crowd grows restless and the arena empties out. But this is real. He's here. He's standing right in front of us and on the same level. As others often attest, he's no giant. In fact he's considerably shorter than me. ("You're shorter than I expected," I'll later read, is a common response from fans.)[42] He's two feet away. He's reaching out, shaking hands, with Pat, with Rachel, with Giles, with Gary, with Valerie, with Nicki. I clasp his cold, clammy shoulder, his shirt dark with perspiration and sponged water. He's still here, singing half a verse at us, a whole verse, and during this time I do what any serious, sane professor of American literature in his mid-fifties does when confronted with an artist he's writing about. I have form for this. With William Styron, after I'd traveled three thousand miles, including taxi, train, plane, and bus, to visit him in Connecticut, I greeted him when he arrived to collect me by car in Danbury, less than twenty miles from his home in Roxbury, with the question: "Did you have a good trip?" With Joyce Carol Oates I was struck dumb on meeting her for lunch in Princeton after four years of correspondence. "How are you?" she asked as I sat there in my blazer and slacks on the hottest day of that summer. "Sweaty," I finally replied. With Bruce Springsteen, who is not just sweaty, as we all are, but truly drenched, I have nothing to say, and he wouldn't hear it if I had. I look at him. He looks at me—actually, no, he isn't really looking at me—I reach out with a clenched fist and, delicately, slowly, clonk his cheek.

It's not every day you punch someone, and even less often that you punch a billionaire rock mega-star of global renown. But please understand (though I'm not sure I can myself) I didn't exactly punch him. I gently put my fist to his cheek, in a brotherly gesture, like a gangsta (maybe, I don't know) gestures to another brother, fist to fist. John Lahr writes of being close enough to him as a journalist at a media event that "we could almost have fist-bumped."[43] Well, his hands were clasping others, including Nicki's. Bumping fists wasn't an option. What on earth was I doing? When an academic meets a writer, when anybody meets anybody, what you *don't* do is, in however brotherly a gesture, put fist to face. Maybe I should ask a psychologist. It was instinctive and, as I see it, a gesture of gratitude, of solidarity, if a little embarrassing. Maybe he momentarily gave me a bemused expression—"catch a subject by surprise," writes Michael Hann, without managing this when interviewing Springsteen, "and you can see them deciding what they think about something"—but more likely he didn't even notice.[44] What he did notice was a girl behind us with a sign saying something like, "Since we lost the Euros last night" (a reference to the soccer tournament Euro 2016, in which France lost in the final to Portugal) "my Daddy says I'll get a hug from the Boss." He gestured to her and we lifted her over us and onto the gangway for probably the longest, biggest hug she'd ever had. Then he was back on stage, no longer with us but enwrapped in the sound and light show of mega-stardom.

That might have been it. That was full-circle enough. You start as a teenager annoying him by calling for "Backstreets" when he's playing his new *River* songs. You end in middle age by fisting this sexagenarian superstar's face, and then you confess to it in writing, so putting your credentials as a serious academic at further risk. But it wasn't over yet. This was the show where the E Street Band blew the circuitry. A few lines into "Ramrod," everything went down and on came the house lights, like the end of a party. The amplifiers blew. The video screens blew. The stage lighting blew. Suddenly you could see thirty thousand people watching some senior citizens and a young saxophonist standing in silence on a bare, black stage less ornate than you'd find at a high-school prom. Yet, oddly, it wasn't silence. Was it the ringing in our ears or a miracle worthy of loaves and fishes that led us to believe, against all likelihood, that above the din the roadhouse rhythm rumbled on? Led by Springsteen, the band, bar Weinberg, left the stage and shuffle past us, left to right, strumming away, Jake's saxophone uttering the occasional phfft. No chance of a voice. But everyone understood. The band played on. We knew what this was about. In the face of adversity, whatever life throws at you,

you carry on. Back on stage the band had a conference with the arena management, and eventually Springsteen took a cardboard sign and wrote on the back, "5 mins." Soon up came the sound, if with little more than house lights, and the show ended without paraphernalia, nothing but the band.

This told me two things. One was that, as the *Tom Joad* and 2017–18 Broadway shows corroborate, Springsteen doesn't need anything more than words and music. The rest is enhancement. The other was that he and his band members are ordinary, traveling minstrels. When we first had contact, Springsteen seemed like a wizard from a foreign land way up on stage weaving spells. Thirty-five years later he was on our level, facing old age just a little ahead of us. When the circuits blew, and the theatrical effects fell away, we were all just human animals making the Big Noise. In a way, it was as if Toto had pulled back the curtain on Oz, but far from dispelling the magic, Springsteen's handling of the power outage made the event all the more human and real. As David Pattie points out, in discussing the question of authenticity, "the performer does not have entire control of the event" any more than the audience is "entirely constructed by their place in the event." Pattie quotes Theodore Gracyk's observation that in rock music the instruments are "almost always several steps removed from the audience. In live performance, speakers deliver a combination of amplified and electronic sounds. We almost never hear the 'original' sounds; when the electricity fails, the music stops." Well, not in Paris, my friend! Paris proved that Pattie is right that, while "mediation is everywhere" in a live event, "so is agency, and so is authenticity." "The fact that it is difficult—in fact, probably impossible—to pin down moments of pure mediation, pure authenticity, or pure agency," he argues, "does not mean that the real has somehow disappeared." True enough, I'd have said before Paris, but that it's *not* impossible revealed itself at that very moment. The mediation had failed. All we had left were those minstrels and a few thousand well-wishers determined that the minstrels would prevail, and they did.[45]

David Shumway, in *Rock Star*, writes of how, with the giant screens, "visual intimacy with the face" enables "the illusion of an emotional intimacy with the performer greater than one produced by being in the same room with him or her." Equally, Auslander argues that "almost all live performances now incorporate the technology of reproduction, at the very least in the use of amplification, and sometimes to the point where they are hardly live at all." Consequently, while "initially, the mediatized form" was based "on the live form," gradually the positions have been reversed, and the live performance has often been an attempt to reproduce "the very mediatized presentations that once took the self-same live event as their models." He thus rejects "the argument for ontological differences between live and mediatized forms." While it's true enough that a person far from the stage and dependent upon a video screen is present "but hardly participates," when it all broke down in Paris there wasn't a vacuum but a new kind of happening. A contributor to *Springsteen & I* suggests "that only the people who saw him in the early days in the small venues, before the mega-crowds, when you could get so close that you were sharing the sweat and the spit of whichever band member you were closest to, can really know the intimacy and the ferocity of those concerts." That may be true, yet however mediated Springsteen's shows are much of the time—but certainly not all of the time—one of the striking things about his concerts is how, even in arenas rather than bars, he fosters togetherness, not just onstage, not just crowd surfing well into his sixties, but by walking down a gangway that's on the same level as the audience, or by deliberately courting relative intimacy, as on Broadway. Whatever else, this emphasizes that, far from being a giant, or, as the line from "The Promise" goes, "way up on the screen," he is physically diminished and, yes, shorter than his stage and screen presence might suggest.[46] When the fuses blew, and the band sauntered round with ordinary light and barely a sound, I thought of Thomas Gencarelli's comment that Springsteen's "music has always been about reaching." "At the end of the monomythic journey, whenever it comes," he writes, "we take that last step of return and find ourselves two steps back: still no more than just human beings, still shy of attaining that greater something, and with only what we have already done and given as a measure of our lives." It was fitting that the lights should blow because Springsteen is always reminding us that they will blow. The illusion will shatter. As he tells David Kemp, "mortality sets back in." You just have to fix the switch, plug in and go again.[47]

While the band did just that, playing on with limited lighting, Nicki left to fetch her coat. Then, during "Tenth Avenue Freeze Out," I received a text with the words, "Get out now!" Given that only a few months earlier, on the night of 13 November, Paris terror attacks had left 130 people dead and hundreds more injured in the northern suburb of Saint-Denis, outside the Stade de France, and in particular at a rock concert in the Bataclan, and given that one member of the couple we were meeting had been at the Stade de France with their son that night, I did as instructed. It turned out that Nicki had misunderstood. They were just ready to leave. They'd had seats and felt enough of a disconnect, they told me later, to have gone for a cup of tea during, of all songs that night, "Point Blank," when spontaneously, the lights of phone after phone, into the thousands, shone like stars in the darkness on behalf, I felt, of the 130. Springsteen writes in *Born to Run* of how, on discovering that the copper beech tree that once stood outside the house on Randolph Street had been cut down, "it was gone but still there. The very air and space above it was still filled with the form, soul and lifting presence of my old friend, its leaves and branches now outlined and shot through by evening stars and sky." By corollary, he feels that we, too, "remain in the air, the empty space, in the dusty roots and deep earth, in the echo and stories, the songs of the time and place we have inhabited" (BTR 504). If we as a European audience sensed that, then it was precisely the kind of moment one seeks at a show. "You cannot book, manufacture or contrive these dates," Springsteen writes of a New Orleans performance after Hurricane Katrina. "It's a matter of moment, place, need, and a desire to serve in our own small way the events of the day." Sometimes there's "a *real* job to do," and "something as seemingly inconsequential as music does certain things very well. There's a coming together and a lifting, a fortifying, that occurs when people gather and move *in time* with one another" (BTR 453). That night, I felt, really did show Springsteen as "a repairman" (BTR 414). I don't know what happened to Pat or Rachel or Valerie. I think she had a pretty good sixty-sixth birthday and they all had a good time. Rachel's child will now be in this world, and maybe named Kathryn, Mary, Bryce, or Bruce or Max. Gary I heard from later, and Giles as well.[48] But since we had to leave, we walked along the Seine sparkling in the moonlight, and, back in Fontainebleau, stayed up the rest of the night recalling the concert, ready for another, two days hence.

On the second night we traveled in by train and had seats up on a second tier with the stage to the right. Where two nights before we'd been momentarily swallowed up in the mayhem of "the Bruce surge," now we had the equivalent of an out-of-body experience. We could see where we'd been. We watched Springsteen saunter down and along between the crowds, and crowd surf back to the stage. It was as if we were watching ourselves from the past, or from outside. I had another curious sensation. On one hand, concerts are about your personal relationship with the music, that feeling that you're the only person there. On the other hand, concerts are about the interaction of the collective, about recognizing that you're a grain of sand on the rock-and-roll beach; that your involvement as part of a cresting wave, however long and intimate it feels, is a fleeting moment in a vast crowd.[49] The second Paris show finished with an acoustic "Thunder Road."

I imagine Springsteen did this for the reasons he gives in *Born to Run* with reference to a low-key encore at Santa Monica Civic Auditorium. "It completed the set for me," he writes, "It might get more response to do a *boom-boom* thing and really rock the joint, but when I walked down the steps afterward, I felt complete. Otherwise, I feel messed up. It's just being honest with the audience and with myself, I guess."[50] The arena emptied, and we took the midnight train back to Melun and the early morning bus to Fontainebleau. Soon enough, on the evening of Bastille Day, we were on the overnight ferry from Le Havre to Portsmouth. I listened all night to a compilation, fell asleep on a couch, and awoke to walk on deck and watch the sun rise to the original, 1970s recording of the same song. It was over, we were older, but what else could we do now? Show a little faith? Find magic in the night? In fact we awoke to news that a truck driver had mowed down more than eighty people along the Boulevard des Anglais in Nice.

So: serious and trivial at once. Not life itself but a simulacrum of life without the risks involved. But, in its connection with my life, it had symmetry. These live shows I'd seen began and ended with *The River*. They began with a teenager calling out for "Backstreets" and Springsteen responding. They ended without a word exchanged, but a gesture: the fist to the cheek, the clasp of the shoulder, the handshake. Minimal need not mean meaningless. A French novelist friend of mine, Thérèse de Saint Phalle, told us when we visited her chateau in our forties with our daughters, twenty years after staying there as a young couple, that we are all "the children of time." That's how I feel about my "relationship" with Springsteen. Parallel lives, twelve years separating our ages, and with two fleeting encounters: the verbal exchange and the physical touch. What's it all about? I was reminded of the moment recently when visiting, bizarre as it may seem, the David Sheldrick Elephant Orphanage in Nairobi; when the newest arrival, eight-month-old Musiara, strolled past the onlookers there was a similar need to touch. It has something to do with connection or verification. Is the need to do this religious? Atavistic? Comradely? Ridiculous? All I know is how much fun it's been. There'll always be London, 4 June 1981. There'll always be Paris, 11 July 2016. Thirty-five years apart, a generation apart, the only common factor, given that physical beings evolve, being a guitar and a baseball shirt. Maybe I hadn't grown up, or he hadn't, but of course we had. We'd simply retained something of the spirit of youth, which is the spirit of life.

* * *

Awakening from my reverie, I'm still driving through darkness. The rain on my glass roof mingles with the applause as another show ends. Given the Paris massacres, any concert there now calls to mind the Bataclan and is an act of defiance and of remembrance. On those two July nights, songs such as "Point Blank" and "Because the Night" seemed to respond to these events, and when the lights from hundreds of cameras came on in the darkness I felt, as I say, that Parisians were thinking this too. Concerts thus have contexts, but time is inexorable. I see the sweat in Springsteen's eyes across the decades. I see him at different ages, skinny and bearded in his twenties; thicker of torso and with receding hair in late middle age. I find myself pondering Dickinson and Stevens again. Both write about dusk, and Stevens also writes of gatherings and of the power of music. Dickinson begins Poem 258 with "a certain Slant of light." In the final stanza, she writes that "When it comes, the Landscape listens—/ Shadows—hold their breath— / When it goes 'tis like the Distance / On the look of Death—." When dusk arrives, certain slants of light pierce the gloom. In *Lonesome*, Kevin Lewis takes solace from what he calls that "moment of haunting light." Pragmatists tend to believe that humans are inherently meaning-makers. David Bromwich calls us "novelists of everyday life." "Everyone is an artist," argues Oates, experiencing a sensation of "'egoless,' almost mystical transport" when "totally immersed in a concentrated action that has some connection with other people." Music enhances this capacity in its listener; "sound makes things happen," posits one theory of music.[51] The mind being creative, we build meaning from sounds, just as from slants of light, and from both fortune and misfortune. Sometimes these meanings only come later. With music, meaning has to do with personal preoccupations at the time of participation. Meaning doesn't exist outside the human; we develop it in relation to the world. This might explain why "a certain Slant of light" evokes, as I write, the moment in open-air concerts when the sun sets. The Paris concerts were indoors, but even indoor concerts mimic the way that, as the day fades, the stage brightens. The darkness erases individual identity. The entrancing magic show becomes the exclusive focus.

"Light the first light of evening," writes Stevens in "Final Soliloquy of the Interior Paramour." Here, in this light, we can think "the world imagined is the ultimate good." For Stevens, such gatherings enable us to "collect ourselves, / Out of all indifferences, into one thing," momentarily enabling us to "forget each other and ourselves" and "feel the obscurity of an order, a whole, / A knowledge, that which arranged the rendezvous." Out of this "We make a dwelling in the evening air, / In which being there together is enough."[52] "The inspiration comes from the music," says Springsteen. The "thing itself" is not "the performer" but "the music—that's where the spirit of the thing is" (TAD 135). This may also be what he means when he refers to "in concert" by its literal meaning of "people working together" (TAD 231). A performance of "Rendezvous" is a pertinent example given Stevens's use of the word. This is a simple song about a man telling a woman of his doomed dream that "their love would last forever." Sung live, it also becomes about the show itself. The singer, band, and audience are the rendezvous. Stevens is writing of the connection that art provides: a deeply personal thing that is shared, a soliloquy. The concert is a drama of paradox. Like other art forms, it provides time away from "real life," but its purpose is to awaken us to what it means to be alive. When Springsteen sings that he'll "prove it all night for you," the proof is in the performance and the "you" is each member of the audience. In such ways can art, for good or ill, change your perspective, actions, and so your life.

This vision of art as a revival mechanism to reinvigorate creator and recipient is an American tradition. Emerson writes of experiencing "a perfect exhilaration" when "all mean egotism vanishes," and it's indeed possible to achieve in everyday life what the Ancient Greeks called *ekstasis,* that "ecstatic moment in which one is lifted out of the mundane and beyond one's ordinary self."[53] If the artist's role is to help others "experience their own inner vitality," then ultimately the train to the "Land of Hope and Dreams" is a round-trip of reinvigoration. You alight where you started, but the place seems different. The Land of Hope and Dreams is not a distant place but life itself. As Thoreau puts it, castles in the air can have foundations built beneath them, and real, practical, daily and long-term consequences. Performances are ephemeral yet can outlast much else in life, whether because recorded or in their effects on participants. The only kingdom we have, as Springsteen puts it in the wistful *Working on a Dream,* is our "Kingdom of Days." Ordinarily we "don't hear the minutes ticking by" or "see the summer as it wanes." We're merely aware of the "subtle change of light" on familiar faces as we each evolve from youthful vitality toward decrepitude. In the end, art provides the only possible afterlife. Springsteen is no longer young, and some of his original band members no longer physically alive. Yet the collective spirit exists in the form of memories of the great performances and in the recordings of shows from long ago. That, to my mind, is the ephemeral, timeless, triumphant nature of Springsteen in performance.

As for the relationship between past and present, in Borges's mesmeric collection of paradoxes, musings, and fables, *Labyrinths,* he has a brief statement titled "Borges and I." There are two Borgeses, he explains, the one on the page and the one who, at the moment of writing, lives. The paradox of his mini-essay is that the speaker purports to be both the living man and the written page. "The other one, the one called Borges, is the one things happen to," writes "Borges." But further down he states: "I live, let myself go on living, so that Borges may contrive his literature." Now, it seems, the biological Borges is referring to the written Borges, who "has achieved some valid pages," even though those pages cannot save him, "perhaps because what is good belongs to no one," but only "to the language and to tradition." Borges the being acknowledges that he must die and that "only some instant" of him can remain. "Little by little I am giving myself over to him, though I am quite aware of his perverse custom of falsifying and magnifying things." The statement concludes with a reiteration of the paradox: "I do not know which of us has written this page."[54] Borges, who serendipitously refers to recognizing himself in "the strumming of a guitar," died the year of *Tunnel of Love.* Yet his work still speaks to us. Surely Baillie Walsh had "Borges and I" in mind when he decided on the title *Springsteen & I.* Springsteen himself echoes Borges's sentiments in sometimes wishing that he, too, could be Bruce Springsteen. After all, to be "Bruce Springsteen" (as opposed to the mortal being) would mean to be immortal, albeit without consciousness. Springsteen is not his fame, and Springsteen the "attachment figure," in Storr's phrase, is not the breathing, mortal being, even to himself. So, as I reach the end of this particular journey, my personal contribution to *Springsteen & I* is to adapt "Borges and I."

The other one, the one called Springsteen, is the one whom things happen to. I walk through the streets of Chippenham and stop to look at Rudy's Bridge and Cochran's memorial, the red of the Gretsch guitar, the black background and white writing all glistening by the roadside. I know of Springsteen from his work and see his name in books and essays. Like him, I felt so transparent in youth that you'd see the wall through me. Like him I hit the road. We share preferences, but sometimes I wonder if he's created mine in a way that I can never create his, for I know him, but he has never known me. It would be an exaggeration to say that ours is a warm relationship, or even a relationship at all. I live my life and do my work, and Springsteen lives his life on the Jersey Shore, and creates his music, and I listen to it, and the existence of people like me across the globe justifies his work. That work can't save him, and can't save me, but it can sustain us. We are destined to perish, definitively, though his work will live on for a while. I take this seriously and not seriously at the same time. I'm quite aware of his perverse custom of falsifying and magnifying things. I recognize myself less in his songs than in many others or in the laborious strumming of a guitar. Years ago I tried to free myself from him and went from the mythologies of the suburbs to the games with time and infinity, but those games belong to the past now, and I shall have to imagine other things. Thus our lives are flights, and we lose everything, and everything belongs to oblivion, or to the printed word or recorded moment. It's the fate of all writers to become their books, singers to become their songs, the photographed or filmed to become their images. But I, and only I, must take responsibility for this chapter and, reaching home now, park the car, and hang on its usual hook, so as not to lose it, the key to the universe. There ain't no cure for the Winterland blues.

Poetry makes nothing happen.
—W. H. AUDEN, "IN MEMORY OF W. B. YEATS"

On the contrary, poetry, or the poetic imagination,
has made everything happen.
—JOYCE CAROL OATES, *New Heaven, New Earth*

5

PRAGMATIC ROMANTICISM

S
ome appraisals of Springsteen describe him as an American romantic. This is invariably meant pejoratively. Geoffrey Himes refers to the early work as "romanticism" that by 1978 Springsteen had "learned too much to ever go back to," and writes that one of his "weaknesses" is "a tendency toward romanticized earnestness." Simon Frith, in 1988, refers to Springsteen's career in terms of the "commercialization of romanticism." Robert Sandall, a rock critic for the *Sunday Times* in Britain, said in the early 1990s, "there's a sense in which we probably always exaggerated Springsteen as a realist" and that "he's much more of a romantic in his approach to America." For Sandall, Springsteen's version of small-town America "is the kind of folksy America that was being dealt with realistically back in the thirties. These small town couples running away with each other into the sunset" don't belong to "real life as we know it" but rather locate him in the "dream world mythology of rock and roll." More recently Ian Collinson refers to *Darkness on the Edge of Town* moving "away from the romantic individualism of his first three albums and towards something approaching realism." Select specific songs, and these comments contain truth. Alex Pitofsky is right about the "vague, abstract references to death" in early work, such as the "melodramatic journey to 'hubcap heaven' in 'The Angel.'"[1] Even Springsteen refers to "Incident on 57th Street" and "New York Serenade" as "romantic stories of New York City," his "getaway from small-town New Jersey" since he turned sixteen

(S 26). He thus apparently accepts Lester Bangs's 1975 concurrence with a friend's comment that "when I listen to Bruce Springsteen, I hear a romanticized version of New York. When I listen to Lou Reed, I hear New York."[2] But Springsteen's fluid pragmatism renders restrictive descriptions of his work outmoded as soon as made. With his vision developing, even as his songs came into being he was always a step ahead of his characters. Just because Wendy is promised a future where she'll "walk in the sun" doesn't mean the writer shares such naivety.

Nevertheless, discussion of Springsteen and romanticism ultimately depends upon what we mean by the term. From a pragmatist viewpoint, such judgments downgrade his writing by way of false oppositions of the kind that, in John Stuhr's words, are merely "distinctions made in thought." To elevate realism over romanticism is a distinction that Dewey, Menand implies, would "find inherently invidious and wish to break down," "a tacit hierarchy" implying that reason is superior to emotion.[3] Sandall's comments relate Springsteen's vision to escapist nostalgia. He designates it a sentimental fantasy about an illusory past.[4] But there are other ways to define romanticism.[5] Even if Springsteen writes of a "land of hope and dreams," and of "the dream world of popular music," such places needn't preclude practical planning and realistic expectations. Tours, for instance, involve huge logistics. Behind the AccorHotels Arena in Paris I found rows of vehicles for Trucking Service, and purple EST trucks with yellow lettering (www.yourock-weroll .com). But these are the foundations for the dream castles built in the night air. Springsteen errs toward idealism, but that isn't necessarily the opposite of realism. True to his pragmatist instinct, as early as 1980 he redefined romanticism as something less about escapism than about the practical effects of how we think. "'Romantic' is when you see the realities, and when you understand the realities," he said, "but you also see the possibilities" (SOS 115). It's intriguing, indeed, to read of him saying, in 1986, that he "looked at *Born to Run* and the things people were saying about it, that it was just a romantic fantasy and all that," and thought, "No, this is me. This is my story." Only then did he realize that the lives of his friends and acquaintances "weren't that way at all" and "look around and see what other stories there were to tell."[6] This dissolves another supposed opposition: that of reality and imagination. Springsteen's life differed because he acted on the possibilities. As Stevens puts it, just as "there is always a romantic that is impotent," so "there is always a romantic that is potent." Springsteen's romanticism transformed his possibilities, lifting him, in Mikal Gilmore's words, "from a life of mundane reality" into "a life of bracing purpose."[7]

One might think that the opposite of realities would be fantasies. It's true that Springsteen's characters often resort to fantasies as a means of escape. But there's a world of difference between a writer portraying people in that situation and believing that fantasy is a long-term solution. What Mikhail Bakhtin notes of the polyphonic novelist applies to Springsteen's narratives. Such an author "ventriloquates" voices, an "oscillation" sometimes near to the author's vision and sometimes far from it. Sceptical of oppositions that may only be mental distinctions, the author champions nuance over category, complexity over simplicity, and interpretation over dogma. Where W. H. Auden states that "poetry makes nothing happen," the pragmatist Oates states that, "on the contrary, poetry, or the poetic imagination, has made everything happen."[8] To see this as a contrast between Old and New World thinking would be to erect another simplistic opposition, but America was imagined into being, and that's had a continued effect on the way American artists think. As Springsteen discovered when he read Allan Nevins and (former Dewey student) Henry Steele Commager's *Pocket History of the United States,* first there was the statement of ideals, and then the attempt to implement those ideals.[9] Of course, it works better in some ways than others, but this is the tradition that leads Oates to uphold the poetic imagination as shaping our worldview and that leads Springsteen to associate realities and possibilities. Such pragmatic realism is melioristic: to imagine and articulate new realities creates the conditions for them to materialize. The key, to quote from his *Live in New York City* "Tenth Avenue Freeze-Out" mock-preacher routine, is that "you've got to work at it." "You" means both the individual and the collective.

Far from being something he'd "learned too much to ever go back to," therefore, Springsteen's romanticism never really went away. It either always contained or else morphed into a pragmatic romanticism, rooted in a clear-eyed understanding of realities and possibilities. If the early E Street Band, in Carlin's words, represented "the American ideals of strength, equality, and community," and if "the sound of such belief" in the post-1960s era "was stunning," the feeling returned in the years of the band's reunion.[10] This took a subtle form on the *Magic* tour. The shows started with mechanical, fairground-style music. Was it an invitation to experience the thrills and spills of fantasy? Not entirely. The seeds of this sound are evident even in *Greetings from Asbury Park, N.J.,* which introduced us to the semi-fantasy world of the boardwalk, out of which he would create a parallel world that would in turn bring that real place to life in the recipient. This, as Christa Wolf writes, is one reason why writers are important. Out of ordinary places they create possibilities that enrich our mental landscapes. If Asbury Park was built and has always operated with fantasy in mind, it's now forever associated with and thus shaped by Springsteen's songs.[11]

The boardwalk, as a venue for escapism, is in a way already "a place that never existed," as Daniel Wolff puts it, "and has proved almost impossible to leave."[12] In "4th of July, Asbury Park (Sandy)," "tired of hangin' in them dusty arcades," the speaker urges Sandy to move on with him. "This pier lights our carnival life on the water" is Springsteen's concise description of the dynamic interaction between the imagined and the actual in a seaside town. The reflected lights in the lapping water remind us of the ephemerality of their boardwalk lives. In *Magic* Springsteen again reminds us that reality and fantasy are symbiotic. He posits the artist as a magician. "Go back through any creative expression and you're trying to pull something out of thin air and make it tangible and visible," he said in the year before *Magic*. "That's why you're the magician" (TAD 304). Since we're all artists, all using language to define our lives, magic is not something apart from life but at its heart.[13] Not least among magicians are politicians—whether inspiring or deceiving, or both. Fantasy is a fact of life—all lives, not just those of the boardwalk or Springsteen, involve a degree of "fraud," as he calls it at the start of *Born to Run*—so we'd better harness it appropriately rather than have others control our lives through magic shows of their own.

The title song of *Magic* refers indirectly to the Bush administration's response to 9/11 as being based on a "romantic" vision of America. This vision was that America and her allies (in then British prime minister Tony Blair's words) stood "shoulder to shoulder" in what the administration called a "war on terror" against an "axis of evil." Such misleading rhetoric has always existed, and not least during the Vietnam era that saw Springsteen come of age. To acknowledge that the notion of a fight between good and evil is a fantasy with real consequences for ordinary people is not to ignore the phenomenon of terrorism. It's merely to illustrate that romanticism is enmeshed within reality. The "war on terror," Richard Gray notes in *After the Fall*, "reinforced this slippage between fact and fantasy" by way of a rhetoric that elided "the real and the artificial." To illustrate this, he quotes *New York Times* journalist Ron Suskind's account of what a senior government aide told him early in the Iraq war: "The aide said that guys like me were 'in what we call the reality based community,' which he defined as people who 'believe that solutions emerge from your judicious study of discernible reality.'" "That's not the way the world really works anymore," the aide continued. Since America was now "an empire," "when we act, we create our own reality." Moreover, "while you're studying that reality," the government would "act again, creating other new realities." Only members of the administration were "history's actors." The role of everyone else, journalists included, was to "be left to just study what we do."[14]

"Magic" makes the same point. "I got a coin in my palm / I can make it disappear." Whatever the magic trick, "this is what will be." The linguistic sleight of hand creates the reality, dictating perception and shaping facts, from the invasion of Iraq through the war in Afghanistan to the toppling of Gaddafi. In our post-truth era of populist movements, from Brexit to the election of a reality television host as president, it resides in the very core of the English-speaking Western world. This works both ways. Through language, the song's implicit subject, we can discover freedom as surely as Houdini escaped his shackles. "Chain me in a box in your river / And I'll rise singin' this song." Therefore, advises the magician, "Trust none of what you hear / And less of what you see." If you trust others' rhetoric, without thought of their agenda, you may become the next victim, falling mentally and perhaps physically for the fraudulent. Propaganda's "shiny saw blade" simply requires "a volunteer," whom they'll cut in half while their victim smiles "ear to ear." Thus the distortions come to seem the reality. What is true in "TV Movie" is true in the "artistic" rhetoric of politicians. "This is what will be." The final verse is uncompromising in its assertion that the magic show on offer during the times of which Springsteen is writing has unleashed horror on innocent and guilty alike, and, as in all wars, most of the victims are innocent. "There's a fire down below," writes Springsteen. "But it's comin' up here." Hell has surfaced. People are displaced, their lives destroyed, forced to leave everything they know and to carry only what they fear, and there are "bodies hangin' in the trees."

"Magic" thus uses implication as a counter to the politicians' tautologies and binary oppositions. Metaphor can deceive or enlighten, but for Stevens the poet's "motive for metaphor" is to shrink from "the A B C of being, / The ruddy temper, the hammer / Of red and blue," and use "intimation" rather than "steel." Through indirection, the writer avoids "the vital, arrogant, fatal, dominant X" of moral certainty. A "war on terror" against an "axis of evil," like the quasi-Orwellian tautology "Brexit means Brexit," is a dogmatic position as fixed and fake as "The A B C of being." "Magic," in contrast, offers a nuanced response, countering the unsubtle romanticism of Us against Other or good against evil characteristic of primitive tribalism and contemporary populism.[15] "All wars are boyish, and are fought by boys," wrote Melville. The old have always persuaded the young to fight their wars through simplistic appeals. Sometimes you have to counter such simplification directly. "Blind faith in your leaders or in anything," Springsteen said in 1985 before a rendition of "War" (on *Live/1975–85*), "will get you killed."[16] But undermining false oppositions is another ploy.

Springsteen's pragmatic romanticism, therefore, is demonstrably complex. Indirection can mask direct critique while, as with "Born in the U.S.A.," declarative statements can contain subtler levels of meaning. A useful contrast to Springsteen's approach with "Magic" is Toby Keith's song on the same subject, "Red, White and Blue (The Angry American)." A rousing, uncomplicatedly romantic tune beloved by Texan Republicans, if not by the Dixie Chicks, its gung-ho lyrics directly address America's enemies about the country's intention to avenge 9/11. In contrast, Springsteen's reference to bodies hanging in trees alerts us to the bigger picture of romanticism in American history. The romanticism of the South led to a belief in the myths of a hierarchical society "gone with the wind" as a result of Yankee invasion. That this southern romanticism was inextricable from the brutalities of racism is starkly documented in the visual evidence of lynching. In turn, this testifies to the intertwining of romanticism and reality, whereby human beings designated as outside the dominant group are destroyed with alacrity. On the album as a whole, a benevolent form of romanticism does exist in the idealistic belief that the country must realign with its founding statements. But through "Magic" and other songs, including "Livin' in the Future," "Last to Die" and "Long Walk Home," Springsteen not only shows the label of romanticism to be misleading, if meant to designate him a pied piper for escapists, but also that his mature idealism links to political realism even while alert to the nuances of all such "-isms."[17]

T he extent to which Springsteen's romanticism is escapist or pragmatic depends upon its consequences. The argument here is a one-time transatlantic disagreement about the relationship of thought to action, pitting William James's pragmatism against Bertrand Russell's logical positivism. While much less the case among neo-pragmatists, who like Dewey view it as "the philosophy of democracy," pragmatism was once seen, in Rorty's words, as "distinctly American." Russell describes it as such but "in tones of contempt," regarding it as "a shallow philosophy, suitable for an immature country." Against Russell's determination to find truth beyond language, scientifically and logically so he thought, pragmatists reject any attempt to be told how things are, beyond language and human agency. For logicians like Russell, "redemption by philosophy is through the acquisition of a set of beliefs that represent the ways things are." The idea that "the only source of redemption is through the human imagination" was for Russell anathema.[18]

Springsteen might be aware of this clash of ideas. In the *New York Times Review* interview, he cites Russell's *History of Western Philosophy* as having turned him on to philosophy.[19] In it, Russell takes issue with James's argument about belief, and shows himself, as a twentieth-century patrician Englishman, to be fundamentally at odds with the American pragmatist impulse. For Russell, James's argument that how we think shapes our lives is mere guesswork. We can't, he counters, simply will the future into being without knowing the consequences. As the inventor of radical empiricism, writes Russell, James became "the recognized leader of American philosophy."[20] But he sees James as thinking in two incompatible ways, "one scientific, the other religious," and takes issue with the latter. "An idea is 'true,'" writes James in *Pragmatism*, "so long as to believe it is profitable to our lives." Therefore, "our obligation to seek truth is part of our general obligation to do what pays." In terms of religion, "if the hypothesis of God works satisfactorily in the widest sense of the word, it is true."[21] If the outcome of a belief is good then something is true about it. Russell objects that, firstly, we must know what is good and that, secondly, we must know what the outcome is before we can decide if the belief is true. If we choose to believe that Columbus crossed the Atlantic in 1492, rather than in 1491 or 1493, we have to ascertain what the effect is of believing one date over another, and must in turn argue that the effect is good and therefore true. As far as Russell is concerned, James would have us believe that Santa Claus exists because the hypothesis is useful. For Russell, James "wants people to be happy" (a trait he shares with Springsteen) and has decided that "if belief in God makes them happy let them believe in Him," but he calls this "benevolence, not philosophy." "James's doctrine is an attempt to build a superstructure of belief upon a foundation of scepticism," he writes, "and like all such attempts it is dependent on fallacies," in James's case the fallacy that you can "substitute belief in God for God" and "pretend that this will do just as well." This, for Russell, is "subjectivist madness."[22]

Yet my sympathies, surely Rorty's—and I suspect Springsteen's if he's read Russell or James—remain with James. This is not merely because it's a more comforting option. Russell's argument is flawed. The will to believe is not guesswork but a pragmatic approach based on past evidence of practical consequences. Moreover, his mockery of James's reasoning is the result of a word-based philosophy that takes no account of emotion. He can't understand that words are as ephemeral as feelings while feelings, even if ephemeral, are facts. The emotions experienced during a concert "are real and they happen," protested Springsteen in 1980 (TAD 104). Not only does a song, created like magic out of nothing, become physically real, but a concert experience, for all the fantasy, is also "real and its results are physical and tangible" (TAD 231). Emotions are real, and the effects are real. Art can change your perspective, and therefore your actions, and therefore your life. Proof of this can be found by viewing this in reverse. Paranoia or anger can lead to intimidation, violence, murder, and death camps. By Russell's logic, to believe that another group of people is evil or threatening or to blame for your circumstances is unconnected with truth. But beliefs demonstrably create truth; such attitudes lead to racism, random violence, and genocide. Truth can therefore be (in James's words) what "*happens* to an idea."[23] Whether in positive, negative, benevolent, or pernicious ways, to recognize the relationship between language and truth enables you to use it.

Oddly, neither Russell nor James shows much interest in music. Russell mentions music on only six of the eight hundred pages of *History of Western Philosophy*. Each reference is fleeting, and none relate to emotional effect. James, as Oliver Sacks notes, devotes one sentence to music in the fourteen hundred pages of *Principles of Psychology*.[24] This is an extraordinary gap in the thinking of both men yet equally characteristic, according to Kathleen Higgins, of contemporary American philosophy. Whether attention to music is likely to produce a positive outlook and to enhance your usefulness depends, of course, on the music. Patsy Cline's "Three Cigarettes in an Ashtray" is likely to leave you feeling grimmer than Glenn Miller's "In the Mood."[25] "Waiting on a Sunny Day"; "Blue Bayou," cowritten with Joe Melson by "that great tragedian" Roy Orbison; or the dark lyrics offset by a swaggering rhythm on the Rolling Stones' "Ventilator Blues" might lift or drop you depending upon your state of mind (BTR 45).[26] But you choose your medicine and poison. Take one labeled "Rosalita" and the effect may depend upon whether you're a would-be rock star or the parent of a daughter. (If you're both, you might offer a mixed response.) Either way, by James's logic but not Russell's, there's something true about music, if like James we take truth to mean useful and life enhancing: "not duplication but addition."[27] Russell becomes ensnared in words rather as a worker might get entangled in his tools. "Words," as the clown reminds us in *Twelfth Night*, "are very rascals since bonds disgrac'd them," and words, as Russell's erstwhile disciple, and ultimately James admirer, Ludwig Wittgenstein, puts it, are the limits of our world. James's use of the word "true" discombobulates Russell because he's tied to the notion that truth is inflexible. But truth is not the same thing as fact, and within the word "true" there are other meanings. The effect of music on people proves James to be describing a truth that the formidably logical Russell is unaware of.[28] Had he owned an iPod or smartphone, chosen judiciously from the menu, and trusted its effects, his *History of Western Philosophy* might have read a little differently. James at least worked out through other means what Russell was deaf to.

T his foray into a philosophical dispute perhaps familiar to Springsteen facilitates a brief survey of songs that show what we might mean by romanticism across the earlier part of Springsteen's career up to and including the *Born in the U.S.A.* era. The reason for focusing on this first section of his career is that, however you define the interlude of *Tunnel of Love*, after this album pragmatic romanticism becomes Springsteen's professional raison d'être. The pertinent question with regard to romanticism in these earlier albums, therefore, is whether the lyrics express escapist or pragmatic romanticism. Does his romanticism evolve over this time? If the E Street Band has become "purpose-based," what's the nature and purpose of romanticism in the earlier albums? A handful of individual songs from the period may provide a sufficient answer.

The *Greetings from Asbury Park, N.J.*, song "Lost in the Flood," for instance, has nothing to do with pragmatic romanticism; it's pure escapism. It involves at least one death, and two shootings, possible fatalities, one by the police, but the violence is caricatured and without consequence: "vague, abstract references to death," to recall Pitofsky's verdict. The narrator is as excited by the action as those he talks to. What happens is unclear but involves "Ragamuffin Gunner" who is admired by girls and warned by Sticker about quicksand. The bald, pregnant nuns running through the Vatican "pleading immaculate conception" make up one of several memorable images but, unless they represent Catholic girls impregnated by the likes of Gunner and Sticker, they seem unrelated to the rest of the song. The next verse switches to Jimmy the Saint, a Sunday street racer who suffers a James Dean fate: "just junk across the horizon, a real highwayman's farewell." The narrator advises a bystander that he's looking not at oil but blood, and wonders what Jimmy thought as "he hit that storm." Next, there's a hold-up and shoot-out. The cops arrive. "The whiz-bang gang from uptown" get involved, as does "that cat from the Bronx," promptly "blown right off his feet." A Hispanic kid comes "blastin' round the corner, but a cop puts him right away." As he lies there screaming, another bystander exclaims that the Hispanic boy's "body hit the street with such a beautiful thud." We're left with the narrator musing on all this violence and mayhem, and wondering if these "poor cats" were "just lost in the flood."

Such lyrics aren't meant for scrutiny. But it's notable that the images belong to popular culture. The scenario bears little relation to actual lives. Just to mention "41 Shots (American Skin)" in relation to "Lost in the Flood" reveals the distance between this early portrayal of violence and Springsteen in artistic maturity. The primary impulse here is making street life into something fantastical, just as the little boy in "Bishop Danced" would seem to have retreated from a hostile world into his imagination. In "Lost in the Flood," the most vivid character is the fantasist Jimmy the Saint. The young Springsteen might have had Dean's death in mind. Certainly Dean's life, films, and death would have influenced individuals Springsteen knew in Jersey. The description of this "pure American brother, dull-eyed and empty-faced," "telling racing stories" on the hood of a Chevy emblazoned with "Bound for Glory in blue, red and white flash paint" anticipates the economy of his later writing. The realism in the song is the recognition that fantasy is an escape from the mundane. Jimmy's expression suggests that the narrator sees beyond those he observes. In "Growin' Up," as the title implies, that gap exists between the narrator and his younger self. The song is about the journey toward maturity. The voice is ironic about the "cosmic kid," but we see that he had the promise that his older self now feels is being fulfilled. The gap between escapist and pragmatic romanticism, suggested by "Lost in the Flood" versus "Growin' Up," is also evident in *The Wild, the Innocent & the E Street Shuffle*. The song "4th of July, Asbury Park (Sandy)" is about moving on from that fantasy world deftly signaled by the image of pier lights reflected in water. Reality and romanticism interlink. If for this narrator the "boardwalk life is through," "Rosalita" shows the way out. Typical of early Springsteen songs in focusing on the writer's life—"emotionally autobiographical" without disguise (BTR 267)—it's about creating something from very little: the magic of art made manifest.

The album that critics usually mean when they refer to Springsteen's romanticism is *Born to Run*. But in fact this album shows further signs of an evolving sense of what the term might signal. "Backstreets" may offer nothing more than escapist romanticism, but "Thunder Road" does. The narrator tells Mary not to waste her "summers praying in vain / for a savior to rise from these streets." Had he read *Madame Bovary,* and had she, too, read Flaubert's novel (and so known what he was talking about), he might have said, Don't be an Emma Bovary; don't dream your life away waiting for a romantic hero. Choose me, instead. "Well now I'm no hero / That's understood," he says. All he has is a car and a guitar, and no doubt callused hands, but he appeals to reality over fantasy. What he actually offers is a vision that might make a difference, whereas having no vision, or wallowing in pure fantasy, will get them nowhere. They have the possibility "to make it real." We forgive the hyperbole because without urgency nothing will happen. He wants Mary to feel that she must go with him now or never. Then the realism appears. "I got this guitar / And learned how to make it talk." His romanticism has a practical basis. He's learned his craft. Nor are the song's two best-known lines as straightforward as they might seem. "It's a town full of losers / and I'm pulling out of here to win" might seem to be the all-or-nothing sentiments of youth. As Julian Barnes writes, it always looks simple. "There is the life, and then there is the not-life; the life of ambition served, or the life of porcine failure." But this character might, like Springsteen, be a little older. Carlin notes that acoustic versions of "Thunder Road" can sound as if the lines are "exhaled like a sigh of defeat."[29] The acoustic conclusion to the second Paris show made the song sound wistful; the older man sang it knowing that in a way he had won, but that time devours us in the name of wisdom.[30] Whether one interprets the lines as working for this particular character or not, whether one sees this as a musician who succeeds or fails, these lines speak to the reality but also the possibilities. If you have the vision, you can hone skills and, refusing the living death of a wasted life, achieve something. Springsteen clearly understood that possibilities didn't mean certainties, and that success always has a flip side. The likes of Whitman, Dewey, and Rorty, in Rorty's words, are never "committed to the view" that things will "inevitably go well," only that "self-creation" is a viable option. "You keep trying, but you don't count on things," Springsteen has said. "It can be a strength. Because I know some people who sweat on winning so much it kills them." To pursue your goal while aware of the odds is pragmatic romanticism (TAD 20).[31]

As for "Born to Run," its theme of romantic escapism would seem obvious, but the meaning of the song depends not just, as in "Thunder Road," on the tone with which it's sung but also upon what you mean by "run." In "What Pragmatism Means," James tells an anecdote of returning from a walk during a camping expedition to find the others engaged in a dispute about a squirrel. Imagine that a live squirrel is "supposed to be clinging to one side of a tree-trunk" while you stand on the other side. You try to catch sight of the squirrel by moving round the tree, but no matter how fast you go, "the squirrel moves as fast in the opposite direction," always keeping the tree between you and therefore never being seen. "The resultant metaphysical problem," writes James, is whether or not you go round the squirrel. His solution is that it "depends on what you practically mean by 'going round.'" If you think in broader terms of north, east, south, and west then, yes, you've gone around the squirrel. If you mean begin in front of the squirrel, then try to move to the side, then behind and so on, then, no, you've not been around the squirrel since it's always facing you. Straightforward language can turn out on inspection to be complex. So it is with "Born to Run." We're all born, and in being born may be destined. The implication is of a positive destiny. John Fogerty notes in "Fortunate Son" that "Some folks are born silver spoon in hand." But, just as "Born in the U.S.A." has an obviously ironic element, "to run" complicates matters. Does it mean to run as in escaping, or is it run as in perpetual motion? Cars run (as in Arcade Fire's "Keep the Car Running") but they don't themselves escape. Does it mean to run for office? No, but you can see how the phrase would look on the badge of a presidential candidate. Donald Trump: Born to Run. Perhaps it means that poor folk have to keep one step ahead, out of the firing line, away from the abyss; that "shuffle" being "the dance you do every day just to stay alive."[32] But the fact is that, in another sense, we're all born to run. We run, as cars run, until our bodies give out. "Born to Run," taken this way, is not mere romanticism but realism. We can't know whether or not the young Springsteen saw this. As John Rockwell notes, "Born to Run" may only be "four-and-a-half minutes long" but took "three-and-a-half-months to finish."[33] That left Springsteen a lot of time to dwell on the meaning. The obvious meaning is in terms of escape. If they run long and far enough, they'll be able to slow down and "walk in the sun," and it's certainly true that, if the song is strummed slowly with close attention to the words, there's scope to exhale these lines, too, as a "sigh of defeat." But the lyrics as a whole, in urging action to implement dreams, can still be understood as a romantic pragmatist's call to arms.

By the time of *Darkness on the Edge of Town*, the preoccupation is no longer to expend energy but to focus it. When Springsteen wrote "Racing in the Street" he may not have read Arthur Schopenhauer, but their preoccupations are similar. Schopenhauer's term for this energy, "wille," is translated as "will" but has wider connotations, including force, urge, and drive. For Schopenhauer, we are simply will. "The striving of matter can always only be checked, but never fulfilled or satisfied," he writes in *The World as Will and Idea*.[34] Throughout nature "the will to live invariably preys on itself," he argues, "and in different forms is its own nourishment."[35] What's true in nature is true in human behavior. "Every person has constant aims and motives," and he or she can always explain "individual actions," but if you were to ask the person why they will at all, or even will "to exist," the person "would have no answer." For Schopenhauer, their likely sense that the question is absurd would reflect their awareness that they themselves are "nothing but will." "Every goal attained is the starting-point of a new lap in the race, and so on *ad infinitum*," he argues. "Aspirations and desires" are our nature; we then find things to aspire to or desire. (As Nietzsche will later echo, "ultimately one loves one's desires and not that which is desired.") "The fulfilment of these masquerades," states Schopenhauer, is "the ultimate objective of our willing," but once attained we invariably discard them "as vanished illusions." Thus, for all our yearning to fulfill an aim, "we consider ourselves fairly fortunate" to have something "to strive after." This allows us "to keep up the game whereby desire constantly passes into satisfaction, and satisfaction into new desire—if the pace of this is swift, it is called happiness, and if it is slow, sorrow—and does not falter and come to the standstill that shows in dreadful, stultifying boredom, in lifeless yearning without a definite object, a deadening languor."[36] Put simply: this is why on the road Springsteen felt at home while off it he felt lost.

What does it mean to race in the street? Springsteen believes, along with Emerson, James, and Rorty, that we work from the inside out. We look at our own and others' lives and find that connection. He may not have been literally a racer on the circuit, but he knew such individuals. On one hand, street racing as a metaphor allows for identification. Springsteen's view is the same as Schopenhauer's: "each of us can only *be one*, while on the other hand he can *know all*."[37] We can intuit other lives by observing our own. All life is energy, but whether your romanticism goes beyond escapism depends upon what you do with your energy. You can spend it on cars souped up for the drag. Maybe you'll win a race. You can agree to meet criminals across the river. Maybe you'll become a noteworthy gangster. You can learn guitar. Maybe you'll find success. But it's still energy expended for the sake of it. While he may not have been a street racer, Springsteen did put energy into getting (physically) nowhere: just back and forth across the stage and from venue to venue. To use energy in a doomed way, unless it's to roam "empty rooms looking for something to blame" (or, worse, to channel your anger into plans for a murderous suicide attack or mass shooting) may be better than dying "piece by piece." On the other hand, while actual street racers achieve little—except, evidently, causing Asbury Park traffic light patterns to be changed—music, craft, and not a little talent, produce tangible, longer-term benefits.[38] Springsteen's ebullient optimism bubbles between the cracks. It proves infectious. It makes his life. It may only amount to repetitive and reciprocated feel-good activity, but feelings change worlds. As a metaphor for that phenomenon, as good as any is "Racing in the Street."

Other pertinent songs from the era include "Badlands," "The Promised Land," and songs from *The Promise*, including "Gotta Get That Feeling," "Breakaway," and "The Promise" itself. The first two are about taking a stand against injustice and asserting change through force of will. To believe that you can achieve your goal is the first step toward doing so. Both songs exude meliorism, that pragmatist belief that you can improve your world and that of those around you. To believe in a "promised land" needn't be naive. It can mean that you know that belief in the future risks disappointment but believe because there are practical reasons for doing so. As for *The Promise*, the romanticism of the cover epitomizes that sense of the American lonesome but with a difference. The cover of *Darkness* shows Springsteen tousle-haired and trapped—before a shabby wall, blinds down against the night (or day), jacket on, jacket off—what does it matter about his clothes or hair? Who's he going to meet? He has the same pose and expression in three photographs, back and front and inside sleeve: alone, indoors, behind blinds, without a guitar, unsmiling. On *The Promise*, with photographs chosen decades later, he's still alone, still guitar-less, but the paint-peeled rooms give way to photographs on a porch, at a gas station, in a car, on the road. It's still the American lonesome but with romanticism restored. In one, Springsteen strikes a pose worthy of Jack Kerouac, the solitary figure literally *On the Road*, beside his car on the dirt track, with the dark skies behind. There are realities but also possibilities.

The Promise occasionally depicts the world of escapist romanticism that Springsteen tried to excise from *Darkness*. "Breakaway" is a melancholy song about the urge to escape, with three examples of willed disappearance. "Gotta Get That Feeling" depicts romantic, impecunious coupledom, and the desire to find release by indulging the emotions. But "The Promise" itself shows that Springsteen is no Beat. Kerouac's alter ego Sal Paradise evades responsibility. He presents himself as shambling after the madly energetic, amoral "con-man," Dean Moriarty, a fictionalized Neal Cassady. But he's a con-man himself, making promises in California to a Mexican girl (interestingly named "Terry"—though some way from the backstreets of the Jersey Shore) and then, feeling the pull of his "own life," just ditching her with the words, "well, lackadaddy, I was on the road again."[39] In contrast to such solipsism, "The Promise" is ultimately about helping others. The lines about "carryin' / the broken spirits / Of all the other ones who lost," and of living on "when the promise is broken," echo with desolation. The breaking of promises, something Springsteen often returns to, must have come close to causing permanent disillusionment. It must have seemed at times that romanticism had no place in reality and that his own promise, to himself and to others, could never be fulfilled. "Thunder Road," the phrase that encapsulates his early romanticism and that finds its way into the song, as Samuel Bagenstos notes, to powerful effect, must always remain a mythic place rather than a real option.[40] The step forward in maturity, as one might expect given Springsteen's comments that with success he felt responsibility for the people he knew, is the song's focus on others—from promise-as-potential to promise-as-vow.

The River offers more of the downbeat, despite or even because of Springsteen's attempts to inject levity. But, as with some of the songs that came to light on The Promise, it also provides a fitful sense that the will to believe is merely in recess. In truth it will take until the 1990s for that faith to rally and until 2001 for Springsteen to refocus his vision. But the spirit is willing. The River swells with solitude and a yearning for companionship. "Two Hearts" posits the idea that "childish dreams must end," but that "to become a man" means to "grow up to dream again." As with Darkness, the direct addresses to his father brim with compassion. "They ain't gonna do to me what I watched them do to you," writes Springsteen in "Independence Day," a pithy line no less effective than Wordsworth's statement in the Intimations Ode: "the things which I have seen I now can see no more." An engaging quality of Springsteen's world is his supremely articulate awareness that he and his father, in being "too much of the same kind," have lived out two possible versions of a life and either, in different circumstances, might have lived the alternative. Had he not discovered the guitar and been able to face these facts directly in time, Springsteen's moodiness could as easily have turned to failure.[41] Hence he can understand the mind-set, as he puts it in "Hungry Heart," that causes you to take "a wrong turn" and just keep going. It's because of this that he knows, in words from "I Wanna Marry You," that "an unfulfilled life, girl, makes a man hard." He can't offer optimism, but he can offer meliorism: "To say I'll make your dreams come true would be wrong," he admits. "But maybe, darlin', I could help them along." To do so, he creates story after story about the kinds of people he knows, from his sister and brother-in-law, whose situation gave rise to "The River," to the girl in "Point Blank," to the man in "Stolen Car" who waits to get caught but never does, and who fears above all, that he "will disappear," just as another fears he'll "fade away."

The closely connected albums, in terms of time and composition, *Nebraska* and *Born in the U.S.A.,* continue in this vein; neither offers much by way of romanticism as escape. The solitary figures in *Nebraska* are lost souls doomed to drive forever ("Open All Night"), or to dream of visiting a father's house only to find strangers there ("My Father's House"), or pleading not to be stopped ("State Trooper").[42] They're not about to "walk in the sun." The muted romanticism we do see is the belief in possibility against the evidence ("Reason to Believe"). *Born in the U.S.A.* is, strangely, one of Springsteen's bleakest albums. He gives us the dead-end life of a Vietnam veteran; a song about a man pleading to be protected from the world; two songs about felons ("Darlington County" and "Working on the Highway"); two about descent into an emotional and economic quagmire ("Downbound Train" and "I'm Goin' Down"); two about desire ("I'm on Fire" and "Dancing in the Dark"); two about how things were better in the past ("Glory Days" and "My Hometown"), and two more that offer a heavily ironic take on escapist romanticism.

"No Surrender" and "Bobby Jean" are elegies for the appealing but unsustainable escapism of youth. As with "Backstreets," their romanticism has no pragmatic element. This may explain Springsteen's ambivalence about "No Surrender," which he "didn't intend to include on the album" until Van Zandt persuaded him to. He was "uncomfortable" with it, he writes in *Songs.* "You don't hold out and triumph all the time in life. You compromise; you suffer defeat; you slip into life's gray areas." For Van Zandt, "the portrait of friendship and the song's expression of the inspirational power of rock music was an important part of the picture" (S 166). But if "No Surrender" refuses compromise, and therefore reality, its partner, "Bobby Jean," pointedly has the singer stranded and alone with his escapist vision, heard only on the radio in some motel room. That the friend might be listening exacerbates the sense of that fragile communication that, decades later, the singer will seek on "Radio Nowhere," where the solitude is existential, the sound "bouncing off a satellite." Were "Bobby Jean" a movie, the final scene would show the friend in that nondescript room, with the singer's voice suddenly not up close but issuing from a cheap radio. The camera would pull back, out the window and up and away. You'd see the motel as a pinprick of light amid other lights, and then not at all, just an outline of the continent, with the big cities glowing but, where the motel must be, just an overwhelming darkness and finally, out in space with planet earth a ball in blackness, no sound at all. "These romantic dreams" in his head are a farewell to that youthful romanticism that imagines escaping beyond the horizon. Springsteen had come to acknowledge that, "seductive" though it may be, the rock-and-roll dream, if it's to mean anything in maturity, needs situating within the context of "finding your place in the world."[43] But without that romanticism in the first place, he'd have achieved little. Overall, therefore, his career vindicates romanticism, defined as the will to believe: a vindication not of escapism but of meliorism, of "seeing the realities but also the possibilities," and therefore a romanticism couched in pragmatic terms.

A man that looks at himself in a glass and finds
It is the man in the glass that lives, not he.
He is the image, the second, the unreal,
The abstraction.
—WALLACE STEVENS, "AMERICANA"

I check my look in the mirror
I wanna change my clothes, my hair, my face.
—"DANCING IN THE DARK"

6

MULTIPLE SELVES

Springsteen's career has always been about fulfilling "possibilities" in the face of "realities." His later career is also about making the most of new realities, including possibilities fulfilled. Success and fame changed the music irreversibly, but with accompanying artistic compensations. One of the remarkable things about his creation of character as his career has progressed has been his willingness to write from female as well as male viewpoints and diverse perspectives in terms of age, ethnicity, and experience. Such attempts may not always convince, but they at least champion human plurality and show an openness to creative risk. We project multiple selves even while, as Tolstoy reminds us, it's easy to assume that the inner lives of other people are less complex than our own.[1] It's a rare and sensitive person who can consistently empathize with other people and embrace multiplicity with verve. But to write convincingly from other mind-sets takes time and dedication. Springsteen barely attempts this early in his career. Decades later, it appears to be second nature. "I chose fiction," writes Australian novelist Patrick White, "as a means of introducing to a disbelieving audience the cast of contradictory characters of which I am composed."[2] Springsteen has presented his cast of selves by writing songs. How he's done so reveals another way in which his work has matured.

To step outside one's own perspective and explore wider contexts and competing viewpoints is a political act. The political is nothing without the personal. Springsteen's path into engagement was perhaps inevitable. Refusing to accept the troubled lives of those whom, in economic terms, he'd left behind, he turned back to observe. His observations led to reflection, wider reading, wider awareness, and ultimately to knowledge of context. As he became more politically savvy, his art deepened and nuanced. His career, however, contains a distinct break. It takes place around the time of Born in the U.S.A., the period when many of his earlier fans, not least his home-state following, felt they'd lost him to the wider public. Once you're a celebrity on that scale, you can't undo the fact, though you can defy expectations. Springsteen began to rethink his purpose and, in time, used his writing in the service of this vision of multiplicity, with all its personal and political connotations. While neither abrupt nor unanticipated, Born in the U.S.A. both brings Springsteen to a wider audience and, with 1984 barely buried, sees him try to step down from that pedestal.[3] It's Springsteen's "Borges and I" moment. When he signed with Columbia Records, Adele asked her son what he'd changed his name to.[4] He didn't change it, but nor did it remain the same. By 1984 Bruce Springsteen had become "Bruce Springsteen." In the public eye, he was a postmodernist rock star with no actual heartbeat or voiding of the bowels: a cartoonish figure, epitomized by the lip-synced "Dancing in the Dark" video, the Action Man pose on the album's inside cover, and— for an example of mass-media by-products—the sepia-tinted, garish cover of the bio-catalogue Bruce Springsteen: Blinded by the Light (1985), where our hero, in superimposed, photo-brushed Technicolor, gazes askance a tequila sunglow and resembles a 1950s B-movie pirate matinee idol.[5] Viewing this cuckoo self, destined to live on in multimedia images and sounds beyond the mortal being, how easily the man might have reflected something similar to Borges's sentiments. The relationship between the public and private self is tangential. The artist, being mortal, must accede his art to the public realm. Therefore what matters, to reprise the title of Marge Piercy's poem, is "to be of use."

Rethinking was a necessity if Springsteen was to retain artistic integrity rather than be consumed by the public image he had colluded in creating. If the "super-duper stardom" (Jim Farber's term) had "trivialized" him (Springsteen's word), he knew he'd desired this to happen.[6] He wrote the pop songs, agreed to the album cover, wore the bandana, and bulked up his muscles. "We all have multiple selves," he half-jokes on the VH1 Storytellers DVD, before telling a story about fans accosting him outside a strip club. He was merely the singer's alter ego, he explained to them. "Bruce does not even know I am missing. He is at home right now doing good deeds" (TAD 303). Fame, one would think, makes the multiplicity of selves we each inhabit and project all the more obvious. As Borges notes, there's the physical, mortal being, and there's the artistic persona, and it's easy to confuse the two. "I get tired of being Elvis Presley" evidently became a refrain of the King. In his posthumously published *The Life and Death of Émile Ajar,* French author Romain Gary, who had secretly used the pseudonym "Émile Ajar," explained that he'd grown weary of being "the famous Romain Gary," and quoted Polish writer Witold Gombrowicz: "there comes a day when a writer is held prisoner by 'la gueule qu'on lui a fait' ('the mug which the critics have given him')—an appearance which has nothing to do with his work or himself."[7] Eduardo Galeano writes of how Argentina's greatest soccer player, Diego Maradona, felt "the burden of being Maradona" and became "overwhelmed by the weight of his own personality." Galeano uses Maradona's actual spinal problems to make of his body a metaphor. "Maradona carried a burden named Maradona that bent his back out of shape." That sense of selves, complicated further by celebrity, and by performance ("I used to do a lot of jumping," Springsteen evidently once told a doctor), is something the singer has commented on periodically and not least in terms of the *Born in the U.S.A.* era.[8]

One of the most poignant stories in *Born to Run,* in this regard, is the tale of how Springsteen and Steve Van Zandt got thrown out of Disneyland for wearing bandanas. They'd planned this visit to the Magic Kingdom with mounting excitement. How, asks Springsteen of Van Zandt, does he feel about having being "thrown out of 'THE HAPPIEST PLACE ON EARTH'"? Is it that they "do not deserve that degree of happiness" (BTR 329)? Of course, stardom on the scale of 1984–85 might look from the outside like precisely that place. But it didn't feel like that. "I had no way of knowing if this was going to be my life, my *whole* life," he writes. "Everywhere I'd go, day after day, country after country, bed after bed, in a *Groundhog Day* of stultifying, inane attention, brought on by my own sacred ambitions crossed by the normal human longing for life and love." He smashes a Takamine guitar against a wall in Gothenburg, plays the first song he learned, "Twist and Shout," with such fury, as he tells it, that the frenzied response cracks "the concrete foundation" of the Ullevi stadium (BTR 336–37). Somehow, this is not happiness. Look in the mirror and what do you see? The mirror has cracked and blackened. The reflection is unrecognizable.

In other words, it seems likely that Springsteen shared with William James the experience of coming to terms with the complicated nature of what we call "self." James's revelation, in John J. McDermott's words, about "the diaphanous and utterly fragile character of the classically alleged, rock-bottom personal self" occurred in his twenties, and shaped his subsequent thought. He experienced a "vastation" (to use "mystic-philosopher" Emanuel Swedenborg's term for "the projecting of an inner self outward") in the late 1860s.[9] Suffering from, in James's words, "philosophic pessimism and general depression of spirits" about his prospects, he recalled an epileptic patient he'd seen in an asylum, "a black-haired youth with greenish skin, entirely idiotic, who used to sit all day on one of the benches, or rather shelves against the wall, with his knees drawn up against his chin, and the coarse gray undershirt, which was his only garment, drawn over them." In a low mood and confronted with this image, James pondered whether his sense of a coherent self and of superiority to this being were really illusions. *"That shape I am,* I felt, potentially," he admits. Thereafter, writes McDermott, he came to "doubt the existence of the traditional 'soul'" and opted "for a more free-flowing movement between the focus of one's own self and the fringe that we visit." Such visits to the "fringe" or, as Erin McKenna and Scott Pratt put it of Springsteen, to "the darkness at the edge," revealed "radically different versions" of James's sense of self. "For, it turns out," McDermott states, "we are actually multiple selves."[10]

"There is a crack in everything," writes Leonard Cohen in "Anthem." "That's how the light gets in." But, although intimations of it can be found earlier, only in the 1990s did Springsteen come to terms with this identity crisis and articulate his motivation for presenting multiple selves through his art. Even before the insight offered in the autobiography, one could second-guess from the music and interviews that the crisis came to a head in the 1980s before Springsteen literally "faced up" to and began to make use of the insight. On one hand, there's the public image he came to be saddled with. Where James was at a low point because of his apparent lack of prospects, Springsteen had achieved all he once hoped for, but seems to have experienced it as his own kind of nadir. The heights of rock stardom took him to rock bottom. Fame on such a level seemed to entrap rather than free him. "I think every fan creates an image of you in his or her head," he said in 1995, "that may not be totally accurate" (TAD 176). Fascination with celebrities, he told Walker Percy's nephew, Will, in 1998, becomes "a problem if a certain part of your life as a writer—your 'celebrity,' or whatever you want to call it—can blur and obscure the story that you're interested in telling" (TAD 228). On the other hand, there's his recognition, akin to James's, of the minimal distance between success and failure, between being able to assert an identity and being seen as social detritus. "I've had an enormous amount of luck and fortune and have worked hard," he said, again in 1995, "but that other thing, I don't know, it never feels that far away, and I think it's as far away as the guy next to you" (TAD 186–87).

Of course, James and Springsteen belong to different eras and different personal circumstances. Had James been alive to review *Born to Run*, he'd no doubt have written much as John Lahr does, of himself as "a preppy, a person Bruce would have sneered at as a Rah-Rah—a clean-cut, college-bound kid full of an optimism born of abundance, who never threw a punch in his life." Springsteen's career has also coincided with the deindustrialization of many western countries, the United States included, and in the view of many commentators, notably Dale Maharidge, "the political failure" of our representatives "to stem this tide" or to steer the economy "in a direction that might serve the majority." In *Someplace like America*, which revisits some of the victims of deindustrialized communities recorded in *Journey to Nowhere*, he writes, "a babbling man with missing teeth sat in a village of shacks in sight of the skyscrapers of Houston." "Amid gibberish," this man tells Maharidge and photographer Michael Wilson how he was once "a trucker who hauled steel in Youngstown." Maharidge admits that if they'd met this man during the previous project "he would have been an example of the newly homeless." But "now he was among the wasted old guard," someone they "would have ignored back in 1983," when they sought out only those "who were more sympathetic," avoiding the old guard "in large part because of public enmity toward the homeless." What Maharidge came to understand in the meantime was how little "separated this man from the workers of the Warren steel mill." In a matter of a few years "the cackling man" had illustrated "the arc of descent a human being can travel."[11] This is what James meant by "*that shape I am*," updated to an age of globalization and what Steve Fraser calls "auto-cannibalism," during which the financial sector, under the guise of "rescue missions" that turned out to be "sophisticated forms of looting," have laid waste to industrial heartlands. The resultant precariat of "free-floating working people," in Fraser's view, have been kept periodically contented through consumerism, or had been until (subsequent to the publication of his book, *The Age of Acquiescence*) they acquiesced no more.[12] Offered scapegoats and simplistic slogans, in Britain they voted to abandon the European Union and "take back control," and, in the States, to "make America great again."

On one hand, there is considerable irony here for Springsteen. Many Trump supporters would have been Springsteen fans. In Fraser's terms, his output, as part of popular culture, would at least superficially exemplify "salvation through repeated momentary sensations of personal well-being," delivering something that "is inherently fleeting: otherwise it wouldn't work commercially." On the other hand, he's had to deal with this before, notably in the *Born in the U.S.A.* era, and his work contains responses to it, not only in that "ironic anthem" itself, but in much of *Tom Joad* and in songs like "I Mow Your Lawn" on *Wrecking Ball.* The precariat have always been his people. Fraser refers to Melville's "deeply angry, often inscrutable workingmen, burning with rage and stubborn impassivity," people, of course, not unlike Doug Springsteen.[13] In political terms, the recent embrace of populist politicians would seem very much to be versions of Bartleby the Scrivener's stubborn phrase when asked to take a reasonable course of action: "I prefer not to." For many Springsteen listeners, the point is that the results are not "inherently fleeting." As Daniel Cavicchi shows, while Springsteen concerts, in one fan's words, are "a sure pick-me-up," for many "the artist has touched them where they live and they are better for this," perhaps because, in the long run, "he is more like a folk singer than a pop star." But many others might well have been the consumers Fraser refers to, finding momentary escapism from a deteriorating economic situation. Much of this, his songs suggest, was on Springsteen's mind in the 1980s when, facing huge success while depicting terrible hardship, this crisis of self came to a head.[14]

To the extent that Springsteen was acutely aware that "lack of work creates a loss of self" (TAD 415), and given his perennial fear of "disappearing" (TAD 254), it seems fair to assume that his version of James's revelation that potentially "*that shape I am*" arose from these two simultaneous recognitions: the awareness of the superficiality of the celebrity persona and of the fragility of the accompanying success. The character of "the classically alleged, rock-bottom personal self," to reprise McDermott's explanation in relation to James, came to seem "diaphanous and utterly fragile." Springsteen became all the more aware that he could *be* that other person. The self he believed himself to be and the self he projected or that was projected onto him illustrated the precarious nature of identity. This would prove scary. He'd started out wanting to be like his heroes, whether the actors on the drive-in screen or the musicians on stage. Yet "to walk like the heroes we thought we had to be" was one thing, to find yourself *being* that supposed hero quite another. "You're a bit of a figment of a lot of other people's imaginations," he said in 1992. "And that always takes some sorting out. But it's even worse when you see yourself as a figment of your own imagination." In youth, he continued, "I had this idea of playing out my life like it was some movie, writing the script and making all the pieces fit. And I really did that for a long time. But you can get enslaved by your own myth or your own image" (TAD 156). Like Julien in *The Red and the Black*, and most ambitious young people, he was "moved like a playwright by his own story."[15] As he put it with reference to Walker Percy's essay, "The Man on the Train," that's fine on screen but problematic in reality. "Our mythic hero," Gary Cooper, "looks like he's walking over that abyss of anxiety, and he won't fail. Whereas the moviegoer, the person watching the movie, is not capable of that. There's no real abyss under Gary Cooper, but there is one under the guy watching the film!" (TAD 229).

James's vastation, according to McDermott, marks a beginning of his pragmatist philosophy. In turn, Springsteen's 1980s mega-fame brings a crisis that, once resolved, leads to his mature period from *Tom Joad* to the present. After his vastation, James thinks of the self as being not something deep and fundamental within us but something that we can adapt, experiment with, and above all present to ourselves and to the world through language and action. He believes we can attain ironic distance from the urge to invent narratives while at the same time recognizing the value and power of this self-conscious awareness of constructed selves. It's on reading philosopher Charles Renouvier's definition of free will, "the sustaining of a thought because I choose to when I might have other thoughts," that James states that his "first act of free will shall be to believe in free will." From there, he notes that "only when habits of order are formed can we advance to really interesting fields of action." This allows him to build a basic tenet of pragmatist philosophy, which has to do with what McDermott calls "a pluralistic approach to inquiry" that's "distinctly American in that it allows everyone to have his or her say."[16] Without forcing too close a link between this and Springsteen's 1980s watershed, a general sense of one feels valid. "What happens is when you have a lot of success your complexity tends to be whittled down into a very simple presentation," he's said (TAD 313). To see oneself from the outside, in terms of the "borderline of caricatures" that he and the band came to be presented as, would seem to have had a fundamental effect on his approach to the notion of self (BTR 326). He became "'Bruced' out."[17] Thereafter, crisis time or not, he married in haste, broke up the band, and escaped the "Bruce Springsteen" he had become. When he "returned to form," as it were, his personal life more settled, and with *Human Touch* and *Lucky Town* behind him, he pointedly presented different personas and dramatized diverse selves.

A run through the idea of the self from his earliest to his latest albums illustrates the way these ideas develop, with key songs marking subtle transitions. As time passes, and with *Tunnel of Love* pivotal, Springsteen becomes more daring and experimental with regard to identities. With the exception of *Human Touch, Lucky Town,* and the later *Working on a Dream*—each of which are akin, in this sense only, to the early work—the shift is from a self-focus or external commentary on others to a willingness to render their voices and inner lives. It's this, as much as active intervention beyond art, that makes Springsteen's career an act of "citizenship" of the kind that Wendell Berry refers to with regard to William Carlos Williams, epitomizing the pragmatist belief in community-oriented art of use to practitioners and recipients alike. Only from 1984 does Springsteen express, and with increasing consistency, his desire for his music to be useful, and see his career in terms of such citizenship. "I wanted to be good at doing something that was useful to other people, and to myself," he told Roger Scott and Patrick Humphries that year. "You play some role in people's lives, whether it's just a night out, a dance, a good time, or maybe you make someone think a little bit different about themselves, or about the way they live, which is what rock 'n' roll music did for me. The interaction with the community is the real reward" (TAD 134). Subsequently, that idea of "usefulness" has often surfaced, from "becoming part of people's lives" (TAD 172) to providing "some service" (SOS 297). Springsteen became comfortable, in maturity, with this notion of multiple selves, intimately tied, as it is in his work, with art as an act of "citizenship."

A n account of the evolution is inevitably schematized, but Springsteen's depiction of selves in early albums differs markedly from his depiction of selves in later albums. The lyrics on *Greetings from Asbury Park, N.J.*, mostly dramatize the perspective of a young man who is a version of Springsteen as he saw or presented himself at the time. They deal with immediate, personal experience. Often he's the observer on the edge of things, as in "Lost in the Flood." In other songs he's the center of the action. In "Blinded by the Light," it may as well be Springsteen who looks "into the sights of the sun." In "Mary Queen of Arkansas" he's "a lonely acrobat" with "the live wire" as his trade. The early self-satire, "Growin' Up," with the literary staple of ironic distance from the younger self, anticipates Springsteen's mature expression of the dangers of the artist taking himself as seriously as he takes his art, but it merely intimates changes to come. As Clarence Clemons notes in *Big Man,* the young Springsteen is more into spinning stories the sounds and words of which are the subject matter. "I sometimes thought of cloudbursts," writes Clemons. "An impossible amount of rain crammed into too little time." "It had that Chuck Berry syncopation, using vowels and consonants like musical notes," but he had no idea "what any of it meant."[18]

The Wild, the Innocent & the E Street Shuffle often uses what will become another familiar mode of storytelling. The authorial voice speaks to a third party about personal dreams. "Rosalita" is about a young artist making his way. "4th of July, Asbury Park (Sandy)" does introduce further characteristics of Springsteen's writing, such as his rendering of ambience and mood, from the "cheap seaside bars" to the "dusty arcade," and his eye for apt detail. When, for example, the protagonist gets his shirt caught on the Tilt-a-Whirl, his sense that he might never escape the fairground ride is implicitly a fear that he'll be trapped in the cycle of this "carnival life." While not as dramatic as Buzz on the *Rebel without a Cause* chicken run, catching his sleeve in the car-door handle and plunging over the cliff, it's a death all the same, just slower. But the song is again one in which the protagonist speaks to a friend or partner of their hopes and dreams, mutual or otherwise. As such it belongs with "Incident on 57th Street" and "Rosalita" as a forerunner of "Born to Run" and "Backstreets," and as a form of self-expression Springsteen will reprise in "No Surrender" and "Bobby Jean" and later songs of mature love, such as "This Life" and "Kingdom of Days."

Years will pass before the possibility of projecting multiple selves fully manifests itself, but the process begins on *Born to Run* with the one-time anomaly, "Meeting Across the River." It's the earliest song told from a first-person viewpoint clearly distinct from Springsteen's own (and no song of this period on *Tracks* counters this observation). The structure and rendition of voice is notably sophisticated. Inspired by film noir, it begins and ends with the request for a ride, hinting at a tragic or tragicomic denouement. What is unsaid intensifies the drama. All that Springsteen includes is "the supremely necessary" that, in William Styron's words to a would-be writer, amounts to "the secret of art." The monologue, as Styron also counsels, is "action," and "kept at a fever pitch of narrative excitement."[19] The small-time crook dominates his silent accomplice. He's leading the unfortunate Eddie further astray. "You gotta promise to not say anything" also suggests that Eddie is not wholly reliable. Nor can he get out of it. The speaker is a bully. They won't be looking for just him this time. The most innovative moment is when he hands Eddie something resembling a gun and advises him conversationally to change his shirt. In a few lines we get to know two ne'er-do-wells, one dominating the other, about to act out an impromptu heist in a criminal underworld they're ill equipped to encounter.

The other narrators on *Born to Run*, as with *Darkness*, seem at most a fraction removed from Springsteen's recognizable persona. Alan Rauch points out that "Born to Run" "is in every sense a dramatic monologue" and that Springsteen's "use of the monologue transforms the audience into active rather than passive listeners," but while he may be ahead of the escapist whose dream is to "walk in the sun," or who feels he's abandoning "a town full of losers" to "win," "Tenth Avenue Freeze-Out," in the "Rosalita" mode, is about the determination to form a band and succeed, and it's essentially Springsteen intending to "find one face that ain't looking through" him, and believing in "The Promised Land."[20] Where distinctions appear, they're of small degree, as in "Night," about a factory worker, and "Racing in the Street," about a fate Springsteen rejects, even if the metaphor might broaden to mean any restless activity, making loud noises included. The same is essentially true of the songs on *The Promise*.

It's worth noting, however, one other place where this willingness to imagine beyond the unitary self emerges, and that's in the androgyny of "Backstreets." Rosalie Fanshel's "Beyond Blood Brothers: Queer Bruce Springsteen" may overstretch the case, but it's valid to argue for Springsteen's "career-long, systematic blurring of the rigid boundaries by which we regulate society." Primarily through glam rock but in ways that go back to "Esquerita and Little Richard in the mid-1950s," argues Auslander, rock has celebrated "the freedom to explore and construct one's identity," not least "in terms of gender and sexuality." The possibilities for the female in the male and the male in the female have always been part of the artist's repertoire as a dramatizer of multiple selves. (Shakespeare's comedies feature female characters, Portia, Nerissa, and Viola for instance, disguising themselves as boys. Given that originally boys would have performed the parts, those actors would have been boys playing women playing boys.) Faced with the singer reminding Terry of "all the movies" they've seen and of trying to "walk like the heroes we thought we had to be," it's hard to sustain a reading of Terry as female. Whether they just realize they're not cut out to be "heroes" or, more than that, fail to fit the model of manhood portrayed on the screen, is open to interpretation. "What makes their lives so forbidden that they must hide on the backstreets?"

asks Fanshel. Why is their "love so hard and filled with defeat"? In asking such questions she at least makes a case for the song being about "erotic brotherhood" and for Springsteen's career as containing a complex portrayal of male selves.[21]

Whether or not androgyny has always been part of Springsteen's artistic worldview, *The River* sees a development in the portrayal of multiple selves. The narrative mode of "Meeting Across the River" becomes the norm, with "song-stories" told from the perspectives of diverse individuals (S 100). McKenna and Pratt note that the title song, by his "own report, represented a transitional moment in his work in which he recognized the value of narrative detail."[22] It distinguishes between authorial self and first-person character. It depicts, moreover, not merely a moment but a story that takes place over time.[23] Rendering others' viewpoints in first or third person, Springsteen's powers of empathy are also more marked. "Independence Day" (written during the time of *Darkness* but not included due to a surfeit of "slow songs") is especially moving for its acknowledgment of the parental viewpoint.[24] Compare it with Cat Stevens's "Father and Son," and it's obvious that, despite supposed dialogue, Stevens's song skews wholly toward the son's viewpoint. The father is portrayed as condescending and uncomprehending. The youth is in no mood to ponder why. The father in "Independence Day" doesn't need to speak. From the tender opening, telling the father to "go to bed" because nothing they say will "change anything now," to the son's plea that he "never meant to take those things away," the son honors his viewpoint. In Springsteen's words, reflecting on the song in the *Ties that Bind* documentary, we're eavesdropping on "a very late night intimate conversation between two people," and "it's a song quite without bitterness." What it does contain, however, is a poignancy all the more painful if the fact that the son is "leaving in the morning from Saint Mary's Gate" means that he's bound for Vietnam.[25]

The first-person voices Springsteen dramatizes in *Nebraska* and *Born in the U.S.A.* are often non-autobiographical. Beyond the tracks that Springsteen tells us "came directly out of" his experience with his family, including "Mansion on the Hill," "Used Cars," and "My Father's House" (S 138), these individuals aren't musicians and don't have art as an avenue toward redemption. In the final song, "Reason to Believe," the singer observes ordinary folk from outside. But prior to this the speakers include petty criminals, murderers, the unemployed, and those whose jobs put them in difficult situations. By this stage, Springsteen is identifying with people however aberrant their behavior or different their life. *Born in the U.S.A.* continues this pattern, with the voices of, for instance, a Vietnam veteran, a possible statutory rapist, a convict, and a father talking to a son. On the songs of that era on *Tracks,* too, "A Good Man Is Hard to Find (Pittsburgh)" is told from the viewpoint of a war widow with a young daughter, "Car Wash" from a girl's perspective, and "Lover Man" by a narrator of unspecified gender. Other *Born in the U.S.A.* songs contain autobiographical elements, but, as with *Nebraska,* we're a long way from the story-of-a-band autobiographies. In "Glory Days" the speaker's encounter with a high-school hero stuck on "boring stories of glory days" shows just how far he's come. "Some day we'll look back on this," we recall from "Rosalita," and here he is, doing just that. In the interplay of words and music the masterstroke, emphasized by Springsteen on record, is the echo of "boring" and "glory." That ironic juxtaposition is the heart of the song.

Then comes an accelerated development toward greater emphasis on multiple selves by way of *Tunnel of Love.* "The writing was not painful, and though some thought so, not literally autobiographical," writes Springsteen. But it did uncover "unresolved feelings" that he'd carried within him "for a long time." "I was thirty-seven years old; I didn't see myself with suitcase in hand, guitar at my side, on the tour bus for the rest of my life. I assumed my audience was moving on, as I was" (S 190). Certainly some songs sound personal given what we know of his life at the time: "Ain't Got You," "Tougher Than the Rest," "Cautious Man," "Tunnel of Love," "One Step Up." But as for Springsteen's portrayal of selves, the key songs are "Two Faces" and "Brilliant Disguise." As so often in his work, allusions to musical lineage provide the basis for complexity that goes beyond the influence. The refrain "two faces have I" pays homage to Lou Christie's 1963 hit, "Two Faces Have I." Equally, Christie's hit of the previous year, "The Gypsy Cried," is echoed in the lines from "Brilliant Disguise," "The gypsy swore our future was right / But come the wee wee hours / Well maybe, baby, the gypsy lied." (Who knows, perhaps this Christie song drew his attention to the possibility of bringing Madam Marie into his lyrical universe.) But "two faces" merely hints at the layers involved. Springsteen presents the idea of split personalities as a fact to endure and apologize for rather than to celebrate. In his swings from elation to depression, warmth to hostility, the speaker feels that he really has two selves. By halfway through the song it's clear that he identifies with his better self. His other self becomes "he," a Hyde to his Jekyll. His ideal self is a decent, spiritual, open man. He prays that his love for the girl will "make that other man go away," yet he knows that in reality he's stuck with his twin. As he kisses the girl, the other man tells him their life is "a lie."

This doppelgänger motif sees Springsteen edge into the grim corridors frequented by Dostoevsky, Poe, and Conrad. In *Crime and Punishment* the murderer, Raskolnikov, has not merely a split personality (his name suggests "schism") but multiple personalities that seem echoed in characters as disparate as his friend Razhumkin (suggesting "reason"), the drunkard Marmaladov, and Porfiry, the perverse examining magistrate who cajoles and terrorizes him into confessing. In turn, in "Brilliant Disguise," Springsteen extends the notion of multiple selves to cover not only the wars between internal selves but the masks people wear in relationships. He wants to know "if it's you I don't trust / 'Cause I damn sure don't trust myself." She plays "the loving woman," while he plays "the faithful man," but this is just the first level of disguise. "Is that you, baby / Or just a brilliant disguise" is rendered without a question mark. The speaker knows not only that it *is* a disguise but that he himself "doubts what he's sure of," within and without. "If there are two people in a room there's a play of some sort going on," Springsteen will say of the song in 2006. "That's human interaction." To talk about it "is a way of dispelling some of the myths that build up around you and which tend to box you in." Hence, "the song is asking, 'Is it me or a brilliant disguise?' And the answer is it's almost always both." Even ten years later, his hesitation in expressing the theme reveals the complexity of his feelings about art and identity. "You know, you've gotta put out an enormous amount of your real self for it to feel real. You can't . . . it's not something . . . for it to feel real, it has to be real," he says. "At least, that's the way that I operate. But it doesn't have to be all, it's not all, you know?" (TAD 313). What's also true, though, is that as Springsteen has come to accept the notion of multiple selves so too his tone has changed from angst to ironic humor. Only in these later years, after the watershed of divorce, remarriage, and parenthood, has he joked publically about multiple selves. It's in that same interview, for instance, that he mock-wishes that he, too, could be the "Bruce" people think he is (TAD 318). That tone is not evident in *Tunnel of Love*.

Where *Tunnel of Love* is introspective, *Human Touch* and *Lucky Town* are largely celebratory of Springsteen's personal arrival at domestic stability. Their reputation is patchy. *Human Touch* began, he writes, as "an exercise" to return to "writing and recording" (S 216). But it also led to the more spontaneous *Lucky Town*. "Once I had written 'Living Proof,'" Springsteen explains, "I wrote and recorded an entirely new record. It was a release from the long process of making *Human Touch*" (S 218). In song after song, many of them based on marriage and new parenthood, Springsteen celebrates what Anna Sergeyevna in Turgenev's

Fathers and Sons describes as "the best thing on earth" (and what Greil Marcus sees as Huck Finn's goal): peace of mind.[26] Complications remain, of course. There's fear mingled with love, and always the possibility of "The Big Muddy." As for "a stable life" driving him to "write more outwardly," as he told Will Percy (TAD 223), it's notable that the penultimate song of *Lucky Town*, "Souls of the Departed," in Springsteen's words, opens with "scenes from the Persian Gulf War and gang warfare in Los Angeles." Springsteen's comment on this is also revealing. The song, he writes, "wrestles with" the family man's "own hypocrisies about the choices he has made for his family in contrast to his beliefs" (S 219).

Springsteen refers to one final song in this gloss on the album, and that's "My Beautiful Reward" and its ambiguous ending, where the man, "searching for something unnameable," and "slipping between life and death, transforms into a bird flying over gray fields" with the cold wind at his back (S 219). The sentiment seems clear. "My Beautiful Reward" is an ironic phrase. Unlike the end of a romantic movie, there's no final place to "walk in the sun," only renewed commitment to one's beliefs, whatever they may be. But the overall tone of *Lucky Town* is captured in "Living Proof," which he describes as being "about the common strength it takes to constitute a family." To view children as "the 'living proof' of our belief in one another" is to side implicitly with James against Russell (S 218): an emotion can yield tangible results. Belief can result in fact. The song vindicates the pragmatic romanticism of *Born to Run* and affirms love as "real." For the love here is very different from the "wild" love that also features in that song, the intoxicating "romantic" love that always spends its force. It's an enduring love that relates to loyalty and mutual commitment, where there's no need any longer for disguise, or at least there's recognition that the existence of multiple selves needn't involve deceit.

By this time the conviction of art's usefulness has become a dominant aspect of Springsteen's thinking. Personal life remains a topic, especially on *Working on a Dream*, with songs celebrating ordinary life, such as "Queen of the Supermarket," and the longevity of domesticity and friendship amid the lengthening shadows of mortality ("Tomorrow Never Knows"). As Dickinson has it: "Presentiment—is that long Shadow—on the lawn— / Indicative that Suns go down— / The notice to the startled Grass / That Darkness is about to pass—" (Poem 764). Or as Oblonsky says in *Anna Karenina*, one can feel that things grow "even brighter toward the end!"[27] Accepting the aging process, and enjoying a domestic plateau, Springsteen now took that originally troubling idea of multiple selves and viewed its positive side. Urgency in the face of galloping time now replaces the urgency of romantic escape. The singular self, at the center of its own world, gives way in emotional maturity to an embracing of selves, and a looking out toward our common experience. Instead of "losers" whom we must abandon to "win," we discover, in words from a Lynyrd Skynyrd song, that "we ain't much different at all." Like William James, the recognition that potentially "*that shape I am*" could lead, Springsteen realized, to a whole new worldview of possibility and productivity. Thus we have his resurgence in songs that imagine the perspectives of all kinds of individuals, whether in non-album songs such as "Streets of Philadelphia" or "Dead Man Walkin'" or through *Tom Joad, The Rising, Devils & Dust, Magic, Wrecking Ball,* and *High Hopes.* These albums show an artist at ease with multiple selves, willing to risk dramatizing the minds of individuals in all sorts of situations, from an AIDS patient to an illegal immigrant, a mother to a hustler, a soldier to a terrorist, a perpetrator to a victim, and—to collapse such language-based categories—all kinds of identities in between.

We ought to hold with all our force, both of hands and teeth, the use
of the pleasures of life that our years, one after another, snatch away
from us. Carpamus dulcia; nostrum est, quod vivis; cinis, et manes, et
fabula fies. (Let us pluck life's sweets, 'tis for them we live: by-and-by
we shall be ashes, a ghost, a mere subject of talk)—Persius, *Sat.*, v. 151.
—MICHEL DE MONTAIGNE, "OF SOLITUDE"

Death don't fuck around. . . . it's waiting around some corner for
all of us, and once you make that turn you're not coming back.
Order the good wine.
—CLARENCE CLEMONS, *Big Man*

7

AFTER SPRINGSTEEN

work to be an ancestor," writes Springsteen (BTR 503). "I know I'm writing
toward an ultimate disappearance," writes poet Tess Gallagher. In *Achieving
Our Country*, Richard Rorty cites an essay by novelist Dorothy Allison. "There
is a place where we are always alone with our mortality," she writes, "where we
must simply have something greater than ourselves to hold onto—God or history
or politics or literature or a belief in the healing power of love, or even righteous
anger. Sometimes I think they are all the same. A reason to believe, a way to take
the world by the throat and insist that there is more to this life than we have ever
imagined." This is very much the pragmatist mode, going back to Nietzsche's
observation that we love our desires rather than what we desire, and dovetailing
with Rorty's own view, elsewhere, that "to accept the contingency of starting
points is to accept our inheritance from, and our conversation with, our fellow
human beings as our only source of guidance."[1] It's not where you start but where
you're at, not what you start with, but that you start: that you find your reason to
believe in whatever you believe in.

For years I've considered Springsteen's work wherever I've been. I first contemplated his music in the summer of 1980 in the Poconos. Since then I've thought
about it in bars and cafés from Buenos Aires to Bucharest, Cincinnati to Catania,
Indianapolis to Istanbul, Kitale to Kansas City, Lisbon to Long Branch, Moscow to
Montevideo. It accompanied me on those buses all over North America, in cars,

on trams, trains, and planes in Europe, Africa, and North and South America. The cliché is the idea of Springsteen as the soundtrack to an individual life. To focus on one individual's music for *life* seems, to say the least, narrow. One of a crowd of musicians, he's mingled with Mozart and Mariza, Coleman Hawkins and Maria Tănase, Ruben Rada and Roberta Sá Delírio. Art works on us in obvious and subtle ways. The more we're exposed to, the more nuanced its effect on our moods and attitudes. Springsteen agrees with Walker Percy's view, in his essay "The Man on the Train," that "the truly alienated man isn't the guy who's despairing and trying to find his place in the world. It's the guy who just finished his twentieth Erle Stanley Gardner Perry Mason novel," or who "just saw the fifth *Batman* picture" (TAD 227). If any one artist, sports team, or movie franchise carries too much weight there's a danger that you live second-hand. Vicarious enjoyment can create the illusion that you've lived yourself when in fact you've devoted yourself to "the dream world" of popular culture. I had this tendency in youth. I was the Great Pretender, the Wanderer, the Duke of Earl. Traveling the country felt in a way like floating through a "giant hologram," as Jean Baudrillard calls America for Europeans, made of music, art, and literature. Perhaps there's no escape from this escapism—"we are all in flight from the real reality," writes John Fowles—or perhaps the drifting of youth is a way the mind acquires experience to form a fruitful vision of the world.[2]

Springsteen's appeal is connected with this. It therefore feels appropriate to focus on his music as a subject in varied settings and in conjunction with other experiences, reading and listening. This is partly because Springsteen himself is, in Heylin's phrase, "a musical magpie," open to eclectic experience, reading included. When, for instance, I recall spending a hot afternoon west of Bergerac in the coolness of Montaigne's tower, contemplating the Latin proverbs carved into the beams, I can connect it to the fact that Springsteen has read a biography of this sixteenth-century philosopher.[3] Curiosity produces some ostensibly unlikely links. But this approach also feels appropriate because Springsteen has performed all over the world, and has spoken of the "rootless existence" of being on the road, and the need to find something stable amid the "transitory." During early touring that meant keeping room keys. In your transitory life you need things to provide "a reminder that you were *somewhere*" (TAD 403). *Born to Run* shows Springsteen to be a fine travel writer. The book opens with his childhood adventures on Randolph Street where, his "belly to the stone, alongside the tiny anthills that pop up volcanically where dirt and concrete meet," he'd be "Hannibal crossing the Alps,

GIs locked in vicious mountain combat and countless cowboy heroes traversing the rocky trails of the Sierra Nevada" (BTR 3). Later he describes actual journeys out West. "The desert at dawn" reveals "the deep blue and purple shadowed canyons, the pale yellow morning sky with all its color drawn out, leaving just the black silhouetted mountains behind." With the sun rising on his back, "the deep reds and browns of the plains and hills" come alive, and his palms turn "salty white on the wheel from the aridity" (BTR 127). But the issue is more profound than mere physical travel. We seek solace against time's attrition through whatever gives our journey substance. This includes creating art, a major motivation for which is to produce something to memorialize our "Kingdom of Days."

To travel and to create are intimately connected. Just as art can center us, so we can feel most alive in a strange city or country and able to see life beyond routine. Hence, on a rainy March day in Berlin, caught in a rainstorm after wandering down Unter den Linden Boulevard from the Brandenburg Gate to Berlin Cathedral, I sheltered in the art bookstore of the Instytut Polski w Berlin on Burgstraße. Looking out across the Spree at the back of the cathedral, I contemplated the fact that Springsteen visited East Berlin in 1981, and again in 1988, when he, too, had strolled Unter den Linden. This part of the city has changed hugely since I first visited in 1994, and would have been very different when Springsteen came here in the 1980s. The second time was to perform what Erik Kirschbaum celebrates, with enthusiastic hyperbole, in *Rocking the Wall* as the "concert that changed the world." A little over a year later, the Berlin Wall came down. Springsteen had told the 300,000 people, many of whom had trampled over barriers the authorities had dismantled, "Ich bin gekommen, um rock and roll für euch zu spielen in der Hoffnung, dass seine Tages alle Barrieren abgerissen warden": "I came here to play rock and roll for you, in the hope that one day all barriers will be torn down." He then sang Dylan's "Chimes of Freedom." Whether or not the concert was all that important, in the words of Imke Handke, a participant found by Kirschbaum, it was clearly "a piece of the mosaic to what happened a year later." For music critic Matthias Döpfner, it shows that "at the right moment and the right place, an artist can do more to change the world than lots of clever speeches by smart people supported with a myriad of logical arguments." For Springsteen, "it was the biggest concert we ever did," exemplifying what he feels his music is about.[4]

I browsed the bookstore with these thoughts in mind. Once again serendipity accompanied me. With no letup in the rain I sat at a table with a few books. The first on the pile was a small volume by Yale professor of the history of art David Joselit. *After Art* is primarily about visual art and architecture. The only immediate link to Springsteen is that it's published in New Jersey. But as I read the book, first in Germany and then back home in a Wiltshire pub within sight of Rudy's Bridge and Cochran's memorial, I began applying Joselit's ideas to Springsteen. His premise is to shift "critical emphasis from art's production (and the corollary of artistic intention) to what images *do* once they enter circulation in heterogeneous networks." An interest in aftereffects is at the heart of a lot of Springsteen commentary. Kirschbaum argues that a concert can help alter the course of history. Daniel Cavicchi's *Tramps Like Us* is subtitled *Music and Meaning among Springsteen Fans*. Baillie Walsh's *Springsteen & I* speaks for itself. But Joselit's particular interest in images provokes further thoughts.[5]

Image, he argues, has "vast power" through its "capacity for replication, remediation, and dissemination at variable velocities." In considering Springsteen's work, image goes beyond Joselit's definitions of "a quantum of visual content (say a digital photograph) that can assume a variety of formats," or "a visual byte, vulnerable to virtually infinite remediation."[6] Such definitions would include photographs of the concert on display in the Stasi Museum, the former headquarters of the secret police on Ruscherstraße, deep in the East Berlin suburbs. But while important as a reminder of the dynamism of the performance these are a lesser part of the package. Without wider resonance, no photograph would count for much. More interesting in thinking about "After Springsteen" are other kinds of images. By this I mean recorded shows and interviews, mental images of shows that participants recall (Kirschbaum testifies that many East Germans "vividly recall the details and atmosphere" of the concert decades later), and, perhaps most important of all, images created by a given song.[7] Since a song is invariably a collage of images, "the video dilemma," as Springsteen puts it, is that you provide physical images on top of mental images, thus dictating or distorting the creative response. "You're robbing people of their imaginations," he says. Since "music is meant to be evocative," you're placing an unnecessary, often counter-productive medium in the way (TAD 137).[8]

Such comments reveal much about Springsteen's approach to his craft. In performance he exudes a "raw energy" that's "contagious," and participants retain moments that exemplify that exuberance.[9] But it's our own images, brought forth by way of evocative phrasing, that produce the most enduring aftereffect. As one might expect, an urge to be useful permeates Springsteen's autobiography, and not least in terms of writerly advice. "The correct detail can speak volumes about who your character is," he counsels, "while the wrong one can shred the credibility of your story. When you get the music and lyrics right, your voice disappears into the voices you've chosen to write about" (BTR 401). In Joselit's words, images "produce power—a current or currency—that is activated by contact." "The more points of contact an image is able to establish, the greater its power will be."[10] As Roland Beiker points out, music as an art form has always been "unique in a variety of ways," not least in "that it can be perceived simultaneously from all directions." But, as Kathleen Higgins notes, "the incredible range of music, a range spanning centuries and the world's cultures," is now easily available to us. We can access it anywhere anytime. We can walk or run with music in our head. We can hear it in the car, on a boat, in bed, in the air, and in any city or on any country road, by any shore, or any river, be it the Spree or the Sewanee, the Wisła or the Willamette, the Potomac or the Plate. If the music aids reflection or shifts mood, it becomes a calming or galvanizing tool. In the twenty-first century, proliferation has accelerated exponentially. In the capitalist world, this has its own raison d'être. Art has become "a fundable hedge," writes Joselit, the value of which "must cross borders as easily as the dollar, the euro, the yen, and the renminbi." As a currency, it must transfer "value easily and efficiently," and, "with the aid of computers, almost instantaneously."[11]

Joselit's ideas amount to a pragmatist theory of art. Giles Gunn argues in *Thinking Across the American Grain* that pragmatism replaces the notion of the canon, whereby culture is seen as "the amassed moral capital of the ages" with a "toolbox" view of culture "as so many sets of directions that show you what can be built with its assistance, or, in other words, that display how the toolbox can be used." Thus, pragmatism construes an artist's importance with regard to the questions that artist continues "to keep alive and insistent." These questions belong to the recipient, upon whom meaning depends. Set against this idea of art as a tool, or as Gunn elsewhere puts it, a currency, is the idea of art as an item of reverence. In a way analogous with religious fundamentalism, to be reverential toward art is akin to adhering to "a doctrine, as laid down in sacred texts," or to assert that "a visual artefact belongs exclusively to a specific site (its place of origin)."[12] In terms of Springsteen, one might think of those who argue that the authentic experience is to attend a concert, and in particular some legendary show. In contrast, those who see art as currency would argue that you can gain from the music in all manner of times and places. A concert may be thrilling, but a given song can have just as deep an effect even if you never see Springsteen perform it. (His attestation to the power of radio backs this up, as does the effect on us of long-dead artists of all kinds.) Both experiences are valid. This is fortunate, since the vaults of the rock-and-roll dead and of original show participants fill as inexorably as such sprawling cemeteries as La Recoleta and Père Lachaise.

To argue that the live experience is the only authentic one is to invoke what Walter Benjamin, in "The Work of Art in the Age of Its Technological Reproducibility," coined the "aura" of performance. The twenty-first century, however, is a very different world from the 1930s, and Joselit argues that we should move on. "The right of possession," he argues, depends not on "cultural commonality or special knowledge" but "on pure empathy." Benjamin may have "produced the most enduring model of how art *belongs* to a place," but it "can hardly account for the revolutions in image production and circulation initiated by media like television, the Internet, and mobile phones." "In order to value the art of our own time," writes Joselit, we can't continue to hold with Benjamin's sense that "in even the most perfect reproduction, *one* thing is lacking: the here and now of the work of art—its unique existence in a particular place."[13] Instead of assuming that "reproduction constitutes an absolute loss—and consequently that commodification, which is premised on large-scale mechanical reproduction, is the worst possible fate for any cultural content," we should recognize that "there are gains as well as losses in the shift from singular artworks to populations of images."[14] Without debunking the idea that a live concert has aura, we can say that its reproduction has enormous and profound benefits. If we talk of "After Springsteen," we should also talk of "Before Springsteen." Few of us saw Elvis Presley perform live—Springsteen didn't—but it doesn't seem to have mattered. As a boy to watch Elvis on the Ed Sullivan show was, ironically, somehow to "see the *real* world," in which what matters is that you "dare" and "watch" and "listen" (BTR 40). "The product of top 40 radio," as he put it, Springsteen has always been the beneficiary of recorded material (S 65). He listened to records, and watched films and TV. Indeed, some of the aura he experienced even had to do with the medium separating the receiver from the actual moment (just as hearing rather than seeing a concert can create a no less dynamic effect).[15] In turn he's exploited this to the benefit of those who wish to loop view the concert experience. The splicing of images that constitutes *Live in Barcelona* makes it arguably superior visually, if not viscerally, to the live experience. There's something to be said for having no one stand on your feet, or edge between you and a view of the stage.

Joselit's celebration of mechanical reproduction directly links to his emphasis on *after*. This pragmatist focus on the audience-listener-participant, moreover, is clear in Springsteen's dislike of aspects of hero-worship, and his sense that what matters is the music. "The status of being *everywhere at once* rather than belonging to a single place," argues Joselit, far from depleting material, "now produces value for and through images." "In place of aura, there is *buzz*." This he likens to coming sufficiently "in phase to produce co-ordinated action." "Several small acts" when "taken individually" "may have no intention," but "buzz indicates a moment of becoming—a threshold at which coherence emerges." Such sentiments are in line with what William James means when he says that pragmatism is "an attitude of orientation."[16] Rather than fixating on an authoritative starting point, individuals encounter and share ideas. Emphasize a starting point, and you encourage the idea of aura. Emphasize process, and you think in terms of buzz. Aura equals fundamentalism and foundationalism. Buzz, like pragmatism, is anti-foundational, suggesting that ideas are not authoritative but open to adaptation. In seeing rock and roll as forward-looking, Elvis Presley as instigating change, and the E Street Band as "a purpose-based organization," Springsteen, too, emphasizes *after*. In doing so he is, in Joselit's terms, thinking "democratically about image circulation," considering the "redistribution of *image* wealth," and using "the currency of art for purposes other than financial profit."[17] Songs and albums anticipate and depend upon ever-changing responses. It being "a commonplace that a piece of music is never the same twice," and that a listener's experience "is never repeated," writes Higgins, "music makes us all Heracliteans."[18] I would say the same is true of art in general, and proof abounds that it profits recipients. "*After* art," writes Joselit, "comes the logic of networks where links can cross space, time, genre, and scale in surprising and multiple ways." While the recipient of any art participates in its afterlife, this is a central thrust of Springsteen's work. Seen this way, explains Joselit, art assembles "a new kind of power," and "the point is to *use* this power."[19]

What Joselit explains, and what Springsteen practices, however, is also traditionally American rather than merely a response to contemporary changes. "Trust thyself," writes Emerson. "Arouse!" shouts Whitman, in "Poets to Come," "for you must justify me." Whitman sees himself as "a man who, sauntering along without fully stopping, turns a casual look upon you and then averts his face." He expects "the main thing from you."[20] The purpose of the apparent intimacy is lost on those who see the actual writer as the focus. The power of art depends upon response. "For it is not for what I have put into it that I have written this book," he writes in "Whoever You Are Holding Me Now in Hand," "Nor is it by reading it that you will acquire it, / Nor do those know me best who admire me and vauntingly praise me."[21] The life force must come from within the participant in the dialogue art facilitates. This idea of reciprocity is at the heart of Stevens's poetry, too, as it is at the heart of Oates's work. As Hannah Arendt notes in her essay "On Violence" (cited by Joselit), "power corresponds to the human ability not just to act but to act in concert. Power is never the property of an individual, it belongs to a group." Hence, writes Joselit, "our real work begins *after* art, in the networks it formats."[22] All writing being a form of art, I have thus appropriated Joselit's ideas about image to Springsteen's work. Springsteen surely knows that, compared with those who truly put themselves on the line, who risk their lives, or who work tirelessly without tangible reward, he's been little more than a hard-working but immensely rewarded entertainer. The image we have of him is not the real man, and the world he offers is a kind of fantasy parallel universe. But he is representative of the kind of person who learns their craft, cultivates their talent, and through force of will rises from obscurity. As Marsh notes, quoting John Berger, this is why he fits the description of a "hero," not an "idol."[23] Through the years he's come to a mature understanding of what it means to matter, of what fuels his own life and the lives of his audience. His art, itself inspired by various sources, has produced the art of others, both literally, in terms of books, stories, artwork, and other music, and in terms of the way others have shaped their lives in part through awareness of that art.

Let me give a literary and then a personal example. Perhaps the best evidence of Springsteen's dialogue with his era is in the patterns that interconnect his work with Bobbie Ann Mason's *In Country.* Mason's novel took full shape when she visited the Vietnam Veterans Memorial in the spring of 1983. The following year saw the production of *Born in the U.S.A.*, which Mason subsequently referenced. But the story would not end there. Mason's novel would seem to have inspired a Springsteen song—"The Wall" on *High Hopes.* Sam's quest to learn about her father, the war he died in, and the experience of her uncle Emmett and other veterans, becomes a narrative about the wider American experience. In the midst of it, Sam asks a veteran if he's seen the memorial. "A big black hole in the ground," he scathingly replies.[24] Sam will eventually reach the memorial with Emmett and her grandmother, Mamaw, and be moved by it. "The Wall," written decades later, acts as a kind of black granite reflection of "Born in the U.S.A." In it, a family member, speaking to a dead relative, reflects on the small recompense this monument is to their loss. It's a long way from the record that saw Springsteen become a household name as a pop icon. He was everywhere on the airwaves in the mid-1980s, with songs that sound made to be the radio and MTV hits they became. People newly exposed to Springsteen's work through these media came to the performances because of that exposure. But rather than being a mere soundtrack to this and other novels, "The Wall" shows how his work came to participate in a conversation. In its remembrance of former band member Bart Hanes and local musician Walter Cichon, both of whom died in Vietnam, and in its specific location at the memorial, it nods to Mason's 1985 novel.[25] With regard to Joselit's ideas here, while something was lost when Springsteen went pop something was also gained. On one hand, many people who appreciated Springsteen before 1984 would agree with Eric Alterman's description of feeling "shunted aside" by "millions of loudmouthed parvenus" attending huge events shorn of "subtlety and spontaneity." On the other hand, hadn't many of us come to Springsteen through media other than the live show? Hadn't we benefited from the age of mechanical reproduction, and don't we now benefit all the more from this, as well as being able to witness live performance? It's not just about the moment of production but the aftereffects. Not only can the influence of one artist create art in another, but that new art can in turn influence the influencer.

As for the personal example of how all this apparent abstraction can translate into personal terms, at a 1981 concert Springsteen finally had to silence my call for "Backstreets" by saying, "We'll get that one for you later." Growing from adolescence into middle age, the beautiful symmetry of life allowed me a second encounter when, with Springsteen on the same floor level, and now perceivable as a human being rather than superhero, I put my fist to his cheek. The British are not very demonstrative, and on the rare occasions when we show affection it can manifest in awkward ways. But what mattered in both cases was human touch—mental in the first instance, physical in the second. Why do we seek to be seen? Why do those up close at a concert feel the need to touch? Why does a performer, indeed, not merely pander to this but enjoy that rapport? To shake a hand or look an individual in the eye is to acknowledge. We can all do this with strangers, students, workmates, employees, neighbors. Acknowledgment is powerfully enabling. One of the odder Springsteen songs, at least on first hearing, is "Queen of the Supermarket." But it's about acknowledgment. When the checkout girl smiles at the speaker, it "blows this whole fucking world apart." A mere smile can touch a person. "After Springsteen" also, therefore, refers to the "After" that came from that gesture at that show all those years ago, for which I suppose I was thanking him with a gesture thirty-five years on. It's not that the sentence, "We'll get that one for you later," had meaning beyond the literal, but that through the years I gave it greater meaning. This, moreover, has happened time after time and all over the world. A word, a look, a gesture, an acknowledgment, can change a life. This is true for good and bad; we must therefore take our responsibilities seriously: "From Small Things (Big Things One Day Come)."

For we have many "after" moments. Writing on Springsteen, I've had in mind a youth in a car with *Born to Run* on his tape deck. He's driving a 1973 Mini. The tape deck is wedged precariously between the steering wheel and windshield. Turning corners it's odds-on that it will slide out and crash down on the passenger side. Listening to "Tenth Avenue Freeze Out," he's heading for night school and, he hopes, college. He dreams he might become a student, learn a few "-isms," and make something of himself. He imagines he might one day write a book, not daring to believe that the inspiration might become the subject. Above all, he hopes to escape. To that end, he flies to America, works at a Christian camp in Michigan, and the next year at a Jewish camp in the Poconos, just outside Stroudsburg, that may even be the same camp Philip Roth describes in his 2011 novel, *Nemesis*. (The camp driver picks up Roth's hero, Bucky Cantor, "at the Stroudsburg station." They zigzag "into the hills" and bounce through woods to a green vista sloping to "the bright metallic sheen of a vast lake."[26] Camps can be similar, but this fits the memory.) Lacking any sense of direction or much sense of what matters to him, he reads voraciously, and listens to whatever music he encounters. At some point in the summer, a counselor from New Jersey named Dogie lends him *Greetings from Asbury Park, N.J.*

He learns more from riding a Greyhound than he ever learned in school. Traveling the country, he talks to people and eavesdrops, but also retreats into his own world through his Walkman, or personal stereo, in the days before MP3s, iPods, and smartphones. All kinds of American music nuance his melancholy, but he also listens to music from his home country, including the Animals, the Who, the Kinks, the Stones, John Lennon's *Rock 'n' Roll* album, and, on that long trip from Vancouver to New York, Supertramp's *Crime of the Century*, haunted by Rudy on his "train to nowhere." Springsteen's music becomes part of a continuum that began with "Summertime Blues" and the Everly Brothers' "Cathy's Clown" and "All I Have to Do Is Dream." It doesn't especially accompany him on the bus journeys.

The Springsteen interest, beginning in 1980, is really suffused with thoughts of rainy streets and driving to night school, and setting up home, starting a family, driving to work: his English life. Enrolled at night school to study history, he finds that *Born to Run* has become synonymous with his studies. It isn't that he sees any great connection between "hiding on the backstreets" and the Thirty Years' War, or "flashing guitars just like switch blades" and writing essays about Elizabeth I, but the music works away at him through those night drives along spooky country roads and the traffic lights of towns, and red taillights, and glistening rain. Springsteen, like an older brother, has something to tell him. There's a saying that the teacher arrives when the pupil needs the lesson. So it's personal. It's as personal as it is for all Springsteen's listeners, and it's just beginning.

Studying harder, becoming more determined, as spring approaches he views life's possibilities in ways he might never have envisaged pre-Springsteen. His concern is not really with America, which is part-real, part-imagined, but with a world of friendship and self-definition. Each visit feeds rather than finishes the fantasy. He's imbued with the country's nostalgic view of itself, one that influences a generation of Europeans slightly older than him. He's conscious that many of his contemporaries reject this romanticism in favor of "seventies cynicism" (BTR 262). But that's okay. He doesn't expect to fit in: outsider here, outsider there. Autumn brings *The River,* but *Darkness* mingles with it, increasing his discontent. "Badlands"—*the* galvanizing song of his youth—appeals to anyone who kicks at restrictions without quite knowing why. He has "a head-on collision" smashing in his guts. He's "caught in a crossfire" he doesn't understand. "Don't waste your time waiting," Springsteen says. "You gotta live it every day." "It" would seem to combine energy, focus, and drive. Looking for those who have "a notion deep inside, that it ain't no sin to be glad you're alive," out "to find one face" that isn't looking through him, the youth buys Penguin Classic paperbacks with foreign names and foreign-sounding authors: Maupassant's *Bel-Ami,* Dostoevsky's *The Brothers Karamazov,* Alain-Fournier's *Le Grand Meaulnes,* and not least *Le Rouge et le Noir.* He reads them on the commute to London for his dead-end job. But above all he has that urge to get out, get away, and "win," which means to define his life.

There have always been then, looking back, two of us in that third row of Wembley Arena in 1981, the one who was there and the one who continued on through time and lived his life. Equally, in Paris, there was the older man and the young self. As part of that reunion, along with periodic selves in between, we've agreed to write this book. We're much like many others in the crowds across the years. A Danish participant in *Springsteen & I* stands in an empty stadium talking of his concert experiences. In his final clip, he says his girlfriend turned to him at a show and said that at some point she felt that she was the only one there and that Springsteen was playing just for her. He replied that he knew exactly what she meant. That was the way it felt that night, or how I recall it. Very much the adolescent, very self-absorbed, I felt that there was no one else at Wembley Arena except Springsteen, the band, and me. No wonder they heard me when I yelled "Backstreets" between songs. Around me, in time, others—who'd mysteriously found their way into the arena—took up my call, until eventually he said, and has continued to say, year on year, decade after decade, "We'll get that one for you later."

A fter Springsteen, then: Bruce Springsteen, the passionate pragmatist, takes the lonesome and turns it into a communal experience, and changes lives just as music changed his life. He'd been inspired, and he sought to inspire. Such a perspective is akin to Wordsworth's lines (quoted by Rorty), that "What we have loved / Others will love, and we will teach them how."[27] To create and to teach, in the broadest sense, are both part of the pragmatist impulse. "If you look at the role of storytellers in communities going back to the beginning of time," said Springsteen in 2010, "they played a very functional role in assisting the community and making sense of its experience, of the world around them, charting parts of their lives, getting through parts of their lives." How he might "perform that function best" has been a key motivation through his career (SOS 369). We evaluate writers in terms of their impact in their own day and their legacy, whether through influence on subsequent writers or continued interest in their work. Springsteen's contemporary impact is obvious, but is he an artist merely of his era or with something to offer eras to come?

Certainly his work deals with mortality. He's not afraid to face his own demise. I was in Rome the summer of *Wrecking Ball*. The title song is ostensibly about the leveling of Giants Stadium, and a metaphor: in Springsteen's words, "an image where something is destroyed to build something new," but also one that suggests "the flat destruction of some fundamental American values and ideas" over the past three decades (TAD 409). It's about the way big business wrecks the lives and cultural activities of ordinary Americans. But it's also a song about transience. Springsteen sings of being raised in Jersey "some misty years ago" and seeing "champions come and go." Once again we have the "guy in a bar telling his story to the stranger on the next stool" mode familiar from country music (S 100), but the "mister" could as easily be a deity, or time swinging that "wrecking ball."[28] The music wields creativity against the destroyer. Eros faces down Thanatos. Life throws up a finger at death. We're defenseless in the face of time except for art in its many forms. When Springsteen sings of the filled arena, and of how tonight "all the dead are here," he calls to mind all those shows from the 1970s through to the present, quelling absence with continuity.

That *Wrecking Ball* summer, I ran daily, through successive limoncello dawns, the sun cracking the umbrella pines and sharpening the spire of Basilica di Santa Anastasia, from Trastevere to the Forum. With barely a person in sight, I ran through cobbled lanes to the shrieks of gulls, the sound of my own footsteps, and soon the cacophony of the Tiber flowing over the weir near Isola Tiberina. Crossing il Ponte Palatino, its weed-wreathed chunk of Roman bridge crumbling against an ever-bluer sky, I ran through Piazza Bocca della Verità, up the short incline of Via della Greca to the grassy swathe of the Circus Maximus and pounded between the pine shadows along the southern side of this vast arena until I entered the wide stone-paved Via di San Gregorio, passed il Arco di Constantino, and reached the thunderous ruins of what Italians call il Colosseo. In its shadow I scrolled to the album's title song and began a succession of circuits. The Colosseum is Rome's most lasting monument to entertainment and to horror. Witness to the deaths of half a million people and two million animals, including nine thousand on the inaugural day, it was a place of unimaginable suffering and cruelty. We've moved beyond that. A rock concert is a life force. But it also contends with a death force. It cannot last, and nor can we. Springsteen talks often of how mortality haunts music. Asked about dealing with the death of Danny Federici and other friends, he says that such issues are "in most great rock music." "The impact of so many great records tells you, 'Oh, there's something else, my friend!'" "I hear death in all those early Elvis records," he says, "in all those spooky blues records. And in records made by young kids—it's in 'Thunder Road.' A sense of time and the passage of time, the passage of innocence. It cuts through all popular music" (TAD 362).[29] Such comments mingled with the lyrics of "Wrecking Ball" as I circled the Colosseum and contemplated "youth and beauty" being "given to the dust." I couldn't truly envisage the Colosseum in its prime, and was no nearer to Springsteen's actual life, or to those of his dwindling band, than to the Romans. But there was a connection. He was getting older. I was getting older. The thing to do was to keep running.

Joyce Carol Oates once described running as having "the illusion that it's timeless." "I just run," she said, "and there's no beginning or end, basically just running. It's a little like dreaming: dreams in succession." Ultimately, perhaps the American lonesome and its connection with the work of Bruce Springsteen comes down to the individual listener's imagination—that narrative dream we experience from infancy through adulthood. Maybe, in my case, it's a lonesome trail, based on a culture that I'm outside of looking in on: a form of romanticism, but a pragmatic one. "The purpose of art is to help us to live and to die well," writes Alain de Botton. Art is "a catalyst of appreciation." It "helps us to develop our powers of empathy by introducing us to people and places far beyond our usual remit." In sum, it's "a form of propaganda for the very best values in human nature."[30] If these are valid definitions, then Springsteen's work fulfills each one. Will the music speak to future generations? It will speak to someone, along with other art, celebrated or obscure. Springsteen sees himself in this continuity. It's not about "glory days," which pass in the blink of an eye. It's certainly not about celebrity. It's about something "money can't buy."[31] It's a process in which we are all invited to participate.

I sat on the grassy bank of the Circus Maximus later one morning, looking out over an arena that was first constructed unimaginable centuries ago. Springsteen, I now know, would play there a few days after Paris, in what was then the future but is now the past. Judging from YouTube, those Springsteen fans I met in the AccorHotels Arena—Gary, Pat and Rachel—saw quite a show. But I knew nothing of that then. I was thinking of Whitman, telling us to look for him "decades hence" beneath our boot soles. I was thinking of an E. M. Forster story, "The Point of It," about a young man with a heart condition who rows hard because you have to say yes to life. "Death don't fuck around," said the shade of Clarence Clemons, nudging me on the grassy bank. "It's waiting around some corner for all of us."[32] The concerts, I reflected, are ultimately one long concert, and, just as I circled the Colosseum, so they go around, in recording, on a loop, no beginning and no end, just intermittences, born to run and run. Listening to those 1970s shows, from before I personally had given much thought to Springsteen, I find myself telling the ghost of the young singer to look after himself. (I think I'm going to throw up, we recall him shout.) But if he heard my voice in the crowd the ghost might say: don't you understand yet? That's the point of it.

"We all wear the things we've survived with some honor, but the real honor is in also transcending them," says Springsteen. "There's a car, it's filled with people. The 12-year-old kid's in the back. So's the 22-year-old. So is the 40-year-old," and "nobody's leaving." "The doors are shut, locked and sealed, until you go into your box." What matters is "who's driving" (TAD 363–64). For me, there's who I am now and there's the young man who first heard Springsteen's music and the increasingly older man in between. I see no reason why non-Americans would consider themselves excluded from the "feeling state" of lonesomeness. But perhaps Springsteen's international appeal has something to do with perceptions that he seems quintessentially American. Perhaps, too, the solitary wanderings I shared with many a youth, then and now, made me predisposed to accept lonesomeness as a cultural norm. To gaze at the American landscape through a tinted bus window, stopping off here and there across the continent for encounters with friends and strangers, all the while seeking a sense of self and glorying in the solitude of travel, the excitement of arrival, and the melancholy of departure, epitomized the lonesomeness Lewis proclaims to be peculiar to Americans. "I was the world in which I walked, and what I saw / Or heard or felt came not but from myself," writes Stevens. "And there I found myself more truly and more strange."[33]

Deeply aware of the degrees of lonesomeness in all lives, but arguably endemic in American culture, Springsteen's artistic response emphasized many of the key elements of pragmatism. With his focus on meliorism, on community, on art as action, and on artistic cooperation, with his qualities of openness and individualism, his provisional rather than categorical stance with regard to identities and perspectives, and his willingness to engage with the pressing or contentious issues of the day, he reflects this perspective. His writing has always involved a lonesomeness that he has sought to quell through the communal, and this has produced an obsession with "people trying to find their way in," and a sustained emphasis on inclusion. This has been, in Dewey's phrase, Springsteen's "intellectual work." All this adds up to a sense that, beyond the power and joy of performance, any writer's enduring impact, if there's to be one, will come outside and beyond his or her own life. In the end, therefore, we must consider his achievement not only in his impact on the generations who have experienced his evolving career, but also in the potential legacy of his work and writing beyond his own time.

The upshot of all this, of course, is that my personal sense of "After Springsteen" is that I wouldn't have had the particular career I've had, for better or worse, had Dogie not introduced me to the music in the summer of 1980, had that not been the summer I decided to become some kind of teacher, and had I not driven back and forth to night school to study, and been up front at the June concert. "After Springsteen" is about the direction lives can go in after being introduced to something that galvanizes them. Springsteen's music and performance were only factors among many others, but they were important. When I think, now, of his music, I think not only of driving through the dark listening to *Born to Run* but also of walking the rainy streets of my hometown listening to *Darkness* and *The River* aged nineteen, of my first year at university trying to play chords from songs on *Nebraska* (not difficult), of taking off again for America to study in upstate New York listening to *Born in the U.S.A.*, setting up home with Nicki as my fiancée, listening to *Tunnel of Love*, becoming a parent to *Human Touch* and *Lucky Town*, traveling to California listening to *Tom Joad*, visiting Ground Zero with *The Rising*, being in Texas when *Devils & Dust* came out, taking my family to a concert at the time of *Magic*, running through Trastevere over the Tiber to circuit the Colosseum listening to *Wrecking Ball*, completing the circle with the *River* tour in Paris, and finally visiting Asbury Park.

Oh Bruce! In my demented memory, I'm back at Wembley Arena, aged twenty, with few prospects and nothing achieved. I'm in the third row and Springsteen, far younger than I am now, has halted the show. He calls back to a roadie who passes him a book. He saunters forward, guitar hanging behind, leans down and hands it to me. I take it and see the cover. It's not any book but this book. Springsteen looks straight at me. He seems to want something.

"Would you sign it, please?"

Because he says please, I do. But he doesn't want it back.

"I told you," he says mysteriously, "it's not about me. I'm a mere catalyst. It's your life. Make something of it."

I nod, look around at the crowd I'm in, and hand this book, in turn, to you.

ACKNOWLEDGMENTS

The origins of this book go back to 1979, when I left art school in England to work at a camp in Michigan. That was my introduction to the United States. The following summer in Pennsylvania I met my first Springsteen fan, David Gelman, as well as Matt Martin, later best man at my wedding to Nicki and a friend to this day. In upstate New York in 1985 Bill Heyen introduced me to the poetry of Wallace Stevens. Bill, who later spoke admiringly of "that haunting song," "Streets of Philadelphia," asked me the pointed question, "Why limit yourself?" That year I also met Marina Vanderput, and thank her, now, for decades of friendship, and her recent hospitality in Rio de Janeiro between drafts of the book. In connection with that, I thank Luisa Pereiro, Sarah-Jane Vokey, and Daniel Supervielle for their Uruguayan welcome to the University of Montevideo, where I learned, among many other things, of the work of Eduardo Galeano. In California in 1997 I met Susan Shillinglaw, who referred to "My Hometown" as her song. In 2002 Susan edited *Beyond Boundaries: Rereading John Steinbeck*. My contribution, "The Ghost of Tom Joad: Steinbeck's Legacy in the Songs of Bruce Springsteen," informs part of chapter 2. Between 2011 and 2013, Susan invited me to be a Steinbeck Festival speaker at the National Steinbeck Center in Salinas. Also speaking in 2013 were Dan Cavicchi and Bob Santelli, both of whom have been supportive of this project. I am especially grateful to Bob for finding time to chat about it on the Jersey Shore during a visit from Los Angeles. Material from "Dead Man Walking: Nat Turner, William Styron, Bruce Springsteen, and the Death Penalty," commissioned by Michael Lackey of the University of Minnesota and published in the *Mississippi Quarterly*, reappears in chapter 4. In chapter 8 I have adapted material from "Rome to Ravello with *Set This House on Fire*," published in the *Sewanee Review*. I tried out ideas for the book in two papers at conferences in Romania: one on Springsteen and spirituality, at the University of Bucharest in 2015; the other on pragmatism and the uses of art, at the 2016 European Association for American Studies Conference in Constanța. I thank participants of both conferences for their feedback.

Thank you to Margaret Lovecraft and her successor as acquisitions editor, James W. Long; to managing editor Lee Sioles, to copyeditor Stan Ivester, to designer Michelle Neustrom, and to all the staff at LSU Press, for their work here and on my previous books. I also appreciate the advice given by Mona Okada of Grubman Shire & Meiselas with regard to the use of lyrics. Bath Spa University provided funding toward the visit to Asbury Park and the Bruce Springsteen Special Collection at Monmouth University and to attend the Paris concerts. I thank Paul Meyer in particular for his support. Eileen Chapman was immensely helpful in facilitating my research work in the archives. I thank her, too, for showing me around Asbury Park and giving me an idea of how it used to be. BSU colleagues Tim Liardet and Lucy Sweetman read the manuscript and offered useful advice. Fiona Peters was responsible for the particular Berlin trip that features in chapter 8. Katie Rickard and Becky Atkins at BSU's Corsham Court campus library have been very helpful. Former BSU colleague Richard Parfitt read the manuscript and introduced me to ideas incorporated here. The insights of David Masciotra and John Massaro proved useful early in the project. Christopher Phillips of *Backstreets* magazine has always been prompt and pertinent in replying to queries. Ken Womack, Jon Stauff, Joe Rapolla, and Michael Waters of Monmouth University all welcomed me to the Jersey Shore. Michael read the manuscript and provided specific information. I thank him for this and him and his partner, Mihaela Moscaliuc, for their hospitality. I thank Tessa and Steve Green for welcoming us to Milly-la Fôret over many years, and Tessa in particular for the fact that her fluent French secured the Paris tickets that helped round out the story in chapter 5. Tanya Tromble, an Alaskan friend now resident in Lascours, has also provided help with the language. Thank you, too, to Bruno and the staff of the Villa Del Bosco Hotel, Catania, Sicily, for a very pleasant stay during a final reading of the manuscript, and to Lanfranco, a bass player who knows all about volcanoes. As one member of the staff, Giuseppe, reminded me, Bruce Zirilli is Italy's greatest rock musician.

I like to think that my brother, Bruce, and sister, Amelia, will find this book an interesting read both on Springsteen and in terms of who I was, who I am, and how I think. I also have in mind my godson, Hamish Grundy, who has studied American history, worked at summer camps, and might find much to identify with here. In Lougratte one summer another nephew, Bradley Walker, taught me how to play "Born to Run," which wouldn't exactly pass muster for live performance but showed me how the song looks on the fret board of my undeserved Fender Stratocaster. Likewise, thank you to former tennis partner, Nick Duff, for teaching me "The Star Spangled Banner," which students subsequently endured at the end of too many semesters. A mention, as well, for my soccer teammates in Corsham, in particular Tim Bligh and Chris Smith, who have expressed interest in this project. But at the heart of everything, always, are three people: my wife, Nicki, who has endured my various obsessions for many decades; my mathematical daughter, Xenatasha, who is also a woman of the new renaissance—thinker, reader, sportswoman, and musician; and my optometrist daughter, Anastasia, a saxophonist of whom Clarence Clemons would be proud.

NOTES

PREFACE

1. Bruce Springsteen, *Born to Run* (New York: Simon & Schuster, 2016), 47. Subsequent endnote and in-text references are to this edition and cited as BTR.

2. William Faulkner, *The Paris Review Interviews*, ed. Philip Gourevitch (New York: Picador, 2007), vol. 2: 57. See also Robert Santelli, "Afterword," in *Racing in the Street: The Bruce Springsteen Reader*, ed. June Skinner Sawyers (Harmondsworth, UK: Penguin, 2004), 386: "He was our Faulkner, our Emerson."

3. Dave Marsh, *Bruce Springsteen: Two Hearts* (New York: Routledge, 2004), 296.

4. See Springsteen, *Born to Run*, 296. "My ranch house was wall-to-wall orange shag carpet. I know, it was Sinatra's favorite color, but I could feel a serial killing comin' on. I decided I needed a permanent home."

5. William Faulkner, *Absalom, Absalom!* (1932; rpt. New York: Vintage, 1972), 378.

6. Bruce Springsteen, "Bruce Springsteen Remembers Madam Marie," 2 July 2008, Box S15, Bruce Springsteen Special Collection, Monmouth University, NJ.

7. Gustave Flaubert, *Madame Bovary*, trans. Alan Russell (Harmondsworth, UK: Penguin, 1986), 121. This is not an exact translation. The French is: "de ses rêves trop hauts, de sa maison trop étroite" (Paris: Gallimard, 1972), 153. This literally means "of her dreams that were too high, of her house that was too narrow."

8. Gustave Flaubert, letter to Louise Colet, 22 September 1846, in *The Letters of Gustave Flaubert 1830–1857*, ed. Francis Steegmuller (Cambridge, MA: Belknap, 1980), 79. Flaubert is quoting Colet's comment back to her.

9. David Kamp, "The Book of Bruce Springsteen," *Vanity Fair*, October 2016, 194. See also 195: "One way or another, I'm always rolling that rock."

10. See Dave Marsh, *Bruce Springsteen on Tour: 1968–2005* (New York: Bloomsbury, 2006), 254, and Eric Alterman, "From *It Ain't No Sin to Be Glad You're Alive: The Promise of Bruce Springsteen,*" in Sawyers, ed., *Racing in the Street,* 375. The fan was evidently New Jersey resident Edwin R. Sutpin Jr. Alterman is citing Gregory J. Volpe, "Rumson Man Inspired Boss," *Asbury Park Press,* 31 July 2002. The Alterman extract is taken from the appendix of the Spanish edition (2003).

11. William Styron, *Set This House on Fire* (New York: Random House, 1960), 10, 18.

12. See Anthony DeCurtis, "Springsteen Returns," in *Bruce Springsteen: The Rolling Stone Files,* ed. Parke Puterbaugh et al. (New York: Hyperion, 1996), 382. DeCurtis tells of how, on the first of two nights of acoustic sets for the Christic Institute, 17 November 1991, Springsteen described these drives and consulting the psychiatrist. For other versions of the story, see Marc Eliot with Mike Appel, *Down Thunder Road: The Making of Bruce Springsteen* (London: Plexus, 1992), 75, and David Remnick, "We Are Alive: Bruce Springsteen at Sixty-Two," *The New Yorker,* 30 July 2012, 28–29, www.newyorker.com/magazine/2012/07/30/we-are-alive. Eliot quotes Springsteen referring to a psychiatrist. Remnick credits the comments to a psychotherapist. Given Remnick's direct contact with Springsteen, this may be the more likely. See also Springsteen, *Born to Run,* 112.

13. Roland Bleiker, "Art After 9/11," *Alternatives* 31 (2006): 85–86.

14. Wallace Stevens, *Opus Posthumous* (1957; rev. ed., New York: Vintage, 1989), 189.

INTRODUCTION

1. Paul Valery, *Pièces Sur L'Art: Autor de Corot,* 1934, epigraph in Simon Schama, *Rembrandt's Eyes* (London: Allen Lane, 1999): "On doit toujours s'excuser de parler peinture. Mais il y a de grandes raisons de ne pas s'en taire. Tous les arts vivent de paroles."

2. Robert Hilburn, *Corn Flakes with John Lennon: And Other Tales from a Rock 'n' Roll Life* (New York: Rodale, 2009), 85.

3. See Theodore Zeldin, *An Intimate History of Humanity* (London: Sinclair-Stevenson, 1994). Zeldin's book is based on oral history and provides portraits of living people and their hopes, desires, and disappointments. They happen to all be French women, but the book's title is in no way misleading.

4. Martha Nell Smith, "Sexual Mobilities in Bruce Springsteen: Performance as Commentary," in *Present Tense: Rock & Roll and Culture,* ed. Anthony DeCurtis (Durham, NC: Duke University Press, 1992), 197–218; Stewart D. Friedman, *Leading the Life You Want: Skills for Integrating Work and Life* (Boston: Harvard Business Review Press, 2014), 142; Gavin Cologne-Brookes, "Written Interviews and a Conversation with Joyce Carol Oates," *Studies in the Novel* 38, no. 4 (Winter 2006): 554; Matthew Continetti, "A Thousand Springsteens Bloom," americasfuture.org.; Fernando Pessoa, *The Book of Disquiet,* trans. Richard Zenith (Harmondsworth, UK: Penguin, 2002), 225, 30.

5. Hilburn, *Corn Flakes with John Lennon,* 85.

6. Bruce Springsteen, *Songs* (1998; rev. ed. New York: HarperEntertainment, 2003), 164. Subsequent in-text references are to this edition and cited as S. Springsteen speaks of "what it means to be alive" in the documentary *Bruce Springsteen: A Secret History,* directed by Steven Goldman (BBC, 1998).

7. Bruce Springsteen, "Keynote Speech," in *Springsteen on Springsteen: Interviews, Speeches, Encounters,* ed. Jeff Burger (New York: Omnibus, 2013), 397. Subsequent in-text references are to this edition and cited as SOS.

8. See, for instance, David R. Shumway, *Rock Star: The Making of Musical Icons from Elvis to Springsteen* (Baltimore: Johns Hopkins University Press, 2014), 192. "The disjuncture between lyrical content and musical presentation," writes Shumway, "is a common feature of Springsteen's work."

9. See Daniel Cavicchi, *Tramps Like Us: Music and Meaning Among Springsteen Fans* (Oxford, UK: Oxford University Press, 1998), 66: "As Fred Schruers wrote in *Rolling Stone* about his interview with Springsteen, 'accuse Springsteen of being a star and he'll flick his hand like he's just been splashed with pigeon shit.'"

10. Roxanne Harde and Irwin Streight, "Introduction: the Bard of Asbury Park," in *Reading the Boss: Interdisciplinary Approaches to Bruce Springsteen,* ed. Roxanne Harde and Irwin Streight (Lanham, MD: Rowman and Littlefield, 2010), 13.

11. Mark Blake, *Stone Me: The Wit and Wisdom of Keith Richards* (London: Aurum, 2008), 54. Richards evidently made the comment in 1986.

12. See his longer explanation on that page, where he describes how, with his eldest son, "over the years, I'd subtly sent signals of my unavailability, of my internal resistance to incursions upon my time by family members . . . my fortress of solitude, where as usual I felt at home, safe, until, like a bear in need of blood and meat, I'd wake from my hibernation and travel through the house for my drink from the cup of human love and companionship. But I always felt I needed to be able to shut it all off like a spigot." "The price I paid for the time lost was just that," he writes elsewhere, "time lost is gone for good" (*Born to Run,* 311).

13. Bobbie Ann Mason, *In Country* (1985; rpt. New York: Harper Perennial, 2005), 187.

14. For Springsteen's view of this period, see *Born to Run,* 326.

15. Stendhal (Marie-Henri Beyle), *The Red and the Black,* trans. Catherine Slater (Oxford, UK: Oxford World's Classics, 1991), 443, 406, 520.

16. Cornel Bonca, "How (and How Not) to Write about 9/11," *Modern Language Studies* 41, no. 1 (2011): 137; Stendhal, *The Red and the Black,* 11; Cormac McCarthy. *The Road* (2006; rpt. London: Picador, 2007), 136; Richard Rorty, "Philosophy as a Transitional Genre," in Christopher Voparil and Richard J. Bernstein, eds., *The Rorty Reader* (Malden, MA: Blackwell, 2010), 479: "The imagination endlessly consumes its own artefacts. It is an ever-building, ever-expanding fire"; Friedman, *Leading the Life You Want,* 148. In a letter of 1813, Stendhal, who seems to have been unimpressed with the play, described Hamlet as "un couillon," which his biographer translates as "pillock." See Jonathan Keates, *Stendhal* (London: Sinclair-Stevenson, 1994), 153.

17. Kevin Lewis, *Lonesome: The Spiritual Meanings of American Solitude.* New York: I. B. Tauris, 2009, xiii.

18. F. Scott Fitzgerald, *The Great Gatsby* (1925; rpt. New York: Scribner's, 1953), 130; Emily Dickinson, Poem 288, *The Collected Poems of Emily Dickinson,* ed. Thomas H. Johnson (London: Faber, 1960), 133. Subsequent references are to this edition, cited by poem number only.

19. See Harry and Michael Medved, *The Hollywood Hall of Shame: The Most Expensive Flops in Cinema History* (London: Angus & Robertson, 1984), 170–85.

20. Dafydd Rees and Luke Crampton, *Q Encyclopedia of Rock Stars* (New York: Dorling Kindersley, 1996), 535. Mr. Skinner was evidently "a legendary antagonist of long-haired students."

21. John Lombardi, "St. Boss: The Sanctification of Bruce Springsteen and the Rise of Mass Hip," *Esquire,* December 1988, 142; June Skinner Sawyers, "Endlessly Seeking: Bruce Springsteen and Walker Percy's Quest for Possibility Among the Ordinary," in Harde and Streight, eds., *Reading*

the Boss, 30; Springsteen refers to his "own localism" as "a strength and something to get away from" in the documentary *Bruce Springsteen: In His Own Words,* directed by Nigel Cole (Channel 4, UK), 2016. On the (well-known) localism of many of the lyrics, see, especially, Kevin Coyne, "His Home Town," in Sawyers, ed., *Racing in the Street,* 366–70.

22. Christopher Phillips and Louis P. Masur, eds., *Talk About a Dream: The Essential Interviews of Bruce Springsteen* (New York: Bloomsbury, 2013), 237. Subsequent endnote and in-text references are to this edition and cited as TAD.

23. *The Spirit of Radio,* Track 5, WBCN-FM, 9 January 1973: "Playing on the radio is something; to know what it's like in the radio. Just open up the little back and we're all right in there."

24. Walt Whitman, "Crossing Brooklyn Ferry," in *Leaves of Grass* (1891–92; rpt. New York: Norton, 1973), 160.

25. Anthony Storr, *Solitude: A Return to the Self* (London: HarperCollins, 1988), xiv.

26. Louis Menand, *The Metaphysical Club: A Story of Ideas in America* (2001; rpt. London: Flamingo, 2002), 236.

27. John Gardner, "A Novel of Evil," in *Critical Essays on William Styron,* ed. Arthur D. Casciato and James L. W. West III (Boston: G. K. Hall, 1985), 246.

28. Richard Ford, "The Boss Observed," *Esquire,* December 1985, 326–29.

29. See "Introduction: The Bard of Asbury Park," Roxanne Harde and Irwin Streight's audacious, light-hearted, but actually rather intriguing comparison of Springsteen and Shakespeare in *Reading the Boss,* 1–20. The review is by Colin Carmin, *Rocky Mountain Review* (Spring 2012), 126.

30. Bruce Springsteen, "No Retreat, No Surrender," Comments at John Kerry Rally in Madison, Wisconsin, 28 October 2004, Common Dreams News Center, Box S15, Bruce Springsteen Special Collection.

31. See Rorty, *The Rorty Reader,* 416. "When people try to associate Americanism and pragmatism," writes Rorty, "it is usually only the classical pragmatists whom they have in mind. The so-called neo-pragmatists do not concern themselves much with moral and social philosophy, nor do they see themselves as presenting anything distinctly American."

32. John J. Sheinbaum, "I'll Work for Your Love: Springsteen and the Struggle for Authenticity," in Harde and Streight, eds., *Reading the Boss,* 240.

33. Marsh, *Bruce Springsteen on Tour,* 11, 14.

34. Randall E. Auxier, "Prophets and Profits: Poets, Preachers and Pragmatists," and Heather E. Keith, "Living in 'My Hometown': Local Philosophies for Troubled Times," in *Bruce Springsteen and Philosophy: Darkness on the Edge of Truth,* ed. Randall E. Auxier and Doug Anderson (Peru, IL: Open Court, 2008), 3–15, 173–82.

35. Robert Coles, *Bruce Springsteen's America: The People Listening, a Poet Singing* (New York: Random House, 2003), 43; Jim Cullen, *Born in the U.S.A.: Bruce Springsteen and the American Tradition* (1997; rev. ed., Middletown, CT: Wesleyan University Press, 2005), xiv–xv, 125. For a skeptical review of Coles's conversations with Percy, see David Hajdu, "Tramps Like Who?" *New Republic* (15 December 2003), newrepublic.com/article/67272/tramps-who. Hajdu challenges the authenticity of Coles's conversations with Percy, and quotes Will Percy telling him that the attributions are "outrageous." See also Steven Weiland, *Intellectual Craftsmen: Ways and Works in American Scholarship* (New Brunswick, NJ: Transactions Publishers, 1991), 86. Coles scholar Weiland defends them, arguing,

"some distortion is perhaps inevitable given Coles' method and purposes and expectations of his readers." What is not in doubt is that the novelist wrote Springsteen "a fan letter—of sorts." The letter, along with Springsteen's eventual response to Percy's widow, is reprinted in Sawyers, ed., *Racing in the Street*, 319–20.

36. "Bruce Springsteen: By the Book," Sunday Book Review, *New York Times*, 2 November 2014: BR8; 30 October 2014, nyti.ms/1p6nB21.

37. William James, "What Pragmatism Means," in *Pragmatism and Classical American Philosophy: Essential Readings and Interpretive Essays*, ed. John J. Stuhr (Oxford, UK: Oxford University Press, 2000), 196; Ralph Waldo Emerson, "Self-Reliance," in *The Complete Prose Works of Ralph Waldo Emerson* (New York: Ward, Lock and Co., 1889), 15.

38. Sleeve notes, *Tracks* (1998).

39. Pessoa, *The Book of Disquiet*, 19; Jorge Luis Borges, *Labyrinths: Selected Stories and Other Writings*, trans. Donald Yates, James Irby et al. (1964; rpt. Harmondsworth, UK: Penguin, 1987), 266.

40. See Borges, *Labyrinths*, 269, on Buddhism and the fictional nature of past and future as constructed concepts in the human mind.

41. Ibid., 266.

42. Simon Frith, "The Real Thing—Bruce Springsteen," in Sawyers, ed., *Racing in the Street*, 137; Clarence Clemons and Don Reo, *Big Man: Real Life and Tales* (New York: Grand Central Publishing, 2009), 134, 339.

CHAPTER ONE

1. Springsteen, in *The Ties That Bind*, directed by Thom Zimny (New York: Thrill Hill), in *The Ties That Bind: The River Collection* (Columbia Records, 2015).

2. Wendell Berry, "A Homage to Dr. Williams," in *The Generation of 2000: Contemporary American Poets*, ed. William Heyen (Princeton, NJ: Ontario Review Press, 1984), 11. See also Bryan K. Garman, *A Race of Singers: Whitman's Working-Class Hero from Guthrie to Springsteen* (Chapel Hill: University of North Carolina Press, 2000), 250. Writing specifically about the *Tom Joad* era and beyond, Garman states that, "to convert democratic promise into reality, Springsteen suggests, individuals must accept social responsibility, practice active citizenship, be vigilant for abuses of power, and subordinate self-interest to the good of the community."

3. D. H. Lawrence, *Studies in Classic American Literature* (1923; rpt. Harmondsworth, UK: Penguin, 1977), 8: "Never trust the artist. Trust the tale. The proper function of a critic is to save the tale from the artist who created it."

4. Joyce Carol Oates, *(Woman) Writer: Occasions and Opportunities* (New York: Dutton, 1988), 39–40: "The writer must accept it as a premise of his existence that certain delusions—one of these, in fact, the delusion of 'self-knowledge'—are necessary or his career; as necessary as delusions of various sorts are, for all of us, generally. The 'life-lie' as Ibsen called it, but Ibsen is being rather cruel: why not erect 'life-*ideal*' as a more beneficent term?"

5. Coles, *Bruce Springsteen's America*, 43.

6. Lewis, *Lonesome*, xv, xviii.

7. Ibid., 15–16. In fact this feeling transcends cultures. The Turkish have "hüzün"; the Spanish "melanchonia"; the Portuguese the music of fado, and the word "melancholy" itself can be given a positive spin.

8. See Remnick, "We Are Alive." See also Phillips and Masur, "Introduction," in *Talk about a Dream*, 8. They cite Springsteen using the word "depression" in 1992 to describe his feelings after "the *Born in the U.S.A.* juggernaut." Perhaps the most revealing early interview he gave about this was to James Henke, again in 1992. See "Bruce Springsteen: The Rolling Stone Interview," in Puterbaugh et al., eds., *Bruce Springsteen*, 401–23, and TAD 151–69. Several biographies address this issue.

9. William Cowper, "Lines Written During a Period of Insanity," *The Oxford Anthology of English Literature: The Restoration and the Eighteenth Century*, ed. Martin Price (Oxford, UK: Oxford University Press, 1973); Sylvia Plath, *The Bell Jar* (London: Heinemann, 1963); William Styron, *Darkness Visible: A Memoir of Madness* (New York: Random House, 1990), 47; Elizabeth Wurtzel, "My Working Class Hero," *Esquire*, June 1996, 72.

10. Marsh, *Bruce Springsteen: Two Hearts*, 371; Springsteen to Mikal Gilmore, "Twentieth Anniversary Special," in Puterbaugh et al., eds., *Bruce Springsteen*, 295–96.

11. Joyce Carol Oates, *We Were the Mulvaneys* (New York: Dutton, 1996), 148. For an intriguing reading of "Highway Patrolman," see Jonathan Caspi, "'Highway Patrolman': An Application of Sibling Theory and Research," in *Bruce Springsteen and the American Soul: Essays on the Songs and Influence of an American Icon*, ed. David Garrett Izzo (Jefferson, NC: McFarland, 2011), 160–72. Caspi, a teacher of sibling relationship and childhood development courses, suggests that Joe is the older sibling and once again getting to be the hero. Frankie's behavior, in other words, is not to be separated from Joe's holier-than-thou attitude.

12. News on Campus, "King's Connection to the Boss," *Pride* (Winter 2011–12): 8. See also Joe De Pugh, "Reminiscence," 11 May 1979, Box S10, Bruce Springsteen Special Collection.

13. Saul Bellow, *Henderson the Rain King* (1959; rpt. Harmondsworth, UK: Penguin, 1981), 157; L. S. Lowry to Edward Mullins, quoted at *Government Art Collection*, www.gac.gov.uk/lowry.html.

14. Willa Cather, *My Ántonia* (1918; rpt. London: Everyman, 1996), 210.

15. Borges, *Labyrinths*, 259.

16. Stevan Weine, "On the Edge," in Izzo, ed., *Bruce Springsteen and the American Soul*, 215.

17. Cecelia Tichi, *High Lonesome: The American Culture of Country Music* (Chapel Hill: University of North Carolina Press, 1994), 102, 83, 87; Lewis, *Lonesome*, 17, 25, 36.

18. Clinton Heylin, *E Street Shuffle: The Glory Days of Bruce Springsteen and the E Street Band* (London: Constable, 2012), 22.

19. Mark Twain (Samuel Langhorne Clemens), *Adventures of Huckleberry Finn* (1884; rpt. New York: Norton, 1977), 229.

20. See Menand, *The Metaphysical Club*, 227, 350. Peirce borrowed the term itself from a passage in Immanuel Kant's *Kritik der Reinen Vernunft* (*Critique of Pure Reason*). Writing of a physician's need to act on behalf of an endangered patient, Kant explains that the physician may know that his decision is based on a contingent belief. "Such contingent belief, which yet forms the ground for the actual employment of means to certain actions," Kant entitles "*pragmatic belief*," a belief based on a degree of "*betting*." Menand also notes, "none of the principle figures who became identified with the term much liked the name."

21. Menand, *The Metaphysical Club*, 95, 88.

22. Ibid., 75.

23. Rorty, *The Rorty Reader*, 421.

24. Quoted in Menand, *The Metaphysical Club*, 58.

25. Rorty, *The Rorty Reader*, 446.

26. Giles Gunn, *Thinking Across the American Grain: Ideology, Intellect, and the New Pragmatism* (Chicago: University of Chicago Press, 1992), 6. The phrases in quotation are from French sociologist Pierre Bourdieu. Gunn refers to James and "all his talk about 'cash values' and truth as 'something that pays,' that saves 'labor.'"

27. Rorty, *The Rorty Reader*, 488.

28. John J. Stuhr, "Introduction: Classical American Philosophy," in Stuhr, ed., *Pragmatism and Classical American Philosophy*, 1–7.

29. Quoted in Heylin, *E Street Shuffle*, 27.

30. See for, instance, Mikal Gilmore, *Nightbeat: A Shadow History of Rock & Roll* (New York: Doubleday, 1998), 224, and in Puterbaugh et al., eds., *Bruce Springsteen*, 436, and Abbe Smith, "The Dignity and Humanity of Bruce Springsteen's Criminals," *Widener Law Journal* 14 (2005): 835.

31. William James, "What Pragmatism Means," in Stuhr, ed., *Pragmatism and Classical American Philosophy*, 194 (James is paraphrasing Charles Sanders Peirce); Wendell Berry, "Homage to Dr. Williams," and Marge Piercy, "To Be of Use," in Heyen, ed., *The Generation of 2000*, 12, 244.

32. Peter Ames Carlin, *Bruce* (New York: Touchstone, 2012), 457.

33. Rorty, *The Rorty Reader*, 418.

34. Ibid., 446.

35. Richard Rorty, *Achieving Our Country: Leftist Thought in Twentieth-Century America* (Cambridge, MA: Harvard, 1997), 102, 13.

36. William James, diary entry, April 30, 1870, quoted in Stuhr, ed., *Pragmatism and Classical American Writing*, 142. See also William James, "Diary," in *The Writings of William James*, ed. John J. McDermott (Chicago: University of Chicago Press, 1977), 7.

37. William James, "The Will to Believe," in Stuhr, ed., *Pragmatism and Classical American Writing*, 239.

38. See Menand, *The Metaphysical Club*, 375, and Rorty, *The Rorty Reader*, 415–16. For Menand, "turn-of-the-century pragmatism" has "deficiencies as a school of thought. One is that it takes interests for granted; it doesn't provide for a way of judging whether they are worth pursuing apart from the consequences of acting on them," and it doesn't address the fact that "wants and beliefs can lead people to act in ways that are distinctly unpragmatic." Rorty points out that, while "philosophy and politics are not that tightly linked," and that in fact, "there is no reason why a fascist could not be a pragmatist," any more than a democrat, the tendency of American pragmatists is toward the democratic. Of Nietzsche and Dewey, for instance, Rorty writes that their "*only* substantial disagreement" is "about the value of democracy." He upholds Dewey's description of pragmatism as "the philosophy of democracy" in that it expresses a "melioristic, experimental frame of mind."

39. Sawyers, "Introduction," in Sawyers, ed., *Racing in the Street*, 1; Greil Marcus, *In the Fascist Bathroom: Punk in Pop Music, 1977–1992* (Cambridge, MA: Harvard University Press, 1999), 48; Anne Douglas, "Bruce Springsteen and Narrative Rock," *Dissent* (Fall 1985): 486; Geoffrey Himes, *Born in the U.S.A.* (London: Continuum 2005), 71–72; Richard Rorty, *Consequences of Pragmatism: Essays, 1972–1980* (Brighton, UK: Harvester, 1982), 166. Springsteen acknowledges, in selecting "Madame

George" on "Desert Island Discs," that without *Astral Weeks* there would have been, in Springsteen's example, no "New York Serenade." "Desert Island Discs" was first broadcast on BBC Radio 4, 23 December 2016, bbc.in/2gWiz8U. On the more general point about our interconnectedness, see also Dale Maharidge, *Someplace Like America: Tales from the New Great Depression* (2011; rev. ed. Berkeley: University of California Press, 2013), 85. Maharidge quotes hobo folk singer Utah Phillips's "Bridges," depicting time as a river into which we deposit and out of which we collect material. "You do 'art' and then let it go into the river," writes Maharidge. "If you are doing it for the right reason and are very, very lucky, the work gets picked up downstream. It becomes a continuation of a story that must be told, a voice speaking over the decades and centuries."

40. This has included putting his money where his mouth is, as the various biographies attest, in his support for charities and other social groups within the communities he visits. See, for example, Marsh, *Bruce Springsteen: Two Hearts,* 493–502, and numerous references in Marc Dolan, *Bruce Springsteen and the Promise of Rock 'n' Roll* (2012; 2nd ed. New York; Norton, 2013).

41. For a detailed, informed, and highly impressive study of Springsteen's political engagement, see David Masciotra, *Working on a Dream: The Progressive Political Vision of Bruce Springsteen* (New York: Continuum, 2010). See also Shumway, *Rock Star,* 203–4. Shumway thinks "Masciotra claims too much" in arguing for Springsteen's "progressive political vision," which he feels "would perhaps be too much to expect of any popular musician," but cites *Wrecking Ball* as an exception when noting "how little the recent economic crisis has found expression in popular music." "Springsteen's willingness to address the human cost of inequality," writes Shumway, "continues to set him apart."

42. Heylin, *E Street Shuffle,* 184, quotes Springsteen referring, in 1981, to "that fantastic book, *American Dreams, Lost and Found* by Studs Terkel." See Studs Terkel, *My American Century* (New York: New Press, 1997), for selections from Terkel's many acclaimed books of oral history. The foreword is by Springsteen's friend and commentator, Robert Coles.

43. Heylin, *E Street Shuffle,* 6.

44. Cullen, *Born in the U.S.A.,* 132.

45. Warren French, *Steinbeck Revisited* (New York: Twayne, 1961), 76.

46. Cullen, *Born in the U.S.A.,* 182.

47. John Steinbeck, *The Grapes of Wrath* (1939; rpt. Harmondsworth, UK: Penguin, 1992), 570.

48. Ibid., 206.

49. Christopher Sandford, *Springsteen: Point Blank* (London: Little, Brown, 1999), 147; Pedro Almodóvar, *All About My Mother (Sobre mi Madre)* (Barcelona: Warner Sogerfilms, 1999).

50. Michael Watts, "Lone Star," in *"Melody Maker" Classic Rock Interviews,* ed. Allan Jones (London: Mandarin, 1994), 55; Joyce Carol Oates, *You Must Remember This* (New York: Dutton, 1987), 401.

51. David Hepworth, Interview with Bruce Springsteen, *The Late Show,* London Weekend Television Productions, 15 June 1992.

52. Frith, "The Real Thing," 132.

53. For detailed discussion of this period, see Garman, *A Race of Singers,* 227–52.

54. See "A Policeman Takes on the '41 Shots' of 'American Skin,' 'Johnny 99,'" in Coles, *Bruce Springsteen's America,* 109–42, for a criticism of *Nebraska* in terms of the emphasis on criminals rather than victims and their families. See also Gilmore, *Nightbeat,* 222, for a different view on how *Nebraska* and *Tom Joad* only superficially resemble one another.

55. See Richard Gray, *After the Fall: American Literature Since 9/11* (Malden, MA: Wiley-Blackwell, 2011) for a book-length discussion of literary responses.

56. Bonca, "How (and How Not) to Write About 9/11," 138.

57. Himes, *Born in the U.S.A.*, 138; Roxanne Harde, "Living in Your American Skin," *Canadian Review of American Studies / Revue Canadienne d'Études Américaines* 43, no. 1 (2013): 135. Harde is disagreeing with Josh Tyrangiel, whose view is that "what's missing on *The Rising* is politics." See Josh Tyrangiel, "Bruce Rising: An Intimate Look at How Springsteen Turned 9/11 into a Message of Hope," *Time* 160, no. 6 (5 August 2002): 52–59.

58. Cullen, *Born in the U.S.A.*, 199; Rorty, *The Rorty Reader*, 198, 480, 486, 454.

59. Greil Marcus, *Mystery Train: Images of America in Rock 'n' Roll Music* (1975; rev. ed. New York: Plume, 2015), 122.

60. Dave Marsh, *Bruce Springsteen: Two Hearts*, 632; Blaise Pascal, *Pensées*, trans. A. J. Krailsheimer (Harmondsworth, UK: Penguin, 1966), 66. : is quoting Springsteen in 1987: "Is making the Loud Noise worth it? That's a question that I feel like I'm constantly asking myself, and the only answer I come up with is, Well, you don't know unless you try." Pascal's thought number 201 is: "The eternal silence of these infinite spaces fills me with dread."

61. Philip Roth, *Nemesis* (2010; rpt. London: Vintage, 2011), 122–23.

CHAPTER TWO

1. Coles, *Bruce Springsteen's America*, 45; Sandford, *Springsteen*, 392; Coles, *Bruce Springsteen's America*, 45.

2. Richard Ford, "2 Comments," *Wall Street Journal*, 20 January 2015, www.wsj.com/articles /richard-ford-on-bruce-springsteens-wild-billys-circus-story-1421777496; "Rock Springs Eternal: Richard Ford on Bruce Springsteen," backstreets.com/newsarchive74.html. Ford's public comments also include "The Boss Observed," *Esquire*, December 1985, 326–29, and "Richard Ford Reviews Bruce Springsteen's Memoir," *New York Times*, 22 September 2016, nyti.ms/2d1S058. See also Elinor Ann Walker, "An Interview with Richard Ford," in *Conversations with Richard Ford*, ed. Huey Guagliardo (Jackson: University of Mississippi Press, 2001), 131–46. In this 1997 interview Ford says that, given that Springsteen's lyrics, phrasing, and music have influenced him, "that must mean that it or he fits into whatever level of culture being a story writer in America is now." He also says that "Independence Day" was "probably the first thing" that instigated his novel of that title (131), and that he avoided reference to Springsteen in *The Sportswriter* because he'd never have been "able to re-authorize the scene" (132). For an extended analysis of Springsteen and Ford, see David N. Gellman, "'Darkness on the Edge of Town': Springsteen, Richard Ford, and the American Dream," in *Bruce Springsteen, Cultural Studies, and the Runaway American Dream*, ed. Kenneth Womack, Jerry Zolten, and Mark Bernhard (Burlington, VT: Ashgate, 2012), 7–24.

3. *Trouble in the Heartland: Crime Fiction Inspired by the Songs of Bruce Springsteen*, ed. Joe Clifford (Dublin: Gutter, 2014); *Meeting Across the River: Stories Inspired by the Haunting Bruce Springsteen Song*, ed. Jessica Kay and Richard Brewer (New York: Bloomsbury, 2005); Tennessee Jones, *Deliver Me from Nowhere* (Brooklyn: Soft Skull, 2005).

4. Storr, *Solitude*, 15–19.

5. Ibid., 122–24. See Remnick, "We Are Alive," 11. Remnick quotes Springsteen saying: "T-Bone Burnett said that rock and roll is all about 'Daaaaddy!' It's one embarrassing scream of 'Daaaaddy!' It's just fathers and sons, and you're out there proving something to somebody in the most intense way possible."

6. William James, *The Varieties of Religious Experience: A Study in Human Nature* (London: W. F. Roper, 1903), 381, quoted in Storr, *Solitude*, 196.

7. See also Springsteen's comments on having read "all the Russians," on "Desert Island Discs," bbc.in/2gWiz8U.

8. Ralph Waldo Emerson, "Self-Reliance," in *The Norton Anthology of American Literature*, ed. Nina Baym et al. (1979; rpt. New York: Norton, 1989, 442). Emerson's phrase doesn't appear in all versions of the essay.

9. Dickinson, Poem 280. "And then a Plank in Reason broke / And I plunged down and down / And hit a World at every turn"; Lewis, *Lonesome*, 174. "For nothing quite so much as the qualities of their respective solitudes," writes Lewis, do we hold up Whitman and Dickinson as "our crucial forebears in the American tradition." "No other native poet," he writes of Whitman, "has done more to open up 'lonesomeness'" as a way "to signify a positive, 'up-lifting' access of illumination and happiness paradoxically experienced" in solitude. Dickinson, in turn, expresses "metaphysical lonesomeness" (24–26, 29, 32, 36).

10. Frederick Douglass, *The Autobiography of Frederick Douglass, an American Slave* (1845; rpt. Harmondsworth, UK: Penguin, 1982), 135.

11. Ibid., 47.

12. Ibid., 56.

13. W. E. B. Du Bois, *The Souls of Black Folk* (1903; rpt. Mineola, NY: Dover, 1994), 156–57; James Baldwin, *The Fire Next Time* (1963; rpt. Harmondsworth, UK: Penguin, 1964), 42–43; Toni Morrison, *Jazz* (1992; rpt. London: Picador, 1993), 114.

14. Douglass, *Autobiography*, 56–58; Du Bois, *Souls of Black Folk*, vi.

15. Alain Locke, "The Ethics of Culture," in Stuhr, ed., *Pragmatism and Classical American Writing*, 672–73, 676.

16. George F. Will, *The Morning After: American Successes and Excesses 1981–1986* (New York: Prentice Hall, 1987), 11; Eric Alterman, *It Ain't No Sin to Be Glad You're Alive: The Promise of Bruce Springsteen* (1999; 2nd ed. Boston: Little, Brown, 2001), 156; Gavin Martin, "Hey Joad, Don't Make It Sad . . . (Oh, Go On Then)," in Burger, ed., *Springsteen on Springsteen*, 218–19.

17. Douglass, *Autobiography*, 79.

18. Ibid., 84, 87.

19. Ibid., 122.

20. Alexander Solzhenitsyn, *One Day in the Life of Ivan Denisovich*, trans. Ralph Parker (Harmondsworth, UK: Penguin, 1963), 143. The extra three days "are for leap years."

21. Kathleen Mary Higgins, *The Music of Our Lives* (Lanham, MD: Lexington, 2011), 123–30.

22. Douglass, *Autobiography*, 79; Michel de Montaigne, "Of Glory," in *The Essays of Montaigne*, trans. Charles Cotton (London: Bell, 1913), vol. 2: 337: "Those discourses are, in my opinion, very true and rationale; but we are, I do not know how, double in ourselves, which is the cause that what we believe we do not believe, and cannot disengage ourselves from what we condemn."

23. Robert Duncan, "Lawdamercy, Springsteen Saves!" in Burger, ed., *Springsteen on Spring-*

steen, 90. This is from a story Springsteen would relate during concerts and can be found in several sources. Duncan refers to an introduction to "Growin' Up" at a 1978 Houston concert.

24. Nathaniel Hawthorne, *The Scarlet Letter: A Romance* (1837; rpt. Harmondsworth, UK: Penguin, 2012), 7–8.

25. Ibid., 248–49.

26. See Cullen, *Born in the U.S.A.*, 157–89. As a result of his work on Springsteen and Catholicism here, Cullen went on to write a book about other Catholic figures, *Restless in the Promised Land: Catholics and the American Dream* (Franklin, WI: Sheed & Ward, 2001).

27. Cullen, *Born in the U.S.A*, 8.

28. Ibid., 250.

29. See *Born to Run*, 179. Of the trauma of experiencing his father's drunken tirades, Springsteen writes: "As a child, my nervousness became so great I began to blink uncontrollably, hundreds of time a minute. At school I was called 'Blinky.' I chewed all of the knuckles on both of my hands night and day into brown rock-hard calluses the size of marbles. Nope, drinking wasn't for me."

30. Herman Melville, *Moby-Dick; or, The Whale* (1851; rpt. Harmondsworth, UK: Penguin, 1972), 93.

31. Keith Richards, *Life* (2010; rpt. London: Phoenix, 2011), 36.

32. "Bruce Springsteen: By the Book," BR8.

33. Marsh, *Bruce Springsteen: Two Hearts,* 615.

34. Melville, *Moby-Dick,* 95.

35. Eleanor Melville Metcalf, *Herman Melville: Cycle and Epicycle* (Cambridge, MA: Harvard University Press, 1953), 283–84. Melville evidently kept this quotation from Johann Friedrich Schiller's *Don Carlos* by his desk.

36. Melville, *Moby-Dick,* 150.

37. "Bruce Springsteen: By the Book," BR8.

38. Melville, *Moby-Dick,* 241.

39. Henry David Thoreau, *Walden and "Civil Disobedience,"* ed. Owen Thomas (1854; rpt. New York: Norton, 1966), 1–5, 62.

40. Ibid., 5.

41. Marsh, *Bruce Springsteen: Two Hearts,* 631.

42. Thoreau, *Walden,* 57, 61, 61; see *Bruce Springsteen and the E Street Band Live in New York City,* DVD, Sony, 2001; Alex Pitofsky, "Springsteen's Intimations of Mortality," in Izzo, ed., *Bruce Springsteen and the American Soul,* 228, reminds us that "the late seventies was the time when he began to shout 'Are you ALIVE?' to fire up audiences."

43. Thoreau, *Walden,* 214.

44. Gilmore, "Twentieth-Century Anniversary Special," in Puterbaugh et al., eds., *Bruce Springsteen,* 298.296.

45. Robert Hilburn, "Out on the Streets," in Sawyers, ed., *Racing in the Street,* 97. See also, Marsh, *Bruce Springsteen: Two Hearts,* 323: "I was very distant from my family for quite a while in my early twenties. Not with any animosity; I just had to feel loose."

46. June Skinner Sawyers, *Tougher than the Rest: 100 Best Bruce Springsteen Songs* (New York: Omnibus, 2006), 246.

47. Ibid., 246.

48. See Lisa Delmonico, "Queen of the Supermarket: Representations of Working Class Women," in Izzo, ed., *Bruce Springsteen and the American Soul*, 51: "Rescue, not gender equality, is Springsteen's fixation, and feminists can justifiably have a field day noting his infantilization of women by use of sexist pet names such as: baby, girl, little girl, little pretty, little darlin', little miss, little honey, little sugar."

49. Marsh, *Bruce Springsteen: Two Hearts*, 372–73.

50. Coles, *Bruce Springsteen's America*, 6, 23.

51. Emily Dickinson, *Selected Letters*, ed. Thomas H. Johnson (Cambridge, MA: Belknap, 1996), 174.

52. "Bruce Springsteen: By the Book," BR8; Walt Whitman, "Song of Myself," in *Leaves of Grass*, 89.

53. Sawyers, *Tougher than the Rest*, 240–41. See her whole entry, 238–42, for a detailed discussion of the song and its sources.

54. Ernie Sandonato, "All Aboard," Box A5, Bruce Springsteen Special Collection.

55. Sawyers, *Tougher than the Rest*, 242.

56. Marcus, *Mystery Train*, 116–17: "There is no chance anyone who wants to join will be excluded. Elvis's fantasy of freedom, the audience's fantasy, takes on such reality that there is nothing left in the real world that can inspire the fantasy, or threaten it."

57. Alterman, *It Ain't No Sin to Be Glad You're Alive*, 188; Gilmore, *Nightbeat*, 221; Springsteen, interview (Channel 4, UK), 18 October 2016. For Springsteen's response to Reagan's appropriation attempts see, among other sources, Marsh, *Bruce Springsteen: Two Hearts*, 483–89. I should note that, on the *Wrecking Ball* version of "Land of Hope and Dreams," Springsteen sings that "you don't need no ticket," you just need to "praise the lord." This information, however, is contradicted by the lyrics sheet, which starts with "grab your ticket" and makes no mention of any need to profess religious belief.

58. Whitman, "Song of Myself," 52–53.

59. Quoted in Menand, *The Metaphysical Club*, 375; Cologne-Brookes, "Written Interviews," 548.

60. Colin Burrows, "What Is a Pikestaff?" review of Denis Donoghue's *Metaphor* (Cambridge, MA: Harvard University Press, 2014), *London Review of Books* 37, no. 8 (23 April 2015): 27. On the question of landscape and travel as metaphor, see Tichi, *High Lonesome*, 174.

61. Baldwin, *The Fire Next Time*, 79; *James Baldwin: The Price of a Ticket*, directed by Karen Thorsen (Nobody Knows Productions, 1989).

62. William James, "A Pluralistic Universe," in Stuhr, ed., *Pragmatism and Classical American Philosophy*, 158–59.

63. Gunn, *Thinking Across the American Grain*, 98–99.

64. Rorty, *Achieving Our Country*, 31.

65. Paul Nelson, "Springsteen Fever," in Puterbaugh et al., eds., *Bruce Springsteen*, 55. Among other sources, for details of Springsteen's lawsuit filed against Mike Appel, Appel's counter-lawsuit, and a comment on "The Promise," see Carlin, *Bruce*, 224–26. For Appel's version, see Eliot, *Down Thunder Road*, 175–228, and elsewhere. *Down Thunder Road* also contains transcripts of Springsteen's deposition in an attorney's office on 16 August 1976 and cross-examination by Leonard Marks, and an appendix of letters and other documentation.

66. See Maureen Orth, Janet Huck, and Peter S. Greenberg, "Making of a Rock Star," in Sawyers, ed., *Racing in the Street*, 56. See also Eliot, *Down Thunder Road*, 186–223 and appendix A, for

a transcript of the court proceedings and related documents. "It's hard to trust anybody anymore," Springsteen is recorded as saying (189).

67. Whitman, "Song of Myself," 89, 52.

68. Ernest Hemingway, *Green Hills of Africa* (New York: Scribner's, 1935), 22; F. Scott Fitzgerald, statement read at the Banquet of the International Mark Twain Society, 30 November 1930, in *F. Scott Fitzgerald on Authorship*, ed. Matthew J. Bruccoli with Judith F. Bauman (Columbia: University of South Carolina Press, 1996), 122: "*Huckleberry Finn* took the first journey *back*. He was the first to look *back* at the republic from the perspective of the west."

69. Marcus, *Mystery Train*, 12–13, 127.

70. Storr, *Solitude*, 28, 197.

71. Twain, *Huckleberry Finn*, 169, 170. See also 279. In his autobiography, an extract of which appears in the 1977 Norton edition, Twain describes Huck as being a bona fide portrayal of a boyhood acquaintance, Tom Blankenship, who became "a justice of the peace in a remote village in Montana, and was a good citizen and greatly respected."

72. Lewis, *Lonesome*, 54.

73. Eddie Cochran was born in Minnesota, but his parents came from Oklahoma.

CHAPTER THREE

1. Eduardo Galeano, *Open Veins of Latin America: Five Centuries of the Pillage of a Continent*, trans. Cedric Belfrage (1973; rpt. London: Serpent's Tail, 2009), xiv. The fuller quotation is: "one writes out of a need to communicate and to commune with others, to denounce that which gives pain and to share that which gives happiness. One writes against one's solitude and against the solitude of others. One assumes that literature transmits knowledge and affects the behavior of those who read." It's included in this edition of Galeano's classic study as an introductory excerpt from his 1978 book, *Days and Nights of Love and War*, trans. Bobbye Ortiz. *Open Veins of Latin America* took on a new lease of life when the president of Venezuela, Hugo Chávez, presented Barack Obama with a copy in 2009.

2. For Springsteen's comments on McCarthy, see "Bruce Springsteen: By the Book," BR8.

3. Baldwin, *The Fire Next Time*, 79.

4. Flannery O'Connor, "A Good Man Is Hard to Find," *The Complete Stories* (London: Faber, 1990), 132. "No pleasure but meanness," says the murderer known as the Misfit.

5. See Sawyers, "Endlessly Seeking," and Michael Kobre, "On Blessing Avenue: Faith, Language, and a Search for Meaning in the Works of Bruce Springsteen and Walker Percy," in Harde and Streight, eds., *Reading the Boss*, 23–39, 41–52, and Gellman, "'Darkness on the Edge of Town,'" in Womack, Zolten, and Bernhard, eds., *Bruce Springsteen, Cultural Studies, and the American Dream*, 9; Ford, "Rock Springs Eternal." Ford is "already known to be a Springsteen fan," the article states, "even if the name of his Pulitzer and PEN/Faulkner award-winning *Independence Day* were any kind of coincidence." On O'Connor, see Irwin Streight, "The Flannery O'Connor of American Rock," in Harde and Streight, eds., *Reading the Boss*, 53–75. None of the collections discuss Springsteen and either McCarthy or Roth. That intersection between lonesomeness and community is also true of music and the visual arts. Useful further contextualization can be found both in Lewis's *Lonesome* and in Tichi's *High Lonesome*.

6. John Hammond, *John Hammond on Record* (New York: Ridge, 1977), 391.

7. Sawyers, "Endlessly Seeking," 23.

8. Will Percy, "Rock and Read: Will Percy Interviews Bruce Springsteen," Sawyers, ed., *Racing in the Street,* 319–20.

9. Kieran Quinlan, *Walker Percy: The Last Catholic Novelist* (Baton Rouge: Louisiana State University Press, 1996), 5, 11, 13.

10. Ibid., 17, 5.

11. Isaiah Berlin, *Russian Thinkers* (1948; rpt. Harmondsworth, UK: Penguin, 1994), 30.

12. Walker Percy, "From Facts to Fiction," in *Signposts in a Strange Land* (New York: Farrar, Straus & Giroux, 1991), 188.

13. Walker Percy, *Lost in the Cosmos: The Last Self-Help Book* (1983; rpt. New York: Picador, 2000), 12–13.

14. Virginia Woolf, *To the Lighthouse* (1927; rpt. New York: Harvest, 1955), 224: "A brush, the one dependable thing in a world of strife, ruin, chaos."

15. Rorty, *The Rorty Reader,* 479–80.

16. Quinlan, *Walker Percy,* 49–56; *Ohio Review,* "Transformations of the Self," in *Conversations with Joyce Carol Oates,* ed. Lee Milazzo (Jackson: University of Mississippi Press, 1989), 49; Henry James, "The Middle Years" (1893) in *Collected Stories* (New York: Knopf, 1999), vol. 2: 123. Marsh, *Bruce Springsteen: Two Hearts,* 23.

17. Walker Percy, "How to Be an American Novelist in Spite of Being Southern and Catholic," in *Signposts in a Strange Land,* 168–85; John Edward Hardy, *The Fiction of Walker Percy* (Urbana: University of Illinois Press, 1987), 224, quoted in Quinlan, *Walker Percy,* 226.

18. Walker, "An Interview with Richard Ford," 132.

19. Erik H. Erikson, *Young Man Luther: A Study in Psychoanalysis and History* (New York: Norton, 1958), 12; Albert Camus, *The Myth of Sisyphus and Other Essays,* trans. Justin O'Brien (1942; Harmondsworth, UK: Penguin, 1975), 2.

20. Albert Camus, *The Fall,* trans. Justin O'Brien (1956; London: Hamish Hamilton, 1957), 66; Richard Ford, *The Sportswriter* (1986; rpt. London: Flamingo, 1987), 22, 47, 69.

21. Ford, *The Sportswriter,* 360, 14.

22. See Sandford, *Springsteen,* 195. Sandford states that Springsteen first sought therapy in the winter of 1981–82.

23. Ford, *The Sportswriter,* 15, 111, 50, 52, 180.

24. Carlin, *Bruce,* 339.

25. F. Scott Fitzgerald, "The Crack-Up," in *The Crack-Up with other Pieces and Stories* (Harmondsworth, UK: Penguin, 1965), 39.

26. Ford, *The Sportswriter,* 104, 230, 38, 73, 59, 103.

27. Ibid., 316.

28. Ibid., 276.

29. Friedrich Nietzsche, *Beyond Good and Evil: Prelude to a Philosophy of the Future,* trans. R. J. Hollingdale (Harmondsworth, UK: Penguin, 1973), 72.

30. Ford, *The Sportswriter,* 44, 53, 250.

31. John Dewey, manuscript page, John Dewey Papers, Special Collections, Morris Library,

Southern Illinois University, Carbondale, 102/58/10, quoted in Stuhr, ed., *Pragmatism and Classical American Writing*, 434.

32. Ford, *The Sportswriter*, 87, 103, 318, 380.

33. Ibid., 381.

34. Albert Camus, "Reflections on the Guillotine," in *Resistance, Rebellion, and Death*, trans. Justin O'Brien (London: Hamish Hamilton, 1961), 125–65; Arthur Koestler, *Darkness at Noon* (1941; rpt. New York: Bantam, 1966); George Orwell, "A Hanging," in *Why I Write* (Harmondsworth, UK: Penguin, 2004), 95–101 (quoting 97–99).

35. William Shakespeare, *Measure for Measure*, III, i, 127–30; Stendhal, *The Red and the Black*, 526; Fyodor Dostoevsky, *Crime and Punishment*, trans. Jessie Coulson (Oxford, UK: Oxford World's Classics, 1980), 152; Richard Wright, *Native Son* (1940; rpt. London: Vintage, 2000), 392, 304.

36. Stendhal, *The Red and the Black*, 501.

37. Camus, "Reflections on the Guillotine," 141–42.

38. Wright, *Native Son*, 374.

39. Ibid., 304.

40. Ibid., 306.

41. Ibid., 426.

42. Michelle Alexander, *The New Jim Crow: Mass Incarceration in the Age of Colorblindness* (2011; rev. ed. New York: New Press, 2012), 162.

43. Wright, *Native Son*, 270.

44. Alexander, *The New Jim Crow*, 174.

45. See "Bruce Springsteen: By the Book," BR8, and Steve Kandell, "The Feeling's Mutual: Bruce Springsteen and Win Butler Talk about the Early Days, the Glory Days, and Even the End of Days," in Burger, ed., *Springsteen on Springsteen*, 323, 326. Butler, of Canadian band Arcade Fire, gives Springsteen a copy of Orwell's *Why I Write*, which contains "A Hanging." Orwell describes being shot in *Homage to Catalonia* (1938; rpt. Harmondsworth, UK: Penguin, 1966), 177.

46. Helen Prejean, *Dead Man Walking: An Eyewitness Account of the Death Penalty in the United States* (1993; rpt. London: Fount, 1996); Smith, "The Dignity and Humanity of Bruce Springsteen's Criminals," 794.

47. Black Lives Matter, blacklivesmatter.com.

48. Joyce Carol Oates, ed., *Prison Noir* (New York: Akashic, 2014), 14.

49. Alexander, *The New Jim Crow*, 6.

50. Ibid., 14, 216.

51. Smith, "Dignity and Humanity in Bruce Springsteen's Criminals," 789–91.

52. Ibid., 794, 798.

53. Springsteen in Zimny, director, *The Ties That Bind*.

54. Camus, "Reflections on the Guillotine," 137.

55. Prejean, *Dead Man Walking*, 3–4.

56. Wright, *Native Son*, 443.

57. For Springsteen's comments on Roth, see "Bruce Springsteen: By the Book," BR8. *American Pastoral*, *I Married a Communist*, and *The Human Stain* "just knocked me off my ass," Springsteen said to Ken Tucker in 2003 (TAD 279).

58. Henry Louis Gates Jr., "Murder She Wrote," *Studies in the Novel*, 38, no. 4 (Winter 2006): 544–45; Greg Johnson, *Invisible Writer: A Biography of Joyce Carol Oates* (New York: Dutton, 1998), xviii; Frederic Oates in conversation with the author, July 1998; Joyce Carol Oates, *Fabulous Beasts* (Baton Rouge: Louisiana State University Press, 1977), 83. The poem is reprinted in *Invisible Woman: New and Selected Poems, 1970–1982* (Princeton, NJ: Ontario Review Press, 1982), 81–82.

59. Oates, "The Nature of Short Fiction; or, the Nature of My Short Fiction," preface to *Handbook of Short Story Writing*, ed. Frank A. Dickson and Sandra Smythe (Cincinnati: Writer's Digest, 1970), xii.

60. Johnson, *Invisible Writer*, 40, 263.

61. Joyce Carol Oates, *The Lost Landscape: A Writer's Coming of Age* (New York: Ecco, 2015), 132.

62. Johnson, *Invisible Writer*, 15, 108, 108.

63. O'Connor, "A Good Man Is Hard to Find," 117–33. The statement is on 132.

64. Tichi, *High Lonesome*, 7.

65. Joyce Carol Oates, "High Lonesome," *High Lonesome: Selected Stories 1966–2006* (New York: Ecco, 2006), 118, 145, 150, 152, 153.

66. José Saramago, *All the Names*, trans. Margaret Jull Costa (New York: Harvest, 1999), 14.

67. Carlin, *Bruce*, 240–41.

68. Joyce Carol Oates, *The Faith of a Writer: Life, Craft, Art* (New York: Ecco, 2003), 24; Oates, unpublished response to the author's written interview question, July 1994.

69. Oates, *(Woman) Writer*, 3–4; W. S. Di Piero, *Memory and Enthusiasm: Essays, 1975–1985* (Princeton, NJ: Princeton University Press, 1989), 255.

70. Carlin, *Bruce*, 243; Oates, *(Woman) Writer*, 4–6, 13. 19, 158, 24; Orth, Huck, and Greenberg, "Making of a Rock Star," in Sawyers, ed., *Racing in the Street*, 56; Eliot, *Down Thunder Road*, 199.

71. Oates, *(Woman) Writer*, 25, 44, 52.

72. Oates, *The Lost Landscape*, 237.

73. Cologne-Brookes, "Written Interviews," 549; Gates, "Murder She Wrote," 544.

74. Cologne-Brookes, "Written Interviews," 553–54, 555; Carlin, *Bruce*, 265–66.

75. See Marsh, *Bruce Springsteen: Two Hearts*, 414, for Springsteen's reference to this: "The John Wayne character can't join the community, and that movie always moved me tremendously."

76. Tichi, *High Lonesome*, 126.

77. Robert Coles, quoted in Lewis, *Lonesome*, 114. The work of Hopper and Springsteen also share the risk of over-exposure, being counterproductive to whatever their original aims may have been. See Springsteen's comments in Steve Pond, "Bruce Springsteen's *Tunnel* Vision," in Puterbaugh et al., eds., *Bruce Springsteen*, 329: "The size is tricky, it's dangerous. You can become purely iconic, or you can become just a Rorschach test that people throw up their own impressions upon, which you always are to some degree anyway. With size, and the co-option of your images and attitudes—you know, you wake up and you're a car commercial or whatever. And the way I think the artist deals with that is just reinvention."

78. Gertrude Stein, *The Geographical History of America: Or the Relation of Human Nature to the Human Mind* (1936; rpt. New York: Vintage, 1973), 53.

* * *

CHAPTER FOUR

1. Garry Mulholland, *Popcorn: Fifty Years of Rock 'n' Roll Movies* (London: Orion, 2010), 16.

2. Rees and Crampton, *Q Encyclopedia of Rock Stars*, 201. There are many sources now available about the facts of the crash. For newspaper headlines from the time, see www.eddie-cochran.info /the_crash.htm.

3. William Faulkner, comment on the Emmett Till murder, 1955. See also *Requiem for a Nun* (1951; rpt. Harmondsworth, UK: Penguin, 1987), 81: "The past is never dead. It's not even past."

4. Thomas Wolfe, *You Can't Go Home Again* (1940; rpt. New York: Harper Perennial, 1978), 391–92.

5. Borges, *Labyrinths*, 262.

6. Walt Whitman, "Crossing Brooklyn Ferry," 160.

7. Hilburn, *Corn Flakes with John Lennon*, 232; Gene Santoro, *Highway 61 Revisited: The Tangled Roots of American Jazz, Blues, Rock, & Country* (Oxford, UK: Oxford University Press, 2004), 225.

8. Marsh, *Bruce Springsteen: Two Hearts*, 288.

9. Maharidge, *Someplace Like America*, 75.

10. Marsh, *Bruce Springsteen: Two Hearts*, 290.

11. See Gilmore, *Nightbeat*, 71. Gilmore quotes Springsteen's remarks to Bob Dylan when Dylan was being inducted into the Rock & Roll Hall of Fame: "When I was fifteen and I heard 'Like a Rolling Stone' for the first time, I heard a guy like I've never heard before or since. A guy that had the guts to take on the whole world and made me feel like I had 'em too. . . . To steal a line from one of your songs, whether you like it or not, 'You was the brother that I never had.'"

12. Ibid., 60, 71. For one striking example of Dylan's evident indifference to his audience, see Erik Kirschbaum, *Rocking the Wall: Bruce Springsteen: The Berlin Concert That Changed the World* (New York: Berlinica, 2013), 66. Dylan played behind the Iron Curtain on 17 September 1987, a few months before Springsteen's concert for 300,000, "but those who saw his lackluster performance that evening in East Berlin described the show as a massive disappointment. Dylan was anything but inspirational. He did not endear himself, either, by leaving quickly with nary a wave goodbye after playing just 14 songs in a little over an hour."

13. Alterman, *It Ain't No Sin to Be Glad You're Alive*, 168–70.

14. Ibid., 211.

15. Clemons, *Big Man*, 239.

16. Bruce Springsteen: "You can change a life in three minutes with the right song," *The Guardian*, Sunday, 30 October 2016, theguardian.com. Springsteen may have picked up this repeated gesture from Iggy Pop. See Steve Waksman, *This Ain't the Summer of Love: Conflict and Crossover in Heavy Metal and Punk* (Berkeley: University of California Press, 2009), 101: "Iggy Pop did not view the rock audience as an organic whole. He was motivated to break through the typically guarded rock-and-roll proscenium by a refusal to see his audience strictly as a mass." "Mass recognition is not what's important to me, what's important is individual recognition," he told Dave Marsh. The cover of Waksman's book features a photograph of Pop pointing at an individual in the crowd.

17. Higgins, *The Music of Our Lives*, 114, 121.

18. Gilmore, *Nightbeat*, 220; Rob Kirkpatrick, *Magic in the Night: The Words and Music of Bruce Springsteen* (2007; 2nd ed. 2009), 110–11.

19. See, for instance, Cavicchi, *Tramps Like Us*, 90: "Many performers have mentioned the high they get from performing; Springsteen used to say that the only place he felt right was on stage. Music listeners, including Springsteen fans, likewise report a similar kind of high, which includes feelings of exhilaration, connection with the performer, and a sense of unity with other participants."

20. "Random Notes," in Puterbaugh et al., eds., *Bruce Springsteen*, 424; Eliot, *Down Thunder Road*, 241.

21. Frith, "The Real Thing," 131, 134, 138; Jim Farber, "Springsteen's *Video Anthology/1978–88*," in Puterbaugh et al., eds., *Bruce Springsteen*, 344. See Springsteen, "Keynote Speech," in Burger, ed., *Springsteen on Springsteen*, 385: "We live in a post-authentic world. And today authenticity is a house of mirrors. It's all just what you're bringing when the lights go down. It's your teachers, your influences, your personal history; and at the end of the day, it's the power and purpose of your music that still matters."

22. David Pattie, *Rock Music in Performance* (London: Palgrave MacMillan, 2007), vii: "The idea that it is somehow possible to capture a moment of authenticity through the medium of performance seems paradoxical at best."

23. See Kurt Loder, "*Tunnel of Love* LP Due from Springsteen," in Puterbaugh et al., eds., *Bruce Springsteen*, 285, on Appel's idea of a traveling tent show.

24. Waksman, *This Ain't the Summer of Love*, 72; Philip Auslander, *Performing Glam Rock: Gender and Theatricality in Popular Music* (Ann Arbor: University of Michigan Press, 2006), 4; Nelson, "Springsteen Fever," in Puterbaugh et al., eds., *Bruce Springsteen*, 51. Waksman cites Auslander's layer theory (73). Nelson suggested in 1978 that Springsteen had "carefully cultivated the Method actor's idiosyncratic timing."

25. See also Roxanne Harde and Irwin Streight, ed., "Introduction: the Bard of Asbury Park," in Harde and Streight, eds., *Reading the Boss*, 1–7.

26. Eliot, *Down Thunder Road*, 105. The information about the lighting is from a post by these-shadows, 12 September 2005, www.greasylake.org/the-circuit/index.php?/topic/38098-born-to-run -30th-anniversary-package/. The Hammersmith Odeon concert is available as part of the *Born to Run* box set.

27. Fred Schruers, "Bruce Springsteen and the Secret of the World," in Puterbaugh et al., eds., *Bruce Springsteen*, 112.

28. Christopher Phillips, "The Real World," in Sawyers, ed., *Racing in the Street*, 380.

29. Storr, *Solitude*, 123, 129; Heylin, *E Street Shuffle*, 220.

30. See Schruers, "The Boss Is Back," and Debby Bull, "The Summer's Biggest Tours Get Under Way," in Puterbaugh et al., eds., *Bruce Springsteen*, 99, 160. For the physical toll paid over the decades, see Springsteen, *Born to Run*, 492–93. "Probably since my forties, some physical problem had come along with every tour," he writes. "One tour it's your knee, then it's your back, then it's tendinitis in your elbows from all the hard strumming." Most serious of all was a near-paralysis of his left arm in his sixties that turned out to be "cervical disc problems" in his neck, leading to major surgery and temporary voice loss.

31. D. H. Lawrence, *Sons and Lovers* (1913; rpt. Harmondsworth, UK: Penguin, 1981), 63, 85, 101, 64; Camus, *The Myth of Sisyphus*, 111: "I leave Sisyphus at the foot of the mountain!" writes Camus. "The struggle itself towards the heights is enough to fill a man's heart. One must imagine Sisyphus happy."

32. Di Piero, *Memory and Enthusiasm*, 238–39.

33. Ibid., 255–56. Springsteen refers on "Desert Island Discs" to wearing his father's work clothes (bbc.in/2gWiz8U). For a more cynical view of this, see Frith, "The Real Thing," 132: "Bruce Springsteen is a millionaire who dresses as a worker." "He makes music physically, as a *manual* worker."

34. Elias Canetti, *Crowds and Power*, trans. Carol Stewart (1962; New York: Noonday, 1984), 15, cited in Waksman, *This Ain't the Summer of Love*, 23.

35. Henke, "Bruce Springsteen," in Puterbaugh ed., *Bruce Springsteen*, 409, and TAD 158: "I had locked into what was pretty much a hectic obsession, which gave me enormous focus and energy and fire to burn, because it was coming out of pure fear and self-loathing and self-hatred . . . It's funny, because the results of the show or the music might have been positive for other people, but there was an element of it that was abusive for me. Basically, it was my drug."

36. On the "Sad Eyes" segue on the 1978 Winterland recording, see also Charles R. Cross, "The Promise," in Sawyers, ed., *Racing in the Street*, 178–81. Heylin, *E Street Shuffle*, 135, quotes the "sad eyes" segue at length.

37. Eliot, *Down Thunder Road*, 104.

38. Kamp, "The Book of Bruce Springsteen," 203.

39. Carlin, *Bruce*, 457, 239, 458. There's also the story a factory worker tells in *Springsteen & I* of traveling from Britain to New York for a concert and being a little disappointed with the seats at the back, and of how someone came up to him who worked for Springsteen and got him the best seats in the house.

40. Caryn Rose, *Raise Your Hand: Adventures of an American Springsteen Fan in Europe* (New York: Till Victory, 2012), 12. Rose invites us to "compare the energy in front of the stage in Barcelona to the loud but mostly stationary crowd in 2001's *Live in New York City* DVD."

41. See Rose, *Raise Your Hand*, 101–2, 111, on the differing responses to Springsteen depending upon whether he's playing in the United States or elsewhere.

42. Marcus, *In the Fascist Bathroom*, 161; Springsteen, "Desert Island Discs," bbc.in/2gWiz8U.

43. John Lahr, "Greaser and Rah-Rahs," *London Review of Books* 39, no. 3 (2 February 2017): 27.

44. Michael Hann, "Bruce Springsteen: 'You can change a life in three minutes with the right song,'" *The Guardian*, Sunday, 30 October 2016. www.theguardian.com › Arts › Music › Bruce Springsteen.

45. Pattie, *Rock Music in Performance*, 20, 35, 39. Pattie is quoting from Theodore Gracyk, *Rhythm and Noise: An Aesthetic of Rock* (London: I. B. Tauris, 1996), 76.

46. Shumway, *Rock Star*, 5; Philip Auslander, *Liveness: Performance in a Mediatized Culture* (1999; rev. ed. 2008), 183, 10, 184, 25. See also Santoro, *Highway 61 Revisited*, 226. On his *Tom Joad* tours, Springsteen was deliberately no more than a "small figure on stage."

47. Thomas Gencarelli, "Popular Music and the Hero/Celebrity," in Susan J. Drucker and Robert S. Cathcart, eds., *American Heroes in a Media Age* (Cresskill, NJ: Hampton, 1994), 298.

48. When I contacted Giles, he told me to view the concert on YouTube (www.youtube.com/watch ?v=DIZ2-Gn3TC0). The two of us are not only briefly visible during Springsteen's walk-around but if you freeze the frame at 2 minutes 49 seconds you'll find proof of my comradely gesture (aka embarrassing moment). The whole 'encounter' is between 2.49 and 2.53 seconds. More importantly, he told me, basically a stranger, the following: "I'm actually a widower. Lost my wife December 2015. Springsteen's music helped me during the long illness and has certainly helped since. I went to eight shows that year. It was something I promised myself I would do during the dark times."

49. For another take on this, see Auslander, *Liveness*, 76, paraphrasing Theodore Gracyk: "The individual listener has the opportunity to commune with fellow fans and to experience an illusory bond with the performer."

50. Hilburn, *Corn Flakes with John Lennon*, 83.

51. Lewis, *Lonesome*, 40; David Bromwich, "The Novelists of Every Day Life," in *The Revival of Pragmatism: New Essays on Social Thought, Law, and Culture*, ed. Morris Dickstein (Durham, NC: Duke University Press, 1998), 370–76; Michael and Ariane Batterberry, "Focus on Joyce Carol Oates," in Milazzo, ed., *Conversations*, 46; Lewis Rowell, "Thinking Time and Thinking about Time in Indian Music," *Communication and Cognition* 19, no. 2 (1986): 233, cited in Higgins, *The Music of Our Lives*, 121.

52. Wallace Stevens, "Final Soliloquy of the Interior Paramour," in *The Collected Poems of Wallace Stevens* (London: Faber, 1955), 524.

53. Ralph Waldo Emerson, "Nature," in *Complete Prose Works*, 311; Lewis, *Lonesome*, 91.

54. Borges, *Labyrinths*, 282–83.

CHAPTER FIVE

1. Himes, *Born in the U.S.A.*, 60, 81; Frith, "The Real Thing," 139; Sandall was speaking as part of David Hepworth's interview with Springsteen, *The Late Show*, London Weekend Television Productions, 15 June 1992. 1992; Ian Collinson, "A Land of Hope and Dreams? Bruce Springsteen & America's Political Landscape from *The Rising* to *Wrecking Ball*," *Social Alternatives* 33, no. 1 (2014): 68; Alex Pitofsky, "Springsteen's Intimations of Mortality," in Izzo, ed., *Bruce Springsteen and the American Soul*, 230–32. Other examples, taken from Sawyers, ed., *Racing in the Street*, include Martin Scorsese, who refers to Springsteen, at a time of punk and new wave, as "something else—deeply romantic, even extravagantly so" (xiii). See also Simon Frith, *Taking Popular Music Seriously: Selected Essays* (Burlington, VT: Ashgate 2007), 271: "Realism inevitably means a non-romantic account of social life," he argues, merging the two, "and a highly romantic account of human nature." But here, too, the word sounds pejorative.

2. Lester Bangs, "Hot Rumble in the Promised Land," in Sawyers, ed., *Racing in the Street*, 75. Bangs continues: "he is so romantic, in fact, that he might do well to watch himself as he comes off this crest and settles into success—his imagery is already ripe, and if he succumbs to sentiment or sheer grandiosity it could well go rotten" (77).

3. Stuhr, "Introduction," in Stuhr, ed., *Pragmatism and Classical American Philosophy*, 3; Menand, *The Metaphysical Club*, 236, 330.

4. That judgment seems clear from his view that Springsteen, at least at that time (pre–*Tom Joad*, but not *Darkness*, *The River*, or *Nebraska*) was depicting a "folksy America that was being dealt with realistically back in the thirties." For many, this might seem a contentious comment in any case; there's nothing folksy about those latter three albums, out when the comment was made, and no couples running away into the sunset, though plenty of doomed yearning to do so.

5. For a detailed study of this, see Russell B. Goodman, *American Philosophy and the Romantic Tradition* (Cambridge, UK: Cambridge University Press, 1990). Goodman has chapters on the links between the Romantics and Emerson, James, and Dewey.

6. Marsh, *Bruce Springsteen: Two Hearts*, 257.

7. Stevens, *Opus Posthumous*, 183; Gilmore, *Nightbeat*, 211.

8. Mikhail M. Bakhtin, "Discourse in the Novel," in *The Dialogic Imagination: Four Essays*, trans. Caryl Emerson and Michael Holquist, ed. Michael Holquist (Austin: University of Texas Press, 1981), 299–300; Stuhr, "Introduction," in Stuhr, ed., *Pragmatism and Classical American Philosophy*, 3; Joyce Carol Oates. *New Heaven, New Earth: The Visionary Experience in Literature* (1974; rpt. London: Victor Gollancz, 1976), 246.

9. See Bryan K. Garman, "The Ghost of History: Bruce Springsteen, Woody Guthrie, and the Hurt Song," in Sawyers, ed., *Racing in the Street*, 223. Nevins and Commager's small, dated volume was just a start, of course. Howard Zinn's *A People's History of the United States* (1980), among countless other books, added nuance.

10. Carlin, *Bruce*, 201.

11. See Christa Wolf, *The Reader and the Writer: Essays, Sketches, Memories*, trans. Joan Becker (Berlin: Seven Seas, 1977), 41–44.

12. Daniel Wolff, *4th of July, Asbury Park: A History of the Promised Land* (New York: Bloomsbury, 2005), 4.

13. See also Springsteen's comment to James Henke on guitars and other paraphernalia in *Talk About a Dream*, 405: "That's part of the magic trick, right? That's the magician's tools."

14. Gray, *After the Fall*, 12.

15. Stevens, "The Motive for Metaphor," in *Collected Poems*, 288.

16. Herman Melville, "The March into Virginia, Ending in the First Manassas," *Battle-Pieces and Aspects of the War* (New York: Harper, 1866), 22.

17. For further thoughts on Springsteen in relation to Keith's song, see Bryan Garman's discussion of *The Rising* in "Models of Charity and Spirit: Bruce Springsteen, 9/11, and the War on Terror," in *Music in the Post-9/11 World*, ed. Jonathan Ritter and J. Martin Daughtry (London: Routledge, 2007), 71–89. Garman contrasts "City of Ruins" with "Red, White and Blue," noting that, "in this evocation, Springsteen prays not for the nation, but for 'this world,' a visionary act that departs from the jingoistic rhetoric of both the American president and Toby Keith" (81).

18. Rorty, *The Rorty Reader*, 415–16, 444, 476–79. What I call pragmatic romanticism, Rorty calls "romantic utilitarianism." He describes the pragmatist rejection of truth beyond language as "romantic polytheism"—the belief in multiple possibilities, in this case that truth can take many forms.

19. "Bruce Springsteen: By the Book," BR8.

20. Bertrand Russell, *History of Western Philosophy* (London: Allen & Unwin, 1961), 766–68.

21. Ibid., 771.

22. Russell, *History of Western Philosophy*, 772–73.

23. William James, Lecture VI, "Pragmatism's Concept of Truth," in *Pragmatism: A New Name for Some Old Ways of Thinking* (New York: Longmans, 1946), 201.

24. Oliver Sacks, *Musicophilia: Tales of Music and the Brain* (2008; rpt. London: Picador, 2011), 319. Orpheus, for instance, Russell tells us, hadn't so prominent an addiction to music in the earlier legends; "primarily he was a priest and a philosopher" (37); the other references are to Plato's *Republic*, where music stands for anything related to the muses, and is to be forbidden (126–27); to the links between mathematics and music traceable to the disciples of Pythagoras, and Puritan objections to music; and to Plotinus, the founder of Neoplatonism, who wrote of the link between "the harmony of the Intellectual Realm" and "the harmony in sensible sounds" (295). It should be noted

that James only makes one reference to music in *Principles of Psychology* (Sacks, *Musicophilia*, 319). For the record, as it were, Dewey joined them in having "little interest in, or appreciation of, music." See Goodman, *American Philosophy and the Romantic Tradition*, 117.

25. See Alterman, *It Ain't No Sin to Be Glad You're Alive*, 21. Springsteen's first gig ever, at Woodhaven Swim Club, 1965, ended with Glenn Miller's "In the Mood."

26. Higgins, *The Music of Our Lives*, xiv. See also 109: "Some depressed people can find a beautiful, sunny day offensive. One's empirical response to art, as aestheticians since Hume have noted, may be aberrant because of one's particular circumstances. But the dynamic features of music and certain features of performance and its effect that listeners commonly recognize do provide a basis for claiming that the emotional character is intersubjective and not arbitrary."

27. William James, "Humanism and Truth," from *The Meaning of Truth*, in *Selected Papers on Philosophy* (London: Dent, 1917), 222: "Truth we conceive to mean everywhere not duplication but addition; not the constructing of inner copies of already complete realities, but rather the collaborating with realities so as to bring about a clearer result."

28. Ludwig Wittgenstein, *Tractatus-Logico-Philosophicus*, trans. D. F. Pears and B. F. McGuinness (1961; rpt. London: Routledge & Kegan Paul, 1974), 56–57: "*The limits of my language* mean the limits of *my* world. . . . The world is *my* world: this is manifest in the fact that the limits of *language* (of that language which I alone understand) mean the limits of *my* world."

29. Julian Barnes, *Flaubert's Parrot* (1984; rpt. London: Pan, 1985), 121; Carlin, *Bruce*, 195.

30. Joyce Carol Oates, "George Bellows' 'Mrs. T. in Cream Silk, No. 1' (1919–23)," in *Tenderness* (Princeton, NJ: Ontario Review Press, 1996), 84: "Time?—devours us / in the name of wisdom."

31. Rorty, *Achieving Our Country*, 23. What you in fact discover as the years pass, Barnes continues, is "that life is not a choice between murdering your way to the throne or slopping back in a sty, that there are swinish kings and regal hogs; that the king may envy the pig; and that the possibilities of the not-life will always change tormentingly to fit the particular embarrassments of the lived life" (121). As Springsteen put it to Mikal Gilmore: "One of the byproducts of fame is you will be trivialized, and you will be embarrassed. You *will* be, I guarantee it" ("Twentieth Anniversary Special," in Puterbaugh et al., eds., *Bruce Springsteen*, 297).

32. Carlin, *Bruce*, 162.

33. John Rockwell, "New Dylan From Jersey? It Might as Well Be Springsteen," in Puterbaugh et al., eds., *Bruce Springsteen*, 21.

34. Arthur Schopenhauer, *The World as Will and Idea*, ed. David Berman, trans. Jill Berman (London: Dent, 1995), 84.

35. Ibid., 74.

36. Ibid., 84–85; Nietzsche, *Beyond Good and Evil*, 88. See also Schopenhauer, *The World as Will and Idea*, 162–72. For Schopenhauer, music is the one art form that, rather than reflecting this "will," embodies it. "This is why the effect of music is so much more powerful and penetrating than that of the other arts, for they speak only of the shadow while music speaks of the essence" (164). When Springsteen refers to his music as not an attempt to "recreate the experience" but "to recreate the emotions and the things that went into the action being taken" (TAD 206), and extols the art over the individual artist as a person, he's offering versions of other points that Schopenhauer makes. "The composer reveals the inner nature of the world, and expresses the most profound wisdom, in a language which his reasoning faculty does not understand," he writes. "Thus in the composer, more

than in any other artist, the person is entirely separated and distinct from the artist" (167). Springsteen's lyrics may reflect aspects of his life, but the music itself—as he shows in paying homage to many other musicians—eventually belongs to no one.

37. Schopenhauer, *The World as Will and Idea*, 37.

38. See Charles R. Cross et al., *Backstreets: Springsteen, the Man and His Music* (New York: Harmony, 1989), 47: "For years the Circuit was the place to be seen and to see others—especially if you had a hot set of wheels. You can't do it fast—the traffic lights are tuned to stop speeding."

39. Jack Kerouac, *On the Road* (1957; rpt. Harmondsworth, UK: Penguin, 1972), 10, 94, 97.

40. Samuel R. Bagenstos, "The Promise Was Broken: Law as a Negative Force in Bruce Springsteen's Music," *Widener Law Journal* 14 (2005): 837–45. Bagenstos describes this as Springsteen's "most despairing song" (837), and the invocation of his "greatest anthem of teenage escapism" as its "most powerful element" (839).

41. William Wordsworth, "Ode: Intimations of Immortality from Recollections of Early Childhood" (1807; rpt. in *The Oxford Anthology of English literature: Romantic Poetry and Prose*, ed. Harold Bloom and Lionel Trilling (Oxford, UK: Oxford University Press, 1973), 176.

42. Heylin, *E Street Shuffle*, 196. Springsteen describes "Stolen Car" as a "ghost story."

43. Gilmore, "Twentieth Anniversary Special," in Puterbaugh et al., eds., *Bruce Springsteen*, 298.

CHAPTER SIX

1. Leo Tolstoy, *Anna Karenina*, trans. Louise and Aylmer Maude (Oxford, UK: Oxford World's Classics 1998), 302: "Everyone, knowing intimately all the complexities of his own circumstances, involuntarily assumes that these complexities and the difficulty of clearing them up are peculiar to his own personal condition, and never thinks that others are surrounded by similar complexities." Ironically, Tolstoy's oversimplifies the matter in a way that also, paradoxically, seems to reinforce his point—making assumptions about everyone else while assuming his own mind to be more complex.

2. Patrick White, *Flaws in the Glass: A Self-Portrait* (1981; rpt. Harmondsworth, UK: Penguin, 1983), 20.

3. See also Gilmore, *Nightbeat*, 220: "Springsteen seemed to step back from rock & roll's center at the same moment that he won it."

4. Peter Knobler, with Greg Mitchell, "Who Is Bruce Springsteen and Why Are We Saying All These Wonderful Things about Him?" in Sawyers, ed., *Racing in the Street*, 38.

5. Patrick Humphries and Chris Hunt, *Bruce Springsteen: Blinded by the Light*. London: Plexus, 1985.

6. David Fricke, "The Long and Winding Road," and Gilmore, "Twentieth Anniversary Special," in Puterbaugh et al., eds., *Bruce Springsteen*, 245, 297

7. Bobbie Ann Mason, *Elvis Presley* (2002; rpt. Harmondsworth, UK: Penguin, 2007), 121; Oates, *(Woman) Writer*, 384.

8. Eduardo Galeano, *Soccer in Sun and Shadow*, trans. Mark Fried (1997; rpt. New York: Nation, 2013), 233; Nicholas Dawidoff, "The Pop Populist," in Sawyers, ed., *Racing in the Street*, 248. Of the *Born in the U.S.A.* era and images, specifically the album cover, Springsteen said in 1996 that he "was probably working out" his "own insecurities." "That particular image," he continues, "is probably the only time I look back over pictures of the band and it feels like a caricature to me" (TAD 203).

9. Emanuel Swedenborg was an eighteenth-century man of science who became a theologian. Swedenborgianism, in Louis Menand's words, "was a religion for liberals" (*The Metaphysical Club*, 89).

10. John D. McDermott, "William James," in Stuhr, ed., *Pragmatism and Classical American Writing*, 141–42; Erin McKenna and Scott Pratt, "Living on the Edge: A Reason to Believe," in Auxier and Anderson, eds., *Bruce Springsteen and Philosophy*, 163. McKenna and Scott discuss McDermott's own contemporary pragmatist philosophy in more detail, and with regard to Springsteen.

11. Lahr, "Greaser and Rah-Rahs," 27; Maharidge, *Someplace Like America*, x, 78.

12. Steve Fraser, *The Age of Acquiescence: The Life and Death of American Resistance to Organized Wealth and Power* (New York: Little, Brown, 2015), 13, 248, 255.

13. Ibid., 322, 80.

14. Cavicchi, *Tramps Like Us*, 77, 142, 14.

15. Stendhal, *The Red and the Black*, 348.

16. McDermott, "William James," in Stuhr, ed., *Pragmatism and Classical American Philosophy*, 142–43.

17. James Henke, "Bruce Springsteen: The Rolling Stone Interview," in Puterbaugh et al., eds., *Bruce Springsteen*, 406, and TAD 155.

18. Clemons, *Big Man*, 46, 254, 47.

19. Edwin T. Arnold, ed., "The William Styron–Donald Harington Letters," *Southern Quarterly* 40, no. 2 (Winter 2002): 118.

20. Alan Rauch, "Bruce Springsteen and the Dramatic Monologue," *American Studies* 29, no. 1 (1988): 31, 33. See Michael Ventimiglia, "Bruce Springsteen or Philosophy," in Auxier and Anderson, eds., *Bruce Springsteen and Philosophy*, 191–92, for a solid argument that even this character is not naive.

21. Rosalie Zdzienicka Fanshel, "Beyond Blood Brothers: Queer Bruce Springsteen," *Popular Music* 32, no. 3 (October 2013): 377, 365, 379; Auslander, *Performing Glam Rock*, 33, 234. In the lengthy live renditions of the song in the 1970s, where Springsteen includes an extended segue into what will eventually become "Drive All Night," for instance in Atlanta and Cleveland in 1978, Terry is clearly female. For further discussion, see Smith, "Sexual Mobilities in Bruce Springsteen," in DeCurtis, ed. *Present Tense*, 197–218. For a contrasting perspective, see Will, *The Morning After*, 10. Will's assessment, on attending a 1984 concert, was that "there is not a smidgen of androgyny in Bruce Springsteen."

22. McKenna and Pratt, "Living on the Edge," in Auxier and Anderson, eds., *Bruce Springsteen and Philosophy*, 170.

23. See Henke, "Bruce Springsteen," in Puterbaugh et al., eds., *Bruce Springsteen*, 407, 410, and TAD 156–58: "People think because you're so good at one particular thing, you're good at many things. And that's almost always not the case." "I reached an age where I began to miss my real life—or to even know that there was another life to be lived. I mean, it was almost a surprise. First you think you are living it. You got a variety of different girlfriends and then, 'Gee, sorry, gotta go now.'"

24. Nelson, "Springsteen Fever," in Puterbaugh et al., eds., *Bruce Springsteen*, 56.

25. Springsteen, in Zimny, director, *The Ties That Bind*.

26. Ivan Turgenev, *Fathers and Sons*, trans. Richard Freeborn (Oxford, UK; Oxford World's Classics), 104.

27. Tolstoy, *Anna Karenina*, 375.

CHAPTER SEVEN

1. Tess Gallagher, "Borrowed Strength," in *The Generation of 2000*, ed. Heyen, 56; Dorothy Allison, "Believing in Literature," in Allison, *Skin: Talking about Sex, Class, and Literature* (Ithaca, NY: Firebrand, 1994), 181; Rorty, *Consequences of Pragmatism*, 161.

2. Jean Baudrillard, *America*, trans. Chris Turner (New York: Verso, 1988), 29; John Fowles, *The French Lieutenant's Woman* (London: Jonathan Cape, 1969), 99.

3. Heylin, *E Street Shuffle*, 118; "Bruce Springsteen: By the Book," BR8.

4. Kirschbaum, *Rocking the Wall*, 99, 118, 131.

5. David Joselit, *After Art* (Princeton, NJ: Princeton University Press, 2013), xiv.

6. Ibid., xv.

7. Kirschbaum, *Rocking the Wall*, 109.

8. The dilemma, he expands, is that "either you illustrate the story, which limits it, or you relay another story in something that's already telling a story, which doesn't make sense, because if you did it right the first time, why are you going to try to do it again?" An exception to this, Springsteen seems to suggest, is as a way into the music for people too young to attend shows. "I'm not really interested in making an ad for my record," he says, but the "most intense audience" for video "is between six and sixteen," and they tap into "a cartoonish thing that the videos employ" (TAD 137). The example he gives is of a boy of about eight coming up to him on the beach and asking him if he wanted to see his "Dancing in the Dark" moves. Springsteen, of course, "said okay" (TAD 137).

9. Carl "Tinker" West quoted in Anders Mårtensson and Jörgen Johansson, *Local Heroes: The Asbury Park Music Scene*, trans. Christophe Brunski (Piscataway, NJ: Rivergate, 2008), 61; anonymous fan quoted in Cavicchi, *Tramps Like Us*, 77.

10. Joselit, *After Art*, xvi.

11. Bleiker, "Art After 9/11," 91; Higgins, *The Music of Our Lives*, xiv; Joselit, *After Art*, 1–2.

12. Joselit, *After Art*, 3.

13. Ibid., 11–14. David Shumway, *Rock Star*, 8, writes that, in contrast, "Benjamin welcomed this destruction of art's aura." In fact, Benjamin's essay allows for both interpretations. See Walter Benjamin, *Illuminations: Essays and Reflections*, trans. Harry Zohn (New York: Harcourt, Brace, Jovanovich, 1969), 223, 226. On one hand, Benjamin writes that "the situations into which the product of mechanical reproduction can be brought may not touch the actual work of art, yet the quality of its presence is always depreciated. . . . its authenticity . . . is interfered with. . . . that which withers in the age of mechanical reproduction is the aura of the work of art." But he also writes, "for the first time in world history, mechanical reproduction emancipates the work of art from its parasitical dependence on ritual. To an even greater degree the work of art reproduced becomes the work of art designed for reproducibility." See also Auslander, *Liveness*, 31, 37–39, and elsewhere, for further discussion of Benjamin's theories in relation to rock music.

14. Joselit, *After Art*, 14–15.

15. Carlin, *Bruce*, 246–47. This was not for want of trying. Not only is there the well-known story of Springsteen scaling the gates of Graceland and heading for the front door only to be told that Presley was at Lake Tahoe, but he also wrote "Fire" with the idea that "he might pitch the song to his boyhood hero as a possible single," and had tickets for a September 1977 concert at Madison Square Garden. Presley died on 16 August.

16. Joselit, *After Art*, 15–19.

17. Ibid., 23.

18. Higgins, *The Music of Our Lives*, 168.

19. Joselit, *After Art*, 89, 91.

20. Whitman, *Leaves of Grass*, 14.

21. Ibid., 115–17.

22. Joselit, *After Art*, 96.

23. Marsh, *Bruce Springsteen: Two Hearts*, 634.

24. Mason, *In Country*, 80.

25. See Will Percy, "Double Take," in Phillips and Masur, eds., *Talk About a Dream*, 219. Springsteen refers to Mason's novels. He writes about the genesis of the song and about Walter Cichon in the sleeve notes to *High Hopes*.

26. Roth, *Nemesis*, 141, 143.

27. Rorty, *Achieving Our Country*, 134. See William Wordsworth's conclusion to *The Prelude*, lines 446–47.

28. See Tichi, *High Lonesome*, 44, who notes that "holding court on a barstool" is "a country mode."

29. See Greil Marcus, "The Old, Weird America," in *A Booklet of Essays, Appreciations, and Annotations Pertaining to the Anthology of American Folk Music, ed. Harry Smith*, ed. Peter Seital (Washington DC: Smithsonian Folkways Recordings, 1997), 16–17. Springsteen is echoing Bob Dylan's comments in the 1960s about folk music. Marcus commandeers Dylan's comments to describe the feeling of listening to these songs, whose singers "sound as if they're already dead." For a more negative take on rock music and death, see Milan Kundera, *The Art of the Novel*, trans. Linda Asher (London: Faber, 1988), 148. "I hate to hear the beat of my heart; it is a relentless reminder that the minutes of my life are numbered." "The tedious rhythmic primitivism of rock; the heart's beat is amplified so that man can never for a moment forget his march toward death."

30. Cologne-Brookes, "Written Interviews," 563; Alain de Botton, "Britain's Useless Galleries Don't Know What Art Is For," London *Times*, Saturday 7 March 2015, 26.

31. Nelson, "Springsteen Fever," in Puterbaugh et al., eds., *Bruce Springsteen*, 59.

32. Clemons, *Big Man*, 239.

33. Stevens, "Tea at the Palaz of Hoon," in *Collected Poems*, 65.

SELECTED BRUCE SPRINGSTEEN DISCOGRAPHY

STUDIO ALBUMS

Greetings from Asbury Park, N.J. Columbia Records, 1973.

The Wild, the Innocent & the E Street Shuffle. Columbia Records, 1973.

Born to Run. Columbia Records, 1975.

Darkness on the Edge of Town. Columbia Records, 1978.

The River. Columbia Records, 1980.

Nebraska. Columbia Records, 1982.

Born in the U.S.A. Columbia Records, 1984.

Tunnel of Love. Columbia Records, 1987.

Human Touch. Columbia Records, 1992.

Lucky Town. Columbia Records, 1992.

The Ghost of Tom Joad. Columbia Records, 1995.

The Rising. Columbia Records, 2002.

Devils & Dust. Columbia Records, 2005.

We Shall Overcome: The Seeger Sessions. Columbia Records, 2006.

Magic. Columbia Records, 2007.

Working on a Dream. Columbia Records, 2009.

Wrecking Ball. Columbia Records, 2012.

High Hopes. Columbia Records, 2014.

LIVE ALBUMS

Bruce Springsteen and the E Street Band Live/1975–85. Columbia Records, 1986.
In Concert/MTV Plugged. Columbia Records, 1993.
Bruce Springsteen and the E Street Band: Live in New York City. Columbia, 2001.
Bruce Springsteen with the Sessions Band: Live in Dublin. Columbia Records, 2007.
London Calling: Live in Hyde Park. Columbia, 2009.

COMPILATION ALBUMS

Tracks. Columbia Records, 1998.
18 Tracks. Columbia Records, 1999.
Greatest Hits. Columbia Records, 1999.
The Essential Bruce Springsteen with Bonus CD. Columbia Records, 2003.
The Promise. Columbia Records, 2010.
Chapter and Verse. Columbia Records, 2016.

BOX SETS

Born to Run: 30th Anniversary Edition. Columbia Records, 2005.
The Promise: The Darkness on the Edge of Town Story. Columbia Records, 2010.
The Ties That Bind: The River Collection. Columbia Records, 2015.

EXTENDED PLAY

Chimes of Freedom. Columbia Records, 1988.
Magic Tour Highlights. Columbia Records, 2008.
American Beauty. Columbia Records, 2014.

ARCHIVES

Bruce Springsteen Live on Air with Bonus DVD *Live Rarities.* Britanya-4Worlds, 2005.
The Spirit of Radio: Legendary Broadcasts from the Early 1970s. Parallel Lines, 2014.
Tower Theater, Philadelphia, PA, 1975. brucespringsteen.net, 2015.
Winterland, San Francisco, CA, 1978. Echoes, 2014.
The Agora Ballroom 1978: The Classic Cleveland Broadcast. Leftfield Media, 2014.
Foxy Night 1978: The Classic Atlanta Broadcast. Leftfield Media, 2015.
Arizona State University, Tempe, AZ, 1980. brucespringsteen.net, 2015.
Nassau Coliseum, New York, NY, 1980. brucespringsteen.net, 2015.

Brendan Byrne Arena, East Rutherford, NJ, 1984. brucespringsteen.net, 2015.

LA Sports Arena, Los Angeles, CA, 1988. brucespringsteen.net, 2015.

The Christic Shows, Los Angeles, CA, 1990. brucespringsteen.net, 2016.

Schottenstein Center, Columbus, OH, 2005. brucespringsteen.net, 2015.

Scotttrade Center, St. Louis, MO, 2008. brucespringsteen.net, 2017.

Wachovia Spectrum, Philadelphia, PA, 2009. brucespringsteen.net, 2017.

HSBC Arena, Buffalo, NY, 2009. brucespringsteen.net, 2016.

Olympiastadion, Helsinki, 2012. brucespringsteen.net, 2017.

Apollo Theater, New York, NY, 2012. brucespringsteen.net, 2014.

Ippodromo delle Capannelle, Rome, 2013. brucespringsteen.net, 2015.

VIDEO ALBUMS

Bruce Springsteen in Concert/MTV Plugged. Directed by Larry Jordan. Columbia Records, 1993.

Blood Brothers. Directed by Ernie Fritz. Columbia Records, 1996.

The Complete Video Anthology/1978–2000. Multiple Directors. Columbia Records, 2001.

Bruce Springsteen and the E Street Band/Live in New York City. Directed by Chris Hilson. Thrill Hill, 2001.

Live in Barcelona. Directed by Chris Hilson. Columbia Records, 2003.

Hammersmith Odeon London '75. Edited by Thom Zimny. Columbia Records, 2005.

Wings for Wheels: the Making of 'Born to Run.' Directed by Thom Zimny. Columbia Records, 2005.

VH1 Storytellers: Bruce Springsteen. Directed by Dave Diomedi. Columbia Records, 2005.

Bruce Springsteen with the Sessions Band: Live in Dublin. Directed by Chris Hilson. Columbia Records, 2007.

London Calling: Live in Hyde Park. Directed by Chris Hilson. Columbia Records, 2010.

The Promise: The Making of 'Darkness on the Edge of Town.' Directed by Thom Zimny. Thrill Hill, 2010.

Springsteen & I. Directed by Baillie Walsh. RSA Films, Mr. Wolf Presents, and Columbia Records, 2013.

Born in the U.S.A.: London 2013 (Bonus DVD with *High Hopes*). Directed by Chris Hilson. Columbia Records, 2014.

The Ties That Bind. Directed by Thom Zimny. Columbia Records, 2015.

SELECTED BIBLIOGRAPHY

BOOKS

Agee, James, and Walter Evans. *Let Us Now Praise Famous Men*. 1941. Rpt. London: Panther, 1969.

Alexander, Michelle. *The New Jim Crow: Mass Incarceration in the Age of Colorblindness*. 2011. Rev. ed. New York: New Press, 2012.

Allison, Dorothy. *Skin: Talking about Sex, Class, and Literature*. Ithaca, NY: Firebrand, 1994.

Alterman, Eric. *It Ain't No Sin to Be Glad You're Alive: The Promise of Bruce Springsteen*. 1999. 2nd ed. Boston: Little, Brown, 2001.

Anderson, Douglas L. Anderson. *Philosophy Americana: Making Philosophy at Home in American Culture*. New York: Fordham University Press, 2006.

Auslander, Philip. *Liveness: Performance in a Mediatized Culture*. 1999. Rev. ed. London: Routledge, 2008.

———. *Performing Glam Rock: Gender and Theatricality in Popular Music*. Ann Arbor: University of Michigan Press, 2006.

Auxier, Randall E., and Douglas L. Anderson, eds. *Bruce Springsteen and Philosophy: Darkness on the Edge of Truth*. Peru, IL: Open Court, 2008.

Bakhtin, Mikhail M. *The Dialogic Imagination: Four Essays*. Trans. Caryl Emerson and Michael Holquist. Ed. Michael Holquist. Austin: University of Texas Press, 1981.

Baldwin, James. *The Fire Next Time*. 1963. Rpt. Harmondsworth, UK: Penguin, 1964.

Barnes, Julian. *Flaubert's Parrot*. 1984. Rpt. London: Pan, 1985.

Baudrillard, Jean. *America*. Trans. Chris Turner. New York: Verso, 1988.

Bellow, Saul. *Henderson the Rain King*. 1959. Rpt. Harmondsworth, UK: Penguin, 1981.

Benjamin, Walter. *Illuminations: Essays and Reflections*. Trans. Harry Zohn. New York: Harcourt, Brace, Jovanovich, 1969.

Berlin, Isaiah. *Russian Thinkers*. 1948. Rpt. Harmondsworth, UK: Penguin, 1994.

Blake, Mark. *Stone Me: The Wit and Wisdom of Keith Richards*. London: Aurum, 2008.

Bloom, Harold, and Lionel Trilling, eds. *The Oxford Anthology of English Literature: Romantic Poetry and Prose*. Oxford, UK: Oxford University Press, 1973.

Borges, Jorge Luis. *Labyrinths: Selected Stories and Other Writings*. Trans. Donald Yates, James Irby et al. 1964. Rpt. Harmondsworth, UK: Penguin, 1987.

Burger, Jeff, ed. *Springsteen on Springsteen: Interviews, Speeches, and Encounter*. New York: Omnibus, 2013.

Camus, Albert. *The Myth of Sisyphus and Other Essays*. Trans. Justin O'Brien. 1955. Rpt. Harmondsworth, UK: Penguin, 1975.

———. *Resistance, Rebellion, and Death*. Trans. Justin O'Brien. London: Hamish Hamilton, 1961.

Canetti, Elias. *Crowds and Power*. Trans. Carol Stewart. 1962. Rpt. New York: Noonday, 1984.

Carlin, Peter Ames. *Bruce*. New York: Touchstone, 2012.

Casciato, Arthur D., and James L. W. West III, eds., *Critical Essays on William Styron*. Boston: G. K. Hall, 1985.

Cather, Willa. *My Ántonia*. 1918. Rpt. London: Everyman, 1996.

Cavicchi, Daniel. *Tramps Like Us: Music and Meaning among Springsteen Fans*. Oxford, UK: Oxford University Press, 1998.

Clemens, Samuel Langhorne. *Adventures of Huckleberry Finn*. 1884. Rpt. New York: Norton, 1977.

Clemons, Clarence, and Don Reo. *Big Man: Real Life and Tales*. New York: Grand Central Publishing, 2009.

Clifford, Joe, ed. *Trouble in the Heartland: Crime Fiction Inspired by the Songs of Bruce Springsteen*. Dublin: Gutter, 2014.

Coles, Robert. *Bruce Springsteen's America: The People Listening, a Poet Singing*. New York: Random House, 2003.

Cross, Charles R., et al. *Backstreets: Springsteen, the Man and His Music*. New York: Harmony, 1989.

Cruickshank, John. *Albert Camus and the Literature of Revolt*. Oxford, UK: Oxford University Press, 1959.

Cullen, Jim. *Born in the U.S.A.: Bruce Springsteen and the American Tradition*. 1997. Rev. ed. Middletown, CT: Wesleyan University Press, 2005.

———. *Restless in the Promised Land: Catholics and the American Dream*. Franklin, WI: Sheed & Ward, 2001.

DeCurtis, Anthony, ed. *Present Tense: Rock & Roll and Culture*. Durham, NC: Duke University Press, 1992.

Di Piero, W. S. *Memory and Enthusiasm: Essays, 1975–1985*. Princeton, NJ: Princeton University Press, 1989.

Dickinson, Emily. *The Complete Poems of Emily Dickinson*. Ed. Thomas H. Johnson. London: Faber, 1960.

Dickstein, Morris, ed. *The Revival of Pragmatism: New Essays on Social Thought, Law, and Culture*. Durham, NC: Duke University Press, 1998.

Dolan, Marc. *Bruce Springsteen and the Promise of Rock 'n' Roll*. 2012. 2nd ed. New York: Norton, 2013.

Dostoevsky, Fyodor. *Crime and Punishment*. Trans. Jessie Coulson. Oxford, UK: Oxford World's Classics, 1980.

Douglass, Frederick. *The Autobiography of Frederick Douglass, an American Slave*. 1845. Rpt. Harmondsworth, UK: Penguin, 1982.

Drucker, Susan J., and Robert S. Cathcart, eds. *American Heroes in a Media Age*. Cresskill, NJ: Hampton, 1994.

Du Bois, W. E. B. *The Souls of Black Folk*. 1903. Rpt. Mineola, NY: Dover, 1994.

Eliot, Marc, with Mike Appel. *Down Thunder Road: The Making of Bruce Springsteen*. London: Plexus, 1992.

Emerson, Ralph Waldo. *The Complete Prose Works of Ralph Waldo Emerson*. New York: Ward, Lock and Co., 1889.

Erikson, Erik. H. *Young Man Luther: A Study in Psychoanalysis and History*. New York: Norton, 1958.

Faulkner, William. *Absalom, Absalom!* 1936. Rpt. New York: Vintage, 1972.

——. *Requiem for a Nun*. 1951. Rpt. Harmondsworth, UK: Penguin, 1987.

Fitzgerald, F. Scott. *The Crack-Up with Other Pieces and Stories*. Harmondsworth, UK: Penguin, 1965.

——. *The Great Gatsby*. 1925. Rpt. New York: Scribner's, 1953.

Flaubert, Gustave. *Madame Bovary*. Trans. Alan Russell. Harmondsworth, UK: Penguin, 1986.

Ford, Richard. *Independence Day*. New York: Knopf, 2004.

——. *The Lay of the Land*. New York: Knopf, 2006.

——. *The Sportswriter*. 1986. Rpt. London: Flamingo, 1987.

Fowles, John. *The French Lieutenant's Woman*. London: Jonathan Cape, 1969.

Fraser, Steve. *The Age of Acquiescence: The Life and Death of American Resistance to Organized Wealth and Power*. New York: Little, Brown, 2015.

French, Warren. *Steinbeck Revisited*. New York: Twayne, 1961.

Friedman, Stewart D. *Leading the Life You Want: Skills for Integrating Work and Life*. Boston: Harvard Business Review Press, 2014.

Frith, Simon. *Taking Popular Music Seriously.* Burlington, VT: Ashgate, 2007.

Galeano, Eduardo. *Open Veins of Latin America: Five Centuries of the Pillage of a Continent.* Trans. Cedric Belfrage. 1973. Rpt. London: Serpent's Tail, 2009.

———. *Soccer in Sun and Shadow.* Trans. Mark Fried. 1997. Rpt. New York: Nation, 2013.

Garman, Bryan K. *A Race of Singers: Whitman's Working-Class Hero from Guthrie to Springsteen.* Chapel Hill: University of North Carolina Press, 2000.

Gilmore, Mikal. *Nightbeat: A Shadow History of Rock & Roll.* New York: Doubleday, 1998.

Goldsmith, Lynn. *Springsteen: Access All Areas.* New York: Universe, 2000.

Goodman, Fred. *Mansion on the Hill: Dylan, Young, Geffen, Springsteen and the Head-On Collision of Rock and Commerce.* New York: Times, 1997.

Goodman, Russell B. *American Philosophy and the Romantic Tradition.* Cambridge, UK: Cambridge University Press, 1990.

Gracyk, Theodore. *Rhythm and Noise: An Aesthetic of Rock.* London: I. B. Tauris, 1996.

Gray, Richard. *After the Fall: American Literature Since 9/11.* Malden, MA: Wiley-Blackwell, 2011.

Guagliardo, Huey, ed. *Conversations with Richard Ford.* Jackson: University of Mississippi Press, 2001.

Gunn, Giles, *Thinking Across the American Grain: Ideology, Intellect, and the New Pragmatism.* Chicago: University of Chicago Press, 1992.

Guterman, Jimmy. *Runaway American Dream: Listening to Bruce Springsteen.* Cambridge, MA: Da Capo, 2005.

Hammond, John. *John Hammond on Record.* New York: Ridge, 1977.

Harde, Roxanne, and Irwin Streight, eds. *Reading the Boss: Interdisciplinary Approaches to Bruce Springsteen.* Lanham, MD: Rowman and Littlefield, 2010.

Hawthorne, Nathaniel. *The Scarlet Letter: A Romance.* 1837. Rpt. Harmondsworth, UK: Penguin, 2012.

Hemingway, Ernest. *Green Hills of Africa.* New York: Scribner's, 1935.

Heyen, William, ed. *Generation of 2000: Contemporary American Poets.* Princeton, NJ: Ontario Review Press, 1984.

Heylin, Clinton. *E Street Shuffle: The Glory Days of Bruce Springsteen and the E Street Band.* London: Constable, 2012.

Higgins, Mary Kathleen. *The Music of Our Lives.* Langham, MD: Lexington, 2011.

Hilburn, Robert. *Corn Flakes with John Lennon: And Other Tales from a Rock 'n' Roll Life.* New York: Rodale, 2009.

Himes, Geoffrey. *Born in the U.S.A.* London: Continuum 2005.

Humphries, Patrick, and Chris Hunt. *Bruce Springsteen: Blinded by the Light.* London: Plexus, 1985.

Izzo, David Garrett, ed. *Bruce Springsteen and the American Soul: Essays on the Songs and Influence of an American Icon.* Jefferson, NC: McFarland, 2011.

James, Henry. *Collected Stories.* Vol. 2. New York: Knopf, 1999.

James, William. *Pragmatism: A New Name for Some Old Ways of Thinking.* 1907. Rpt. New York: Longmans 1946.

———. *Selected Papers on Philosophy.* London: Dent, 1917.

Johnson, Greg. *Invisible Writer: A Biography of Joyce Carol Oates.* New York: Dutton, 1998.

Jones, Allan. *"Melody Maker" Classic Rock Interviews.* London: Mandarin, 1994.

Jones, Tennessee. *Deliver Me from Nowhere.* Brooklyn: Soft Skull, 2005.

Joselit, David. *After Art.* Princeton, NJ: Princeton University Press, 2013.

Kaye, Jessica, and Richard Brewer, eds. *Meeting Across the River: Stories Inspired by the Haunting Bruce Springsteen Song.* New York: Bloomsbury, 2005.

Kerouac, Jack. *On The Road.* 1957. Rpt. Harmondsworth, UK: Penguin, 1972.

Kirkpatrick, Rob. *Magic in the Night: The Words and Music of Bruce Springsteen.* 2007. 2nd ed. New York: St. Martin's, 2009.

Kirschbaum, Erik. *Rocking the Wall: Bruce Springsteen: The Berlin Concert That Changed the World.* New York: Berlinica, 2013.

Koestler, Arthur. *Darkness at Noon.* 1941. Rpt. New York: Bantam, 1966.

Kundera, Milan. *The Art of the Novel.* Trans. Linda Asher. London: Faber, 1988.

Lawrence, D. H. *Sons and Lovers.* 1913. Rpt. Harmondsworth, UK: Penguin, 1981.

———. *Studies in Classic American Literature.* 1923. Rpt. Harmondsworth, UK: Penguin, 1977.

Lewis, Kevin. *Lonesome: The Spiritual Meanings of American Solitude.* New York: I. B. Tauris, 2009.

Mack, Stephen John. *The Pragmatic Whitman: Reimagining American Democracy.* Iowa City: University of Iowa Press, 2002.

Maharidge, Dale. *Journey to Nowhere: The Saga of the New Underclass.* 1985. Rpt. New York: Hyperion, 1996.

———. *Someplace Like America: Tales from the New Great Depression.* 2011. Rev. ed. Berkeley: University of California Press, 2013.

Marcus, Greil. *In the Fascist Bathroom: Punk in Pop Music, 1977–1992.* Cambridge, MA: Harvard University Press, 1999.

———. *Mystery Train: Images of America in Rock 'n' Roll Music.* 1975. Rev. ed. New York: Plume, 2015.

Margolis, Joseph. *Reinventing Pragmatism: American Philosophy at the End of the Twentieth Century.* Ithaca, NY: Cornell University Press, 2002.

Marsh, Dave. *Bruce Springsteen on Tour: 1968–2005.* New York: Bloomsbury, 2006.

———. *Bruce Springsteen: Two Hearts.* New York: Routledge, 2004.

Mårtensson, Anders, and Jörgen Johansson. *Local Heroes: The Asbury Park Music Scene.* Trans. Christophe Brunski. Piscataway, NJ: Rivergate, 2008.

Masciotra, David. *Working on a Dream: The Progressive Political Vision of Bruce Springsteen.* New York: Continuum, 2010.

Mason, Bobbie Ann. *Elvis Presley*. 2002. Rpt. Harmondsworth, UK: Penguin, 2007.

———. *In Country*. 1985. Rpt. Harper Perennial, 2005.

Masur, Louis. P. *Runaway Dream: Born to Run and Bruce Springsteen's American Vision*. New York: Bloomsbury, 2009.

McCarthy, Cormac. *The Road*. New York: Knopf, 2006. Rpt. London: Picador, 2007.

Melville, Herman. *Battle-Pieces and Aspects of the War*. New York: Harper, 1866.

———. *Moby-Dick; or, The Whale*. 1851. Rpt. Harmondsworth, UK: Penguin, 1972.

Menand, Louis. *The Metaphysical Club*. 2001. Rpt. London: Flamingo, 2002.

Milazzo, Lee, ed. *Conversations with Joyce Carol Oates*. Jackson: University of Mississippi Press, 1989.

Montaigne, Michel de. *The Essays of Montaigne*. Trans. Charles Cotton. London: Bell, 1913.

Morrison, Toni. *Jazz*. 1992. Rpt. London: Picador, 1993.

Mulholland, Garry. *Popcorn: Fifty Years of Rock 'n' Roll Movies*. London: Orion, 2010.

Nietzsche, Friedrich. *Beyond Good and Evil: Prelude to a Philosophy of the Future*. Trans. R. J. Hollingdale. Harmondsworth, UK: Penguin, 1973.

Oates, Joyce Carol. *Fabulous Beasts*. Baton Rouge: Louisiana State University Press, 1977.

———. *The Faith of a Writer: Life, Craft, Art*. New York: Ecco, 2003.

———. *High Lonesome: Selected Stories 1966–2006*. New York: Ecco, 2006.

———. *Invisible Woman: New and Selected Poems, 1970–1982*. Princeton, NJ: Ontario Review Press, 1982.

———. *The Lost Landscape: A Writer's Coming of Age*. New York: Ecco, 2015.

———. *New Heaven, New Earth: The Visionary Experience in Literature*. 1974. Rpt. London: Victor Gollancz, 1976.

———. *We Were the Mulvaneys*. New York: Dutton, 1996.

———. *(Woman) Writer: Occasions and Opportunities*. New York: Dutton, 1988.

———. *You Must Remember This*. New York: Dutton, 1987.

———. ed. *Prison Noir*. New York: Akashic Book, 2014.

O'Connor, Flannery. *The Complete Stories*. London: Faber, 1990.

Orwell, George. *Homage to Catalonia*. 1938. Rpt. Harmondsworth, UK: Penguin, 1966.

———. *Why I Write*. Harmondsworth, UK: Penguin, 2004.

Pascal, Blaise. *Pensées*. Trans. A. J. Krailsheimer. Harmondsworth, UK: Penguin, 1966.

Pattie, David. *Rock Music in Performance*. London: Palgrave MacMillan, 2007.

Percy, Walker. *Lost in the Cosmos: The Last Self-Help Book*. 1983. Rpt. New York: Picador, 2000.

———. *The Message in the Bottle: How Queer Man Is, How Queer Language Is, and What One Has to Do with the Other*. New York: Farrar, Straus & Giroux, 1975.

———. *Signposts in a Strange Land*. New York: Farrar, Straus & Giroux, 1991.

Pessoa, Fernando. *The Book of Disquiet*. Trans. Richard Zenith. Harmondsworth, UK: Penguin, 2002.

Phillips, Christopher, and Louis P. Masur, eds. *Talk About a Dream: The Essential Interviews of Bruce Springsteen*. New York: Bloomsbury, 2013.

Plath, Sylvia. *The Bell Jar*. London: Heinemann, 1963.

Prejean, Helen. *Dead Man Walking: An Eyewitness Account of the Death Penalty in the United States*. 1993. Rpt. London: Fount, 1996.

Price, Martin, ed. *The Oxford Anthology of English Literature: The Restoration and the Eighteenth Century*. Oxford, UK: Oxford University Press, 1973.

Puterbaugh, Parke, et al., eds. *Bruce Springsteen: The Rolling Stone Files*. New York: Hyperion, 1996.

Pyle, Barbara. *Bruce Springsteen and the E Street Band 1975*. London: Reel Art Press, 2016.

Quinlan, Kieran. *Walker Percy: The Last Catholic Novelist*. Baton Rouge: Louisiana State University Press, 1996.

Rees, Dafydd, and Luke Crampton. *Q Encyclopedia of Rock Stars*. New York: Dorling Kindersley, 1996.

Richards, Keith. *Life*. 2010. Rpt. London: Phoenix, 2011.

Ritter, Jonathan, and J. Martin Daughtry, eds. *Music in the Post-9/11 World*. London: Routledge, 2007.

Rorty, Richard. *Achieving Our Country: Leftist Thought in Twentieth-Century America*. Cambridge, MA: Harvard University Press, 1998.

———. *Consequences of Pragmatism: Essays, 1972–1980*. Brighton, UK: Harvester, 1982.

———. *Contingency, Irony, and Solidarity*. Cambridge, UK: Cambridge University Press, 1989.

———. *The Rorty Reader*. Ed. Christopher J. Voparil and Richard J. Bernstein. Malden, MA: Wiley-Blackwell, 2010.

Rose, Caryn. *Raise Your Hand*. New York: Till Victory, 2012.

Roth, Philip. *Nemesis*. 2010. Rpt. London: Vintage, 2011.

Russell, Bertrand. *History of Western Philosophy*. London: Allen & Unwin, 1961.

Sacks, Oliver. *Musicophilia: Tales of Music and the Brain*. 2008. Rpt. London: Picador, 2011.

Sandford, Christopher. *Springsteen: Point Blank*. London: Little, Brown, 1999.

Santelli, Robert. *Greetings from E Street: The Story of Bruce Springsteen and the E Street Band*. San Francisco: Chronicle, 2006.

Santoro, Gene. *Highway 61 Revisited: The Tangled Roots of American Jazz, Blues, Rock, & Country*. Oxford, UK: Oxford University Press, 2004.

Saramago, José. *All the Names*. Trans. Margaret Jull Costa. New York: Harvest, 1999.

Sawyers, June Skinner. *Tougher than the Rest: 100 Best Bruce Springsteen Songs*. New York: Omnibus, 2006.

———, ed. *Racing in the Street: The Bruce Springsteen Reader*. Harmondsworth, UK: Penguin, 2004.

Schama, Simon. *Rembrandt's Eyes*. London: Allen Lane, 1999.

Schopenhauer, Arthur. *The World as Will and Idea.* Trans. Jill Berman. London: Dent, 1995.

Seital, Peter, ed. *A Booklet of Essays, Appreciations, and Annotations Pertaining to the Anthology of American Folk Music, ed. Harry Smith.* Washington DC: Smithsonian Folkways Recordings, 1997.

Shillinglaw, Susan, and Kevin Hearle, eds. *Beyond Boundaries: Rereading John Steinbeck.* Tuscaloosa: University of Alabama Press, 2002.

Shumway, David R. *Rock Star: The Making of Musical Icons from Elvis to Springsteen.* Baltimore: Johns Hopkins University Press, 2014.

Smith, Harry. See Seital, Peter.

Smith, Larry David. *Bob Dylan, Bruce Springsteen, and American Song.* Westport, CT: Praeger, 2002.

Solzhenitsyn, Alexander. *One Day in the Life of Ivan Denisovich.* Trans. Ralph Parker. Harmondsworth, UK: Penguin, 1963.

Springsteen, Bruce. *Songs.* 1998. Rev. ed. New York: HarperEntertainment, 2003.

———. *Born to Run.* New York: Simon & Schuster, 2016.

Statham, Craig. *Springsteen: Saint in the City: 1949–1974.* London: Soundcheck, 2013.

Stein, Gertrude. *The Geographical History of America: Or the Relation of Human Nature to the Human Mind.* 1936. Rpt. New York: Vintage, 1973.

Steinbeck, John. *The Grapes of Wrath.* 1939. Rpt. Harmondsworth, UK: Penguin, 1992.

Stendhal (Marie-Henri Beyle). *The Red and the Black.* Trans. Catherine Slater. Oxford, UK: Oxford World's Classics, 1991.

Stevens, Wallace. *Collected Poems.* London: Faber, 1966.

———. *Opus Posthumous.* 1957. Rev. ed. New York: Random House, 1989.

Storr, Anthony. *Solitude: A Return to the Self.* London: HarperCollins, 1988.

Stuhr, John J., ed. *Pragmatism and Classical American Philosophy: Essential Readings and Interpretive Essays.* Oxford, UK: Oxford University Press, 2000.

Styron, William. *Darkness Visible: A Memoir of Madness.* New York: Random House, 1990.

———. *My Generation: Collected Nonfiction.* New York: Random House, 2015.

———. *Set This House on Fire.* New York: Random House, 1960.

Symynkywicz, Jeffrey. *The Gospel According to Bruce Springsteen: Rock and Redemption from Asbury Park to Magic.* Louisville, KY: Westminster John Knox, 2008.

Terkel, Studs. *My American Century.* New York: New Press, 1997.

Thoreau, Henry David. *Walden and 'Civil Disobedience.'* Ed. Owen Thomas. 1854. Rpt. New York: Norton, 1966.

Tichi, Cecilia. *High Lonesome: The American Culture of Country Music.* Chapel Hill: University of North Carolina Press, 1994.

Tolstoy, Leo. *Anna Karenina.* Trans. Louise and Aylmer Maude. Oxford, UK: Oxford World's Classics, 1998.

Twain, Mark. See Clemens, Samuel Langhorne.

Waksman, Steve. *This Ain't the Summer of Love: Conflict and Crossover in Heavy Metal and Punk*. Berkeley: University of California Press, 2009.

White, Ryan. *Bruce Springsteen: Album by Album*. London: Carlton, 2014.

Whitman, Walt. *Leaves of Grass*. Philadelphia: David McKay, 1891–1892. Rpt. New York: Norton, 1973.

Wiersema, Robert J. *Walk Like a Man: Coming of Age with the Music of Bruce Springsteen*. Vancouver: Greystone, 2011.

Will, George F. *The Morning After: American Successes and Excesses 1981–1986*. New York: Prentice Hall, 1987.

Wittgenstein, Ludwig. *Tractatus-Logico-Philosophicus*. Trans. D. F. Pears and B. F. McGuinness. London: Routledge & Kegan Paul, 1961.

Wolf, Christa. *The Reader and the Writer: Essays, Sketches, Memories*. Trans. Joan Becker. Berlin: Seven Seas, 1977.

Wolfe, Thomas. *You Can't Go Home Again*. 1940. Rpt. New York: Harper Perennial, 1978.

Wolff, Daniel. *4th of July, Asbury Park: A History of the Promised Land*. New York: Bloomsbury, 2005.

Womack, Kenneth, Mark Zolten, and Mark Bernhard, eds. *Bruce Springsteen, Cultural Studies, and the Runaway American Dream*. Burlington, VT: Ashgate, 2012.

Woolf, Virginia. *To The Lighthouse*. 1927. Rpt. New York: Harvest, 1955.

Wright, Richard. *Native Son*. 1940. Rpt. London: Vintage, 2000.

Zeldin, Theodore. *An Intimate History of Humanity*. London: Sinclair-Stevenson, 1994.

Zinn, Howard. *A People's History of the United States*. New York: Harper & Row, 1980.

ESSAYS, REVIEWS, AND INTERVIEWS

Arnold, Edwin T., ed., "The William Styron–Donald Harington Letters." *Southern Quarterly* 40, no. 2 (Winter 2002): 98–141.

Bagenstos, Samuel R. "The Promise Was Broken: Law as a Negative Force in Bruce Springsteen's Music." *Widener Law Journal* 14 (2005): 837–45.

Bleiker, Roland. "Art After 9/11." *Alternatives* 31 (2006): 77–99.

Bonca, Cornel. "How (and How Not) to Write about 9/11." *Modern Language Studies* 41, no. 1 (2011): 132–40.

Botton, Alain de. "Britain's Useless Galleries Don't Know What Art is For." London *Times*, Saturday 7 March 2015, 26.

Cologne-Brookes, Gavin. "Written Interviews and a Conversation with Joyce Carol Oates." *Studies in the Novel* 38, no. 4 (Winter 2006): 547–65.

Douglas, Anne. "Bruce Springsteen and Narrative Rock." *Dissent* (Fall 1985): 485–89.

Fanshel, Rosalie Zdzienicka. "Beyond Blood Brothers." *Popular Music* 32, no. 3 (October 2013): 359–83.

Ford, Richard. "The Boss Observed." *Esquire,* December 1985, 326–29.

———. "Richard Ford Reviews Bruce Springsteen's Memoir." *New York Times,* 22 September 2016. nyti.ms/2d1S058.

———. "Rock Springs Eternal: Richard Ford on Bruce Springsteen." backstreets.com/news archive74.html.

———. "2 Comments." *Wall Street Journal,* 20 January 2015. www.wsj.com/articles/richard -ford-on-bruce-springsteens-wild-billys-circus-story-1421777496.

Gates, Henry Louis Jr. "Murder She Wrote." *Studies in the Novel* 38, no. 4 (Winter 2006): 544–45.

Harde, Roxanne. "Living in Your American Skin." *Canadian Review of American Studies / Revue Canadienne d'Études Américaines* 43, no. 1 (2013): 125–44.

Kamp, David. "The Book of Bruce Springsteen." *Vanity Fair,* October 2016, 192–205.

Lahr, John. "Greasers and Rah-Rahs." *London Review of Books* 39, no. 3 (2 February 2017): 27–29.

Lombardi, John. "St. Boss: The Sanctification of Bruce Springsteen and the Rise of Mass Hip." *Esquire,* December 1988, 139–53.

Rauch, Alan. "Bruce Springsteen and the Dramatic Monologue." *American Studies* 29, no. 1 (1988): 29–49.

Remnick, David. "We Are Alive: Bruce Springsteen at Sixty-Two." *The New Yorker,* 30 July 2012, 1–39. www.newyorker.com/magazine/2012/07/30/we-are-alive.

Smith, Abbe. "The Dignity and Humanity of Bruce Springsteen's Criminals." *Widener Law Journal* 14 (2005): 787–835.

Tyrangiel, Josh. "Bruce Rising: An Intimate Look at How Springsteen Turned 9/11 into a Message of Hope." *Time* 160, no. 6 (5 August 2002): 52–59.

WEBSITES

www.backstreets.com
www.brucespringsteen.net
www.greasylake.org
www.springsteenlyrics.com

INDEX